How Turner *Painted*

JOYCE H. TOWNSEND

How Turner *Painted*

MATERIALS & TECHNIQUES

with over 200 illustrations

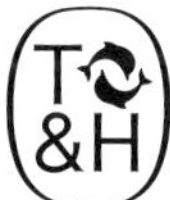

Joyce H. Townsend is senior conservation scientist at Tate, London. She is
the author of numerous books, including *Turner's Painting Techniques* and,
with Tony Smibert, *Watercolour Manual: Lessons from the Great Masters*.

Tony Smibert is Visiting Artist Researcher at Tate, London. As an artist,
he has had over fifty solo exhibitions around the world. In 2016, he was
made a Member of the Order of Australia.

Nicola Moorby is an independent art historian specializing in British
art of the 19th and early 20th centuries.

On the cover: *Front Snow Storm – Steam-Boat off a Harbour's Mouth*, exhibited
1842. Oil on canvas, 91.4 × 121.9 (36 × 48). Tate, London. Photo Tate, London 2019.
Back Turner's 'Chelsea' palette, used at the end of his life, ?1840s. Tate, London.
Photo Tate, London 2019

On p. 2: *Shields Lighthouse, c.* 1823–26. Watercolour on paper, 23.4 × 28.3
(9¼ × 11⅛) Tate, London. Photo Tate, London 2019 (detail; full work ill. p. 23)

First published in the United Kingdom in 2019 by Thames & Hudson Ltd,
181A High Holborn, London WC1V 7QX

First published in the United States of America in 2019 by
Thames & Hudson Inc., 500 Fifth Avenue, New York, New York 10110

Reprinted 2022

How Turner Painted: Materials & Techniques © 2019
Thames & Hudson Ltd, London
Text © 2019 Joyce H. Townsend

British Library Cataloguing-in-Publication Data
A catalogue record for this book is available from the British Library

Library of Congress Control Number 2019934307

ISBN 978-0-500-29483-3

Printed and bound in China by Toppan Leefung Printing Limited

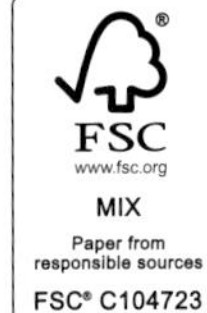

CONTENTS

FOREWORD

NICOLA MOORBY

'The only secret I have got is damned hard work.' So retorted Turner when quizzed as to the secrets of his success. 'I know of no genius but the genius of hard work,' he would add. Over half a century later, Thomas Edison would famously agree that 'genius is one per cent inspiration and ninety-nine per cent perspiration', reminding us that even the most naturally gifted individuals need to underpin their talent with hard graft.

Art, like any other discipline, is a labour-intensive process – it needs to be worked at. Despite the common perception that true artists are born with their ability, technical proficiency is, in truth, hard won. A spectacular, flawless painting unveiled at an exhibition belies a secret history of trial and error, and moments of inspired ease and brilliance are far less common than periods of unremitting slog. To use a musical analogy, a virtuoso soloist performing in a concert will, no matter how innate their musicality or instinctive their aptitude for their instrument, have undergone intensive behind-the-scenes preparation beforehand, comprising training, practice, rehearsal and intense creative scrutiny.

It is exactly the same for artists. Establishing how they express themselves within their chosen medium is hard work. Techniques may be learned or inherited from other colleagues, but the greatest practitioners evolve their own methods, honing their skills and pushing the boundaries of their materials through hours and hours of personal and private struggle. Turner was just such a man, and, although frequently described during his lifetime as a genius and a magician, his achievements were, in fact, the reward for a life of exceptionally prolonged and dedicated hard work.

There have been many books devoted to what Turner painted – the subject matter, the symbolism, the historical, literary and contemporary references and meanings within his pictures, as well as his highly distinctive trademark style. Numerous publications have discussed why and when he painted, the circumstances that drove his career choices and the cultural context that framed his achievements. Thanks to extensive research into his British and European travels, we even know a great deal about where he went to gather the visual material that fed into his paintings.

By contrast, there have been far fewer studies about how Turner painted, and how the conscious selection of specific materials and the unique ways that he chose to apply them combined to create his signature look. The modern era has recognized the formalist and abstract qualities of his work without fully interrogating the technical processes by which he arrived at his painterly conclusions. Yet Turner's practical abilities were as innovative as his artistic vision, and evolved as the result of everyday toil: a quiet, intimate and dogged communion with paper, pencil, paint and canvas, which yielded a surety and expertise that even other artists envied.

Often the greater part of an artist's professional journey is undertaken within the private space of the studio. More than any other 19th-century practitioner, we have the chance to analyse Turner's working methods because of the vast quantity of material that he left behind. An unprecedented amount of physical evidence survives in the form of the Turner Bequest, now housed at Tate, the contents of his London studio as he left it upon his death in 1851.

The Turner Bequest comprises thousands of preparatory sheets and sketchbook pages in pencil and watercolour, and hundreds of canvases touched with oil. Sketches, drawings, studies, trials, colour beginnings, layouts, experiments, from embryonic compositions to finished pictures, with every intermediary and developmental stage in between – in short, a visual archive of a lifetime of daily grind. Largely unseen and unknown while Turner was alive, this accumulated mass of material helps us to chart his pursuit of technical excellence.

While Turner's finished paintings are so complex that often they obscure the secrets of their making, the preparatory and unfinished works are easier to decipher, making it possible to follow the progress of the artist's brushstrokes. It is as though we were standing and looking over his shoulder as he worked. They also allow us to spot patterns within his working methods – oft-repeated ways of approaching a problem, for example, or particular tricks of the brush that, once identified, become as distinctive as a handwritten signature. Whereas in the past these sketches would have been considered simply incomplete, nowadays we place almost as much value on them as we do on his finished works. Taken as evidence of Turner's truest and most authentic artistic sensibilities, the process has become as significant as the end result.

We also have the good fortune to have surviving examples of Turner's tools and equipment: his paintboxes, brushes, palettes and other painting paraphernalia, preserved since the moment he laid them down for the final time. Dr Joyce H. Townsend is the acknowledged expert on these materials and the bespoke ways that Turner used them within his work. In this book, she combines her extensive knowledge gleaned from technical examination and materials analysis with an insightful understanding of and sensitivity towards his modus operandi. She pieces together the clues and reveals for us how Turner was able take base pigments mixed with oil or water and apply them with such skill and flair that he seemed to create effects spun from nature itself.

Whether steam, spray, sea or sunlight, Turner's paintings appear as though he has dipped his brush in the very stuff he sought to represent.

To understand the alchemy behind this transformation is to unlock the innermost secrets at the heart of his genius. It also helps to explain how a relatively untutored boy from London rose from obscurity to become one of the most celebrated, prodigious and radical artists of the 19th century. The story of how Turner painted is ultimately the story of how he became Britain's greatest and most beloved artist.

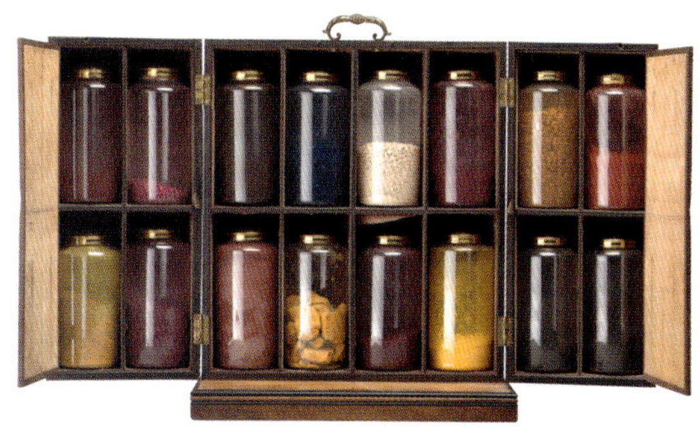

AN ARTIST AHEAD OF HIS TIME

To understand the painting processes of J.M.W. Turner (1775–1851) and the materials he used is to understand the options available to his contemporaries, for Turner was the most innovative artist of his time. Best appreciated long after his lifetime, like all great artists, he was the first and most fearless adopter of the new painting materials produced in abundance during the early decades of the Industrial Revolution.

This book is based on findings from the technical examination and materials analysis of his watercolours, oil paintings and studio materials over many years, made during my work as a senior conservation scientist at Tate Britain, London.[1] It is not about the analytical processes used,[2] nor the frames first used for the paintings (which formed the subject of a separate study in the case of Tate works),[3] but is intended to convey the skill, imagination and mastery of Britain's most well-known landscape artist, to engender greater understanding and appreciation of his paintings, watercolours and sketched ideas, and to inform about his working methods.

Many of the examples discussed form part of the Turner Bequest at Tate Britain, which includes the largest collection of his works in the world: some three hundred oil paintings and 37,000 sheets of paper, ranging from pencil sketches to finished watercolours. (All of the paper-based works can be viewed online in good resolution, as can nearly all of the oils.[4]) Other collections have also been drawn upon, as roughly a third of Turner's oil paintings and over 1,000 works on paper are today in public collections in the UK, the US, Australia, and a few other regions.[5]

Turner lived in the right place – the artistic and artists' quarter of London – and at the right time. The Royal Academy of Arts had been founded in 1768, only seven years before his birth, and one of its aims was to promote the status of artists. In effect, it was a professional body that enabled full members to display their works in oil to the public, but gave lesser opportunities to watercolourists and sculptors. British oil painters stood on the highest step of the hierarchy of artists and subject matter, and they were not restricted by guilds, as in earlier centuries, nor challenged by rival imaging processes such as steel-plate engraving, colour-printing or photography, all of which would be developed during Turner's long life (he lived to the age of seventy-six, painting to the last).

Trade founded on Britain's pre-eminence as a naval power and successful seafaring nation expanded during the first half of the 19th century. The growing number of individuals with self-made wealth would create new patrons for artists working at that time, purchasing paintings, watercolours, prints and illustrated travel books, and commissioning watercolours of picturesque and romantic scenery in Europe – to name only the main sources of Turner's excellent professional income by the standards of the day.

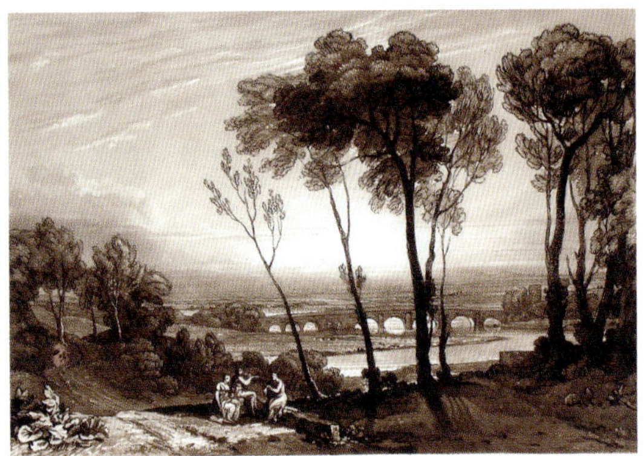

J.M.W. Turner and Charles Turner, *The Bridge in Middle Distance*, 1808. Indianapolis Museum of Art

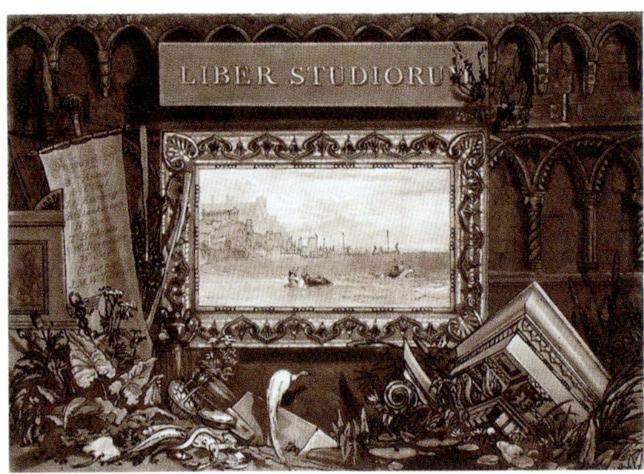

J.M.W. Turner and J.C. Easling, Frontispiece to *Liber Studiorum*, 1812. Indianapolis Museum of Art

Like previous generations of successful artists, Turner responded to new opportunities. He made use of the reproductive technology of copperplate engraving and mezzotint for *Liber Studiorum*,[6] a series of studies published in parts from 1808 (above, left and right). It was projected to include one hundred images, issued in groups by subject, but never quite reached that number. This promoted his work to a wider audience, though one with less to spend. He became a competent engraver and an intelligent client – and probably a rather annoying and highly demanding one, too – of the many professional engravers with whom he would work throughout his life.

In the 1820s the development of steel engraving increased the number of copies that could be made from a single plate. By this time, Turner was creating fully finished and coloured watercolours to be engraved (opposite, top right), as distinct from the brown monochrome subjects of the earlier *Liber Studiorum*, and then selling the originals with the reproductive rights and/or limited editions of prints after his work (opposite, top left and right). By later middle age, he could easily afford to paint pictures like *Norham Castle, Sunrise* (opposite, bottom), which were too advanced to sell well in his own lifetime, but are today regarded as among his most iconic works, and sometimes seen as anticipating Impressionism, Abstract Expressionism and other '-isms' that developed long after his death.

It is not surprising that Turner's range of subjects included the sea in all its moods, ships as transport and bringers of victory against the French,[7] and industrial subjects, as well as the landscape and topographical subjects he typically depicted in watercolour at the start of his career. Equally unsurprisingly, he moved from sketching to painting in watercolour, and then to the higher-status medium of oil while still in his teens. In his early years as an oil painter Turner explored the lofty and highly regarded subject of history painting, and even painted a self-

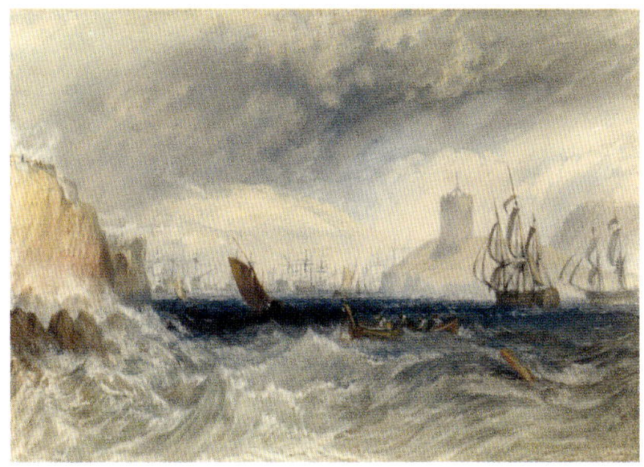

Catwater, Plymouth, 1800–20. Allport Library and Museum of Fine Arts, Hobart

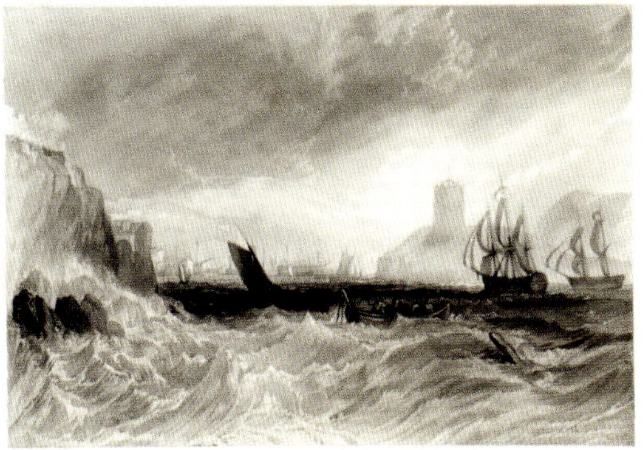

Catwater, Plymouth, from *The Ports of England* series, engraved by Thomas Lupton, 1826–28. Tate, London

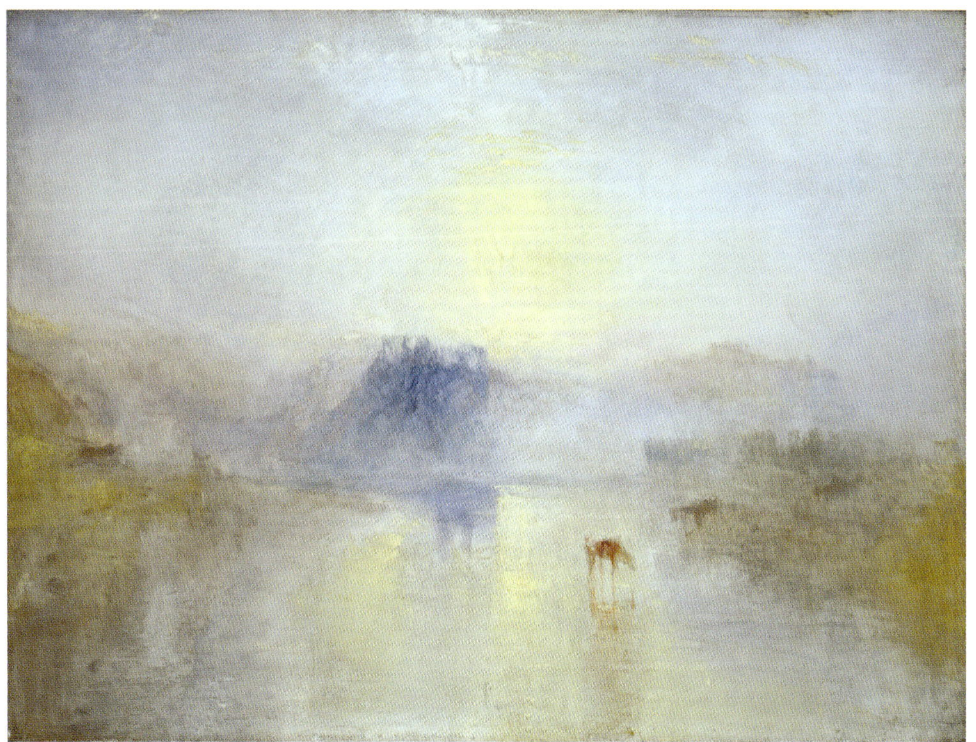

Norham Castle, Sunrise, c. 1845. Tate, London

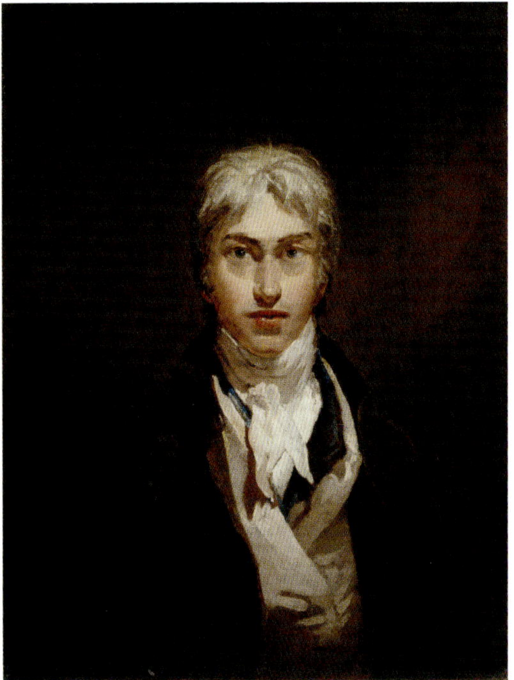

Self-portrait, c. 1799. Tate, London

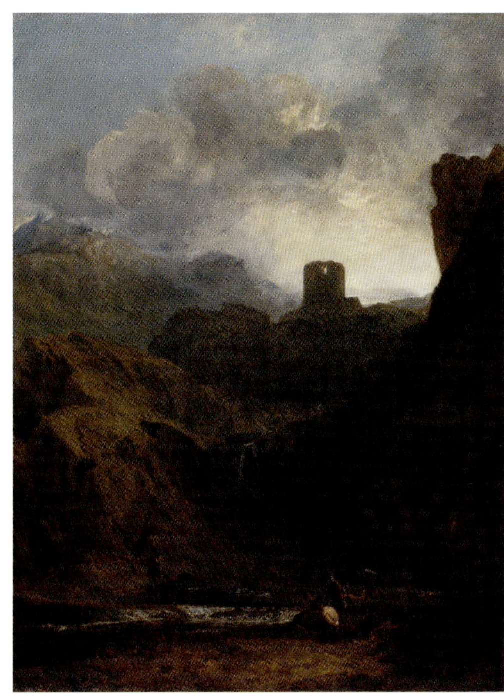

Dolbadarn Castle, North Wales, 1800. Royal Academy of Arts, London

portrait to project exactly such an aspiring individual (above left), although he never sought to paint portraits, and painting figures never became his best skill. He would become the youngest ever Royal Academician at the age of twenty-eight, cannily presenting as his diploma work *Dolbadarn Castle, North Wales* (above right), a far more traditionally rendered subject than he would paint in the years to come.

In later life, Turner would achieve the highest prices yet recorded for oils, through obsessively hard work, self-confidence, an astute assessment of emerging markets and a talent that was obvious from a very young age. If he had to choose between family life and improving his artistic skills, he would always put his art first. He would have many longstanding friendships, but never adopted the conventional middle-class life – or, indeed, marriage – of many of his patrons.

Turner's family was not wealthy. At the time of his birth, his father William worked as a barber and wig-maker in Covent Garden, London, where virtually all the suppliers of artists' materials (known as colourmen) lived within easy strolling distance, and where many successful artists of the previous century had lived and worked. The parental premises were thus well situated for an intelligent lad looking to make useful contacts in the

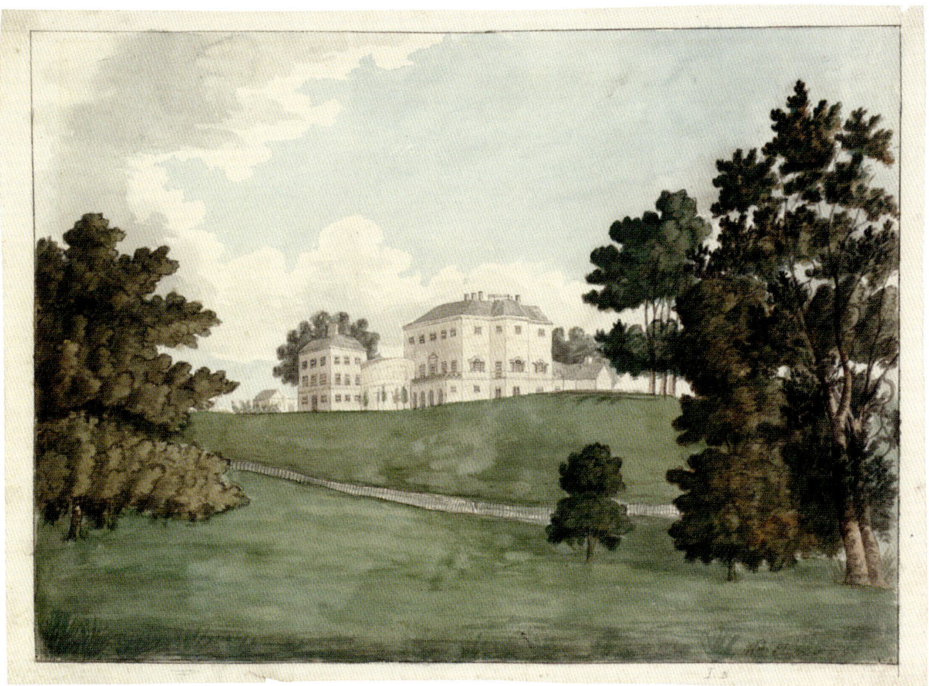

View of Nuneham Courtenay from the Thames, 1787. Tate, London

profession of painting, a career choice approved of by William Turner. Many artists at this period were born into similar financial circumstances, though often without the parental approval, and looked to support both themselves and their education from their mid-teens, as Turner did.

Turner's choices for training and selling opportunities were good ones. He sold drawings and watercolours in the family shop; enrolled in the Royal Academy Schools in 1789, drawing from both plaster casts and live models (essentially the only teaching offered there); learned perspective at evening classes taught by the architectural draughtsman Thomas Malton (1748–1804); and,

possibly, attended the last of influential *Discourses* lectures given by Sir Joshua Reynolds (1723–1792) in 1790 and visited the studio of the painter Philippe-Jacques de Loutherbourg (1740–1812).[8]

In addition, it is very likely that in his late teens Turner worked on dramatic subjects for theatrical scene-painting – on a large scale and at a rapid pace, as plays had only short runs. As well, he joined an informal group of young artists at the home of the physician and art collector Dr Thomas Monro, where they were given facilities, meals, interaction with peers and a ready purchaser. The gifted but short-lived artist Thomas Girtin (1775–1802) had a similar social background, training with Turner under Malton and Monro, and becoming his friend; as a result, their work is sometimes difficult to distinguish.[9]

In later life, Turner would keep up to date with developing ideas, befriending not only the chemist and colourman George Field, who wrote books on colour theory and developed new and better red lake pigments, but also such leading scientists as Humphry Davy and Mary Somerville. The Royal Society was situated in the same building as the Royal Academy, and artists could attend lectures there. Early in the 19th century, Turner followed the work of David Brewster in optics; some decades later, he annotated his own copy of Johann Wolfgang von Goethe's *Theory of Colours* (1810), translated and published in English in 1840. Turner's interest in research into magnetism is said to have inspired some of his compositions.[10]

Turner's earliest works in watercolour reveal his innate talent, even when he was working in a traditional style. *View of Nuneham Courtenay from the Thames* (ill. previous page), painted when he was about twelve years old, reveals an excellent understanding of perspective and colour balance, as well as some more conventional representation that he would soon dispense with (black, rather than reflective, windows, for example). There are also signs of the beginnings of innovation in the realistically depicted clouds. His skills developed rapidly after this promising beginning. Turner always knew his worth, and he frequently positioned himself as not merely a contender for greatness, but also as an equal of the acknowledged masters of oil painting.[11]

His father William became his studio assistant and, in effect, his business manager, facilitating access to the gallery when Turner was travelling, arranging for the delivery of finished paintings to purchasers and for supplies of materials to be at hand, both in the gallery and in the artist's house on the Thames at Twickenham, where they both lived and where Turner entertained his friends. This flexible business model doubtless contributed to Turner's success. When William died in 1829, at the age of eighty-four, his son became more reclusive and relied increasingly on longstanding domestic staff. He did not marry, though he is credited with two daughters and with a number of relationships with women, whom he never painted as recognizable individuals and who did not work in the family painting enterprise as his father had.

Turner was blessed with good health and stamina, which enabled him to undertake long and arduous trips throughout his life to gather material. In his late teens, he travelled to many parts of England and Wales; waking early to cover impressive distances on foot, he would take to the hills to obtain good views of rugged scenery, financing these tours with commissions for watercolours of country seats. When looking at a map of the UK today, it is possible to spot hundreds of towns and regions where Turner travelled and painted; indeed, there is scarcely a region where he did not sketch.

Turner was never without a sketchbook (opposite), and early on formed the habit of sketching in pencil outdoors,[12] often onto off-white paper, with intermittent experiments into the use of colour-washed paper or a second graphic medium, such as white chalk or else black or irongall ink. Such sketches helped to fix in his mind impressions of scenery, regions and building styles, as well as providing a source of images he would draw from decades later. Once indoors for the evening, he would add watercolour to some of the more developed sketches or *aides-mémoire*. He probably dried the paper, along with his clothes and boots, in front of the fire, though some of the early works on paper show rain spatters that attest to his ability to get the most from an interesting view, whatever the weather. His sketchbooks include some odd words and notes, including colour annotations concerning weather and sunsets. If Turner had been alive today, it is easy to imagine him making good use of smartphones and tablets, as modern artists who draw inspiration from landscape do now.

When temporary peace with France made cross-channel travel possible early in the new century, Turner made numerous sketches in the Louvre of significant artworks. In his life-long travels through western Europe, he mostly sketched scenery, groups of people in local costume or incidents that he saw, both indoors and out. He tended to begin a new sketchbook for each trip, but sometimes reused an old one, turning it over and working from the back. His trips have been studied both in the field and via his bank accounts,[13] and it is possible even today to line oneself up with a rapid landscape sketch in a remote area, look around for a convenient rock on which to sit or rest a foot, and find the same rock that Turner must himself have used.[14]

The compositions developed from these sketches, whose subjects are still recognizable in

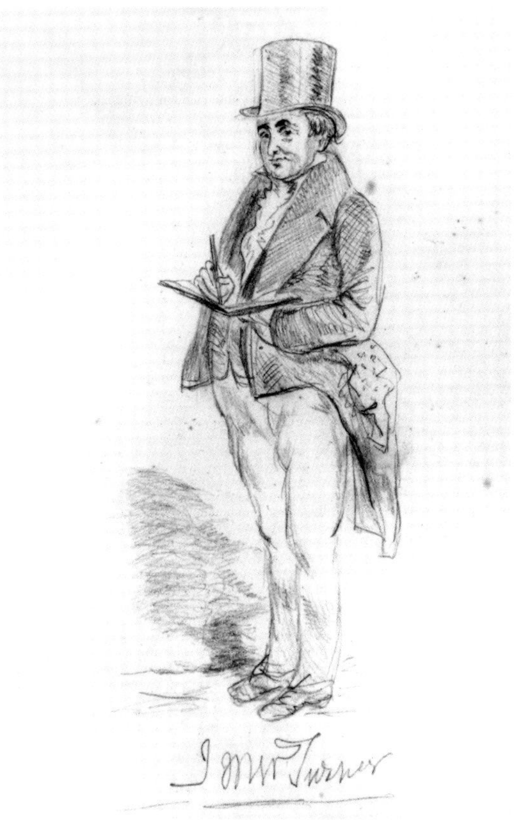

Charles Martin, *Joseph Mallord William Turner*, 1844. National Portrait Gallery, London

situ, were always developed into more picturesque, often more dramatic, scenes, with an increased number of romantic and sublime mountains. The foregrounds would include human incidents that had in reality occurred in another place and time, yet were brought in with consummate skill, where some local or bright/contrasting colour was clearly (to Turner) demanded. This is an engraver's skill, and one that was admired by John Ruskin:

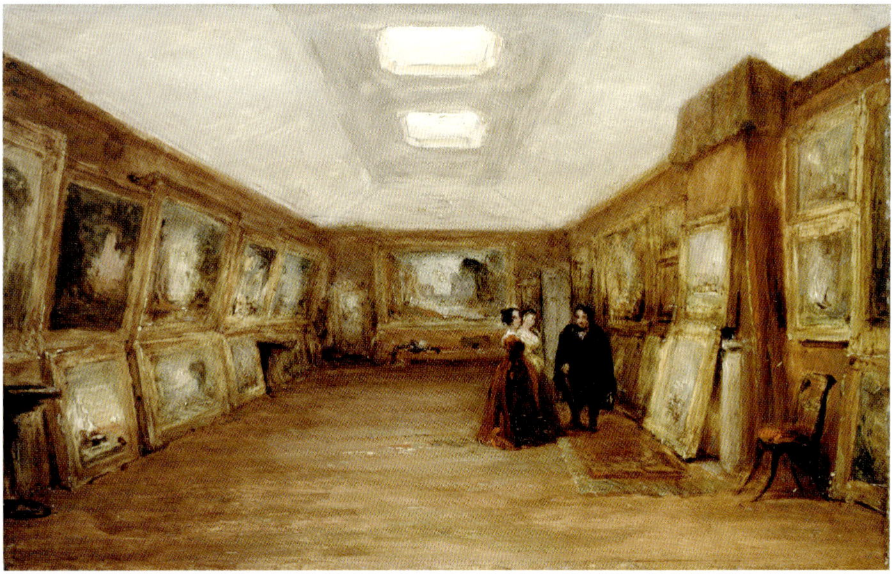

George Jones, *Interior of Turner's Gallery: The Artist Showing his Works*, 1852.
Ashmolean Museum, University of Oxford

It is one thing to know where a piece of blue or white is wanted, and another to make the wearer of the blue apron or white cap come there, and not look as if it were against her will.[15]

The importation of dramatic weather experienced on an entirely different occasion, perhaps a violent storm or an especially lovely sunset, requires the skill of a poet. This poetic facility existed inside Turner's head, even if it did not flow in words with equal felicity, as when he chose to exhibit oil paintings, especially in the early years, with excerpts from his never-completed poem, *The Fallacies of Hope.*

Connoisseurs, patrons and art critics had very clear ideas of what they expected to see at the Royal Academy's annual exhibition, where Turner exhibited regularly from 1796. He also exhibited work at the newly created British Institution, founded in 1805, and built his own gallery in Queen Anne Street as an extension to his house and workspace, for showing work to potential clients outside the exhibition season. It was sketched by George Jones (1786–1869), a fellow artist and friend, after Turner's death (above). It is not known exactly how Turner arranged and rearranged the paintings there over the years. We do know that the walls were red, but not the exact tone.[16]

Reynolds's lectures had hugely influenced public taste.[17] He had styled history painting as the loftiest art, because pictures should have a historical narrative (with an emphasis on the classical world) or tap into national pride. The wealthy upper classes, who had long been the main purchasers of art, knew and understood classical languages and subjects, and successful artists reflected their tastes and experiences back to them. Compositions were admired for their large scale and breadth of content and allusion – one reason why landscape painting, and particularly small-scale watercolours of landscapes, were regarded as inferior to oil paintings. The modern world of industrialization, political unrest and social change could only be painted through the lens of historical precedent. Past masters of the genre were revered and emulated. To Turner, and many others, the most significant of these was Claude Lorrain (*c.* 1600–1682), considered by the generations that followed as incapable of being surpassed. This was an artist worth learning from, and emulating.

Romantic themes that imbued the viewer with wonder and an admiration akin to a religious experience grew in popularity in the years following Reynolds's death in 1792. Turner's art, therefore, had to respond to these dual aspects of the zeitgeist, and this explains why he moved from watercolour to oil at a young age: oil paintings had far more prestige. It is also the reason that his earliest works resemble those of his contemporaries more than his later works do. Turner had to prove himself first, before showing the world that he could match and often surpass the best of the masters. He excelled at painting landscapes, but to be perceived as a serious member of that profession, he had to apply himself diligently and successfully to the understanding and use of classical allusions and historical analogies.

The all-important audience and potential purchasers for a young artist's work looked for skill in composition and a high level of technical competence, as well as the correct and thoughtful application of classical and historical references. Imagination and creativity were all very well, but at best these were among the core aims of painting, rather than the only ones. Tonal harmony and a clear subject, preferably an elevating one that would uphold public morality and boost national pride, were key. Finely honed comparisons of the British present to past eras of peace and prosperity were also acceptable.

As an artist, Turner was continually inventive and willing to try new materials and ways of working. Because he tried out almost every artist's material invented in his lifetime – unusual, when one compares the practice of his contemporaries, as well as successors – one cannot state that he 'always' did anything or 'invariably' used any one material. *How Turner Painted* will describe the wide range of materials, tools and techniques that he employed often and with unconscious competence to create images of breathtaking beauty.

It is because his studio contents survive in the Turner Bequest, including unfinished works never shown in his lifetime, that we can see how the artist went about creating a composition. Apart from the sketchiest essays on canvas, made with only a few brushstrokes, it is always possible to visually 'crop' his compositions, and to find that the reduced image is still powerful. Balance of colour and form is the key to Turner's method, and he was a supreme colourist.

ONE

INNOVATIVE WAYS OF USING WATERCOLOUR

Turner's papers

All paper was handmade in Turner's lifetime, in sheets made in a variety of standard dimensions, ranging downwards from those large enough for maps and full-scale engravings of paintings. Papers were predominantly off-white in tone, and available in a huge range of thicknesses, roughness and absorbency. The dimensions of the larger sheets were based round the biggest and heaviest paper-making tray that could be held in two hands and dipped into a vat of wet fibres.

Wove paper had been invented before Turner's birth (right). It has none of the lines of texture imposed by the wires in the paper-maker's tray, which occur in laid paper, and is instead quite uniform, 'taking' paint similarly on both sides. Turner virtually always used this type, much of which was of medium weight and fairly smooth, with some examples being thinner and slightly more transparent.

Paper could be bought in bulk directly from a paper mill, where it would have been produced for anything from wrapping for food (which had to be absorbent) or ammunition (which required strength, as well as absorbency) to fine writing paper (which had to hold ink crisply on the surface without letting it flow in and smear). What was not made in large quantities was paper intended for drawing upon. This left aspiring artists to seek out paper types and tones from a far wider choice than we find today, with no standardized descriptions of colour or texture, or guarantees

that the perfect paper would be available again in the future. The manufacturing process was slow, and only successful over the cooler months. Stationers supplied paper in smaller quantities, or would bind up sketchbooks to order when provided with paper by the artist.

Absorbency was controlled by the amount of water-repelling 'size', made from animal glue, present in the slurry of fibres used for making the paper. Dipping each sheet into a vat of size as it was created and dried provided a surface coating of water repellency sufficient to keep the printer's ink crisp. When such paper was used by an artist working with paint made from coloured pigments suspended in water and gum, the surface size became disrupted and ultimately washed off, whether by soaking the whole sheet,

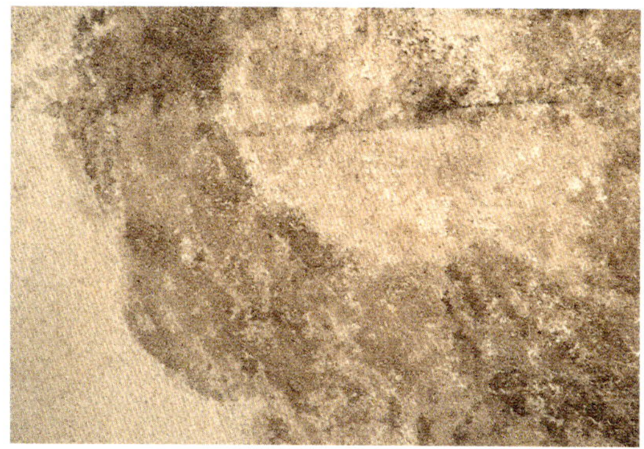

Micrograph of *Bridge and Cows*, showing the regular texture of wove off-white paper (detail; full work ill. p. 34)

applying a wet brush to certain areas or simply applying paint locally and repeatedly, with plenty of brush action.

Turner's papers were mostly well sized with gelatine-based animal glue. This was good for drawing upon with pencil, and gave the most options for varying the effect of the brush when it first made contact with the paper. These ranged from laying down rather dry washes that left a hard edge as they dried, to pre-wetting the whole sheet so that the pigment settled softly between paper fibres without leaving any tide lines, to scratching at the drying surface so that the still-wet paint flowed into the less-sized bulk of the paper, thus varying the intensity of colour or revealing the colour of the paper. To survive the scratching and scraping of Turner's working processes, the paper had to be strong. Sizing could be uneven, creating spots of greater or lesser absorption of colour to be integrated into the evolving image. The degree of sizing added can be assessed by shaking the sheet and listening to the rustling sound it makes; well-sized paper will sound louder.

The main ingredient for paper-making at the time was linen, obtained from rags that came from worn-out clothing. Cotton fibres from the same source were also mixed in. Standard cheap paper was 'whitey-brown', because the rag mixture always ended up as that colour naturally, whereas high-quality papers made from carefully sorted pale rags were whiter. Off-white paper, therefore, came in a wide range of tones, which in the years following production would alter gradually, as it was washed or exposed to light, dirt and dust. It is easy to see that a paper made as 'off-white' or 'cream' (the terms tended to be used interchangeably) was distinct from buff, brown or coloured, but it is impossible to say with certainty whether it began its life darker or lighter than it is now. If the paper has been badly treated, or exposed to light for decades, it becomes darker (opposite, left) and, in the worst cases of over-exposure, straw-coloured. Papers were not routinely bleached during manufacture in Turner's day, but washing, bleaching and other treatments over time, all difficult to detect today, can lighten the colour.

Turner's papers have been studied in detail: there are thousands of sheets in the Tate's collection.[18] In a majority of cases they are off-white or cream, since that is the colour he most often chose, after his earliest years, for his numerous sketchbooks, some of which were likely bound from his personally selected papers cut down to the size he specified. The three hundred or so sketchbooks thus account for many thousands of 'works'. Each sheet has a watermark created during the paper-making process, which enables identification of the maker, and sometimes the period of production to within a few years. When the sheet has been trimmed, however, these watermarks may be chopped through, and only appear sporadically in the sketchbooks.

There are numerous examples in Turner's sketchbooks of high-quality, smooth, off-white wove papers, made by Whatman, many with the date 1794 or 1801 incorporated in the watermark.[19] The company, which supplied the best variety of papers in Britain, traded near Turner's childhood homes, so he had access to the best from his earliest years, just as he did for other painting materials.

Shields Lighthouse, once covered by a window mount that protected a substantial border of paper on all sides

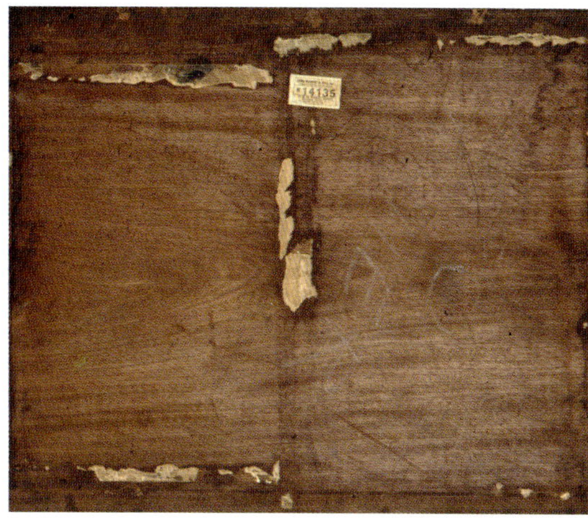

Reverse of *George IV's Departure from the 'Royal George'*, used by Turner as a sketching board (full work ill. p. 44)

In later life, he would choose middle-weight, off-white wove papers, straight from the mill and supplied in bulk. These were produced as writing papers of good quality, but were not the most expensive product available.

Using the paper

When Turner worked on loose paper, rather than in a sketchbook, it was usually torn from sheets, against a straight edge, into halves, quarters and eighths. This means that large numbers of his watercolours are now in fairly standard formats, and some can even be linked together by their common paper support. Sized paper contracts quite powerfully when fully wetted, so these standard formats can vary in length and height by a few millimetres, even if they had not been trimmed of their neatly torn edges in the 19th century, as many works in the Turner Bequest were.

Turner learned from an early age to work within this format without allowing the evolving composition to outgrow the paper (it was the same with his canvases, many of them in standard formats). This was not a skill that was universal among watercolourists, some of whom pasted extensions to their papers; Turner himself virtually never needed to do this.

Painting in watercolour on a single sheet of paper had traditionally been done by taping the sheet to a board on all four sides, or by gluing it down round the edges. This was necessary because the glue size responds strongly to its first wetting. Unrestrained paper would 'cockle' as it dried, developing wavy deformations out of plane, sometimes a few millimetres high. The paper would then need to be humidified or dampened and flattened in a press afterwards, which would be very tedious for a busy artist.

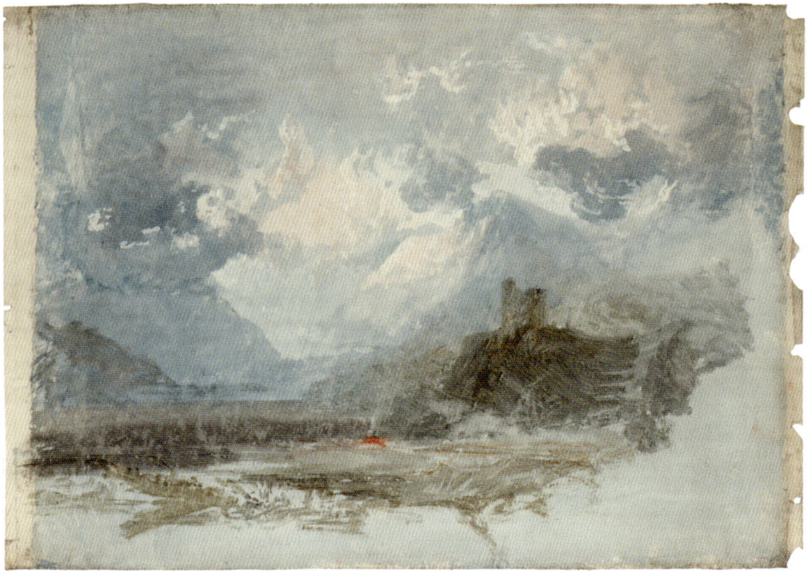

Dolbadarn Castle: Colour Study, ?1799–1800, Tate, London. This has gelatine stopping out
for the dramatic clouds

Turner occasionally glued his paper down at all edges, using the back of a panel support with an unfinished painting on the front. After painting, he would loosen the paper with a knife and rip off several sheets. The torn edges, held down with animal glue (the same glue he would dilute with water and use for stopping out, perhaps), can still be seen (p. 23, right). Some sheets were nearly as big as the board; others were torn in half, with both halves glued down. Whatever he was painting, intense washes of madder and blue paint were left behind when the paper was pulled away from the board. The edges of *Dolbadarn Castle: Colour Study* (above) were taped down, possibly to make it easier to apply the untypical initial wash of blue.[20]

In fact, a smooth drawing board, unmarred by paper residues, can be used just by smoothing a wet light- to medium-weight paper down on top. This restrains it sufficiently, if the composition is worked across the whole sheet while it remains damp. There were eyewitness accounts of Turner plunging small boards with handles on the back into a bucket of water to keep the paper wet. The later application of fine details in wet paint after the paper had dried – the size already soaked into submission, or washed off – would not make the paper cockle. This sounds a better method for a fast-working artist like Turner than gluing, taping or pinning paper to a board. (The latter is not a method he used, since we do not see any pin-holes, even in the untrimmed papers.)

Light-blue papers were a frequent choice from the 1820s, especially for sketches made while Turner stayed with his friends at Petworth House in West Sussex (ill. p. 119), and when he made watercolours from his French travels in the 1830s. These papers were often French and Dutch in origin. Some, like the off-white papers he had used on earlier tours, were likely purchased from paper mills as he travelled, chosen with the same care he exercised at home.

When he was buying in Britain, Turner purchased stout blue papers made by Bally, Ellen and Steart on many occasions: these were quality papers in the colour range he liked, carefully sized during production, and suitable for the rather ferocious brushing and scraping that occurred when he was working fast and creatively. His blue papers were coloured with fibres that came from blue rags (above right), and usually included fibres from a few other rags of different colours, giving each sheet a unique tone.

In the early years, Turner used some light brown or buff papers, rarely dark brown and only occasionally flecked, producing papers that were usually greyish. Very textured or low-quality paper is rare but not unknown, and he clearly tried out many different types, as he honed his preferences and learned how to get the most from well-sized, strong papers that could survive a lot of punishment – if the mood took him – without ripping when wet. Turner did occasionally use oil paint on paper, which would need a preparatory layer to protect it, just as canvas does. On these occasions, he worked at a smaller scale and with smaller brushes than on canvas, and did not develop

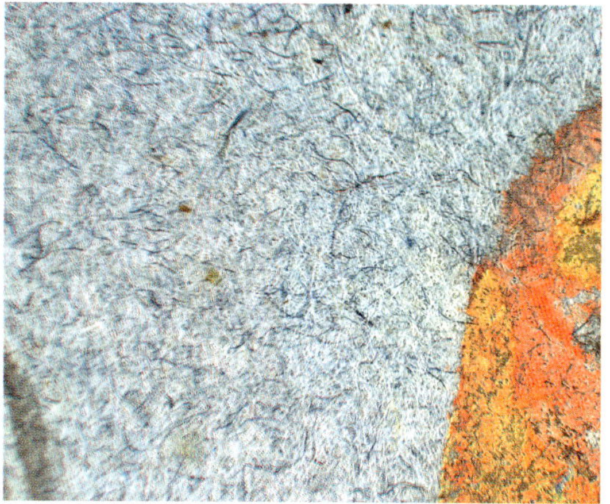

Micrograph of the blue paper of *A Family Seen from Behind* (full work ill. overleaf), made from off-white and blue rags, and close to its original tone

such studies into a painting for exhibition, instead leaving aside some unfinished studies of the sea (below). He sometimes used millboard, an inexpensive compressed paper product that lent itself to outdoor work, because it was rigid, like modern canvas boards, and easier to transport home.

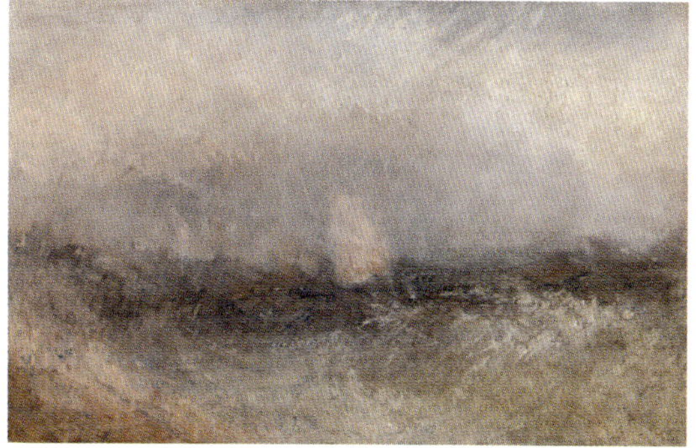

Off the Nore, 1840–45. Yale Center for British Art, New Haven

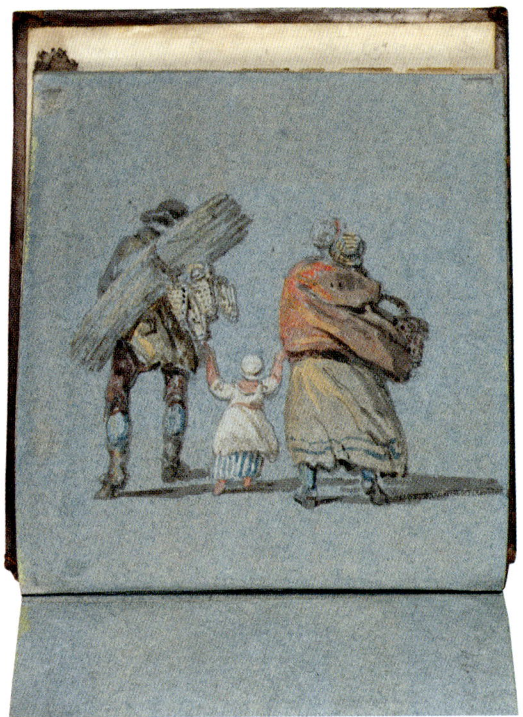

A Family Seen from Behind: A Man with a Bundle and a Woman Carrying an Infant; a Small Girl between them, 1796. Tate, London

Drawing had been key to the development of a traditional 'watercolour drawing', and instruction manuals would continue to proscribe it, followed by colouring in, throughout Turner's lifetime. His earliest work includes light underdrawing to establish the composition, but he quickly began to use freely applied washes of colour for some clouds, then whole skies, and soon trees and small details, bypassing the need to draw first. Turner painted onto most papers directly in watercolour, without any coloured wash to tone them, and hardly any of his papers were purchased with a pre-applied ground to smooth the texture. At least one early sketchbook has a range of colour-washed papers bound in, with pale, dull red and mid-blue interspersed with sheets of the same off-white paper; pale lilac- and green-washed papers, rather than dipped papers with the colour on both sides, can be seen in another. The washes were hastily applied and rather uneven, which does not matter unduly since the sketchbooks were small in scale, but seem too uncontrolled to have been added by Turner himself.

When he selected a coloured paper, or a washed paper like these, he would use the colour as an integral part of the sketch. On some sketching tours, he might acquire grey or buff papers during the trip as his supplies ran low. These darker tones were sometimes sketched upon with ink, white chalk or a single colour of paint, such as yellow ochre, often together with a graphite pencil.

For off-white papers, and when he did not employ much or any pencil underdrawing, it is noticeable that the first brushload of colour Turner applied was more often a warm yellow or brown than a cool tone. If the first colour applied was brown, the next was likely to be a true colour for the depicted scene, rather than another brown or a neutral tone. For blue papers, the first brushload of colour was frequently yellow to establish a colour contrast, and the first few brushstrokes to establish the composition were generally transparent (above left). Heavier and often more localized and controlled strokes of opaque white gouache followed.

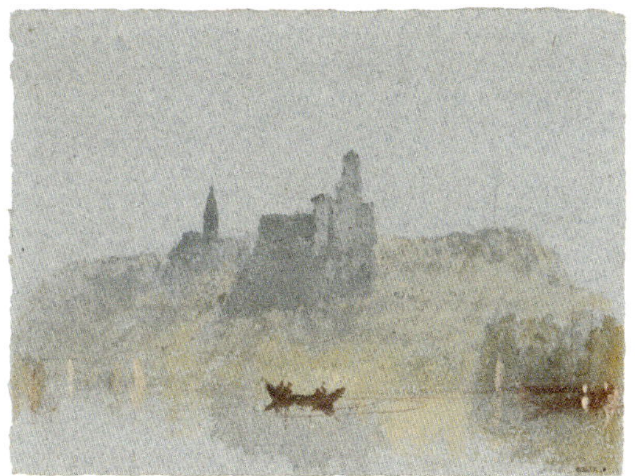

St-Florent-le-Vieil, Northern France, c. 1826–28.
Tate, London

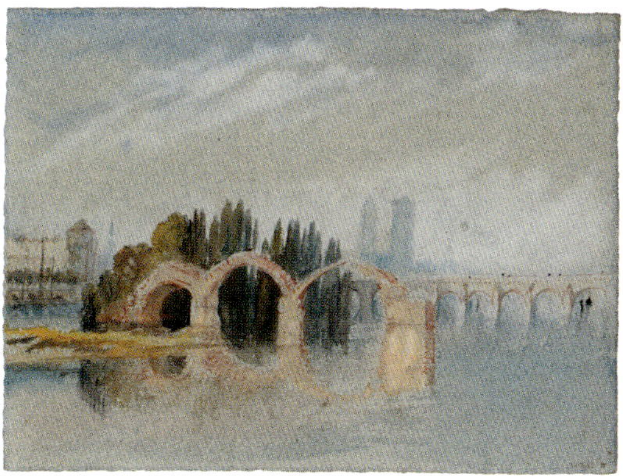

Ruins of the Old Pont Eudes, Tours, c. 1826–28.
Tate, London

Turner also combined the yellow and red pigments he had already used as transparent washes with such white or, less commonly, blue pigments if needed for sea or sky. The blue of the paper could be used directly for sky or water in a swift sketch (above left), or rapidly worked with transparent blue washes to add nuances of tone to such areas.

Clouds always required opaque paint, for example in *Ruins of the Old Pont Eudes, Tours* (above right). Here, the two bridges, trees and more distant buildings to the left were freely painted in watercolour washes with careful placing, since the reflection of the nearer bridge and the trees, and the buildings on the far bank, define the full reach of the river, represented by the blue paper and a few light-blue watercolour washes. Less pale blue washes and thin applications of white gouache define the sky. The pigments used include vermilion (sometimes combined with lead white for paler pink areas), mid-chrome yellow, yellow and brown ochres (combined with black for the

trees) and possibly cobalt blue. This process of using colour is almost as quick and instinctive as sketching, and in many of Turner's sketches on blue paper would have been faster than working on the same subject on off-white paper.

Traditional watercolour practice involved transparent washes of colour, none applied so thickly as to obscure the colour of the paper, and rather static compositions, such as topographic views. It had been employed for battlefield planning and land surveying in just this way, as a means of documentation. Some of the coloured pigments employed for this purpose, such as blue indigo and sap green, had such poor tinting strength that they were incapable of producing intense or opaque-looking colours. Earth tones that could produce dark reddish-brown to greenish-brown hues were also used thinly; black was employed for shadows as a light grey wash; intense (and more costly) colours such as crimson lakes or vermilion were reserved only for details that demanded them, such as military uniforms.

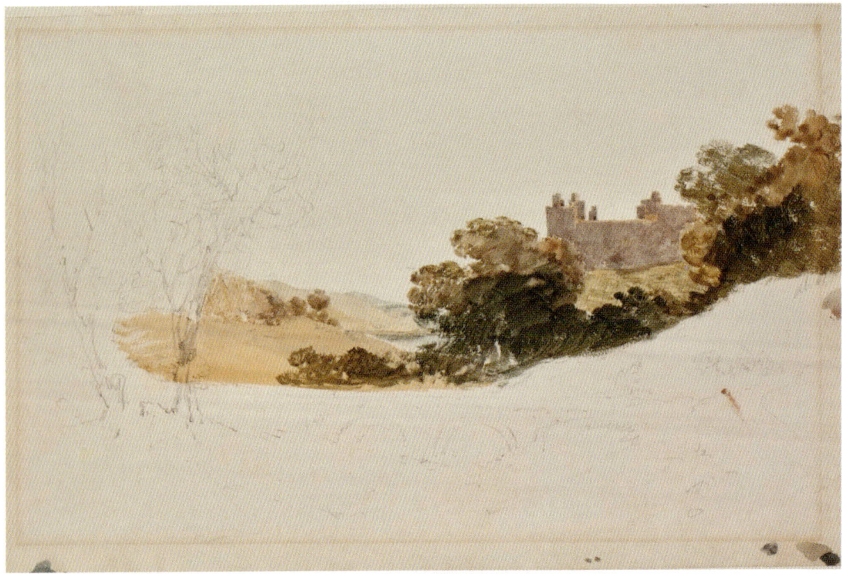

Linlithgow Palace, Scotland, 1801. Indianapolis Museum of Art

Such traditional methods never included the additive process of applying white paint for highlights. Turner's very early watercolours have a similar appearance, but soon he began to leave areas of the paper unpainted whenever his composition included clouds, fallen masonry or patches of sunlight to contrast with deep shadows. He developed subtractive processes that involved the selective removal of applied colour to reveal the paper by washing and scratching out. Such processes mandate a deliberate choice of paper colour from the outset – a choice the artist rarely offered himself when painting in oil.

Watercolour materials

Turner's earliest watercolours include all of the limited range of pigments used by most watercolour artists. These would be applied as pale transparent washes in the 18th-century style, generally to an underdrawing in graphite pencil, as seen in *Linlithgow Palace, Scotland* (above). His friend Thomas Girtin used the same range, which is why the work of these two talented young artists can look similar. They probably explored new techniques together, discovered exciting shades of pigments and the colourmen who were selling them, and learned from one another.

It is only towards the end of his life that we can ascertain from which artists' colourmen Turner obtained his materials. He purchased hard watercolour blocks from the firms of Winsor & Newton, Reeves and Newman, and the latter was reported by Turner's executors as his regular supplier (see also 'Painting as cookery'; p. 43).

These companies, like all the colourmen, stamped the name of their firm or a recognizable trade symbol on one side of the block, and often the name of the pigment on the other. A few of these can still be read on Turner's improvised travelling palettes, two examples of which survive today (ill. p. 110). Formed from leather, which would be wrapped over the wet blocks after use, they are compact when folded, more or less water-proof and fit into a pocket. Opened out, they hold about two dozen watercolour blocks, glued onto canvas or a stiff card printed with an invitation to the prestigious annual dinner at the Royal Academy. Both palettes were used extensively, the blocks clearly replaced with new ones as needed, so that only a few makers' inscriptions can still be identified.

While still in his teens, Turner began to make significant use of the more brightly coloured pigments (see right), vermilion and mars orange (a synthetic ochre). Vermilion had long been used, though sparingly, by watercolourists, since it was essential for illustrating natural-history specimens, such as flowers and tropical birds. For summer skies, he added washes of clear, bright blue, employing first indigo, and later Prussian blue in the 1800s. The new cobalt blue proved to be equally good, its greenish tone perfect for depicting noon and afternoon skies. For the redder blue of an evening sky, he turned to smalt or natural ultramarine, both glassy pigments that give intense colours when the pigment particles are large. Turner obtained these two colours with enormously large particles, when compared to those used later in the century, suggesting that he sought out colourful examples.

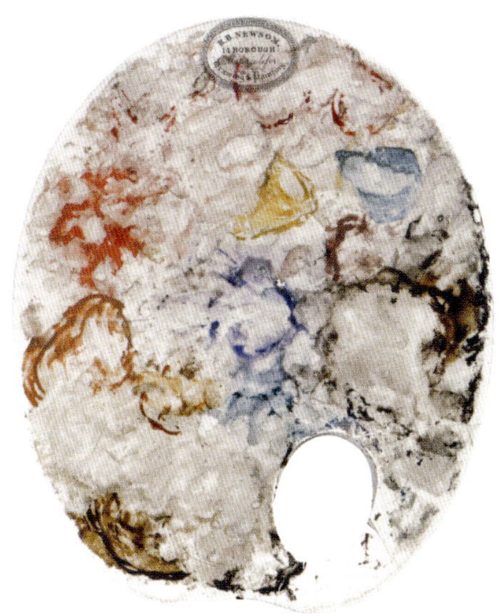

Watercolour palette owned by J.M.W. Turner. Royal Academy of Arts, London

In his youth Turner would use any of the brown earth pigments mixed with indigo blue for dull greens, and the same browns with Prussian blue for brighter tones. For the brightest shades of green, he would mix Prussian blue and yellow ochre. Mixing black and a bright yellow also gives a range of olive tones, which are good for landscapes. Such mixtures are known as optical greens. Optical purples are made from mixtures of blue and red: indigo with red ochre or Indian red for a brownish purple; Prussian blue for a more intense slate colour; or Prussian blue and one of his many shades of red lakes for the purple clouds that form just when the sun is setting (see *Richmond, Yorkshire* [ill. p. 97], which includes a mulberry-coloured madder lake with iron in the substrate, Indian yellow and Prussian blue).

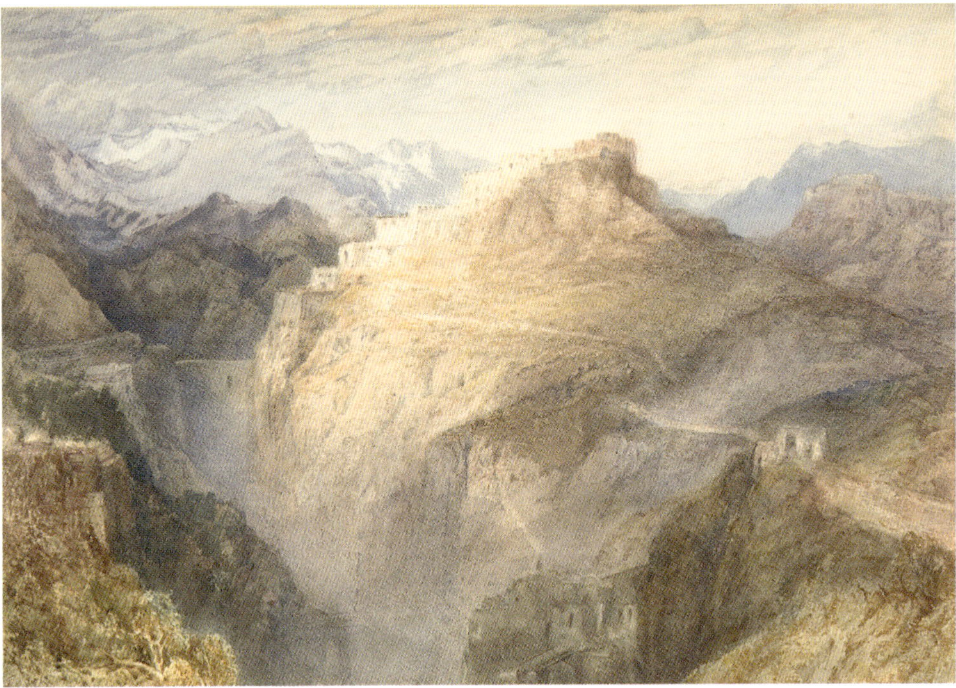

Fort of L'Essillon, Val de la Maurienne, France, 1836. The Metropolitan Museum of Art, New York

Nuanced grey clouds can easily be created using such mixtures of the type seen in *Fort of L'Essillon* (above). This method gives such a wonderful variety of tones that many artists accustomed to using optical greens never, or rarely, made use of the newly invented pure-green pigments. Turner simply added such greens to his stock, and then applied them as pure colours. He would not live long enough to see the invention of pure purple pigments, which could explain why he used such a variety of red lakes, all excellent for optical purples in watercolour.

The blue papers Turner used regularly from the 1820s (ill. p. 119), with bright opaque reds like vermilion and mid-toned opaque yellows like chrome yellow, soon led him to apply these primary colours to white paper, with more transparent washes. Vermilion worked equally well for this, as did both mid-toned and pale-lemon chrome yellow. For off-white papers, the best blue as a complementary colour is ultramarine; smalt is also good. Natural ultramarine, which Turner always used in preference to the manufactured variety, was expensive, but not much is needed for a sky. This became his favourite combination for warm and cool washes on white paper, and was likely used for *A Yorkshire River* and *Inverary Pier, Loch Fyne: Morning* (opposite, above left and right).

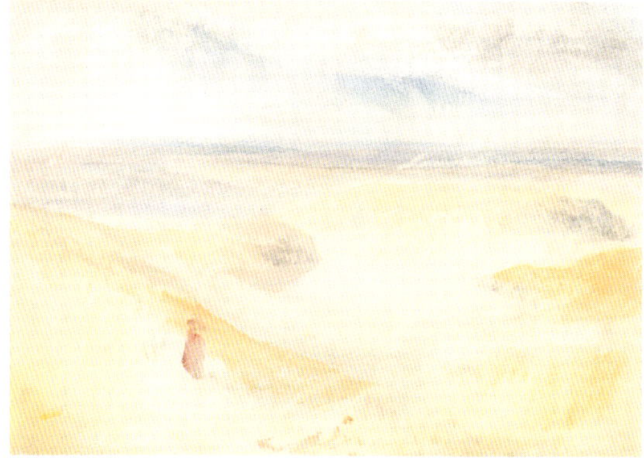

A Yorkshire River, c. 1827. National Gallery of Art, Washington, DC

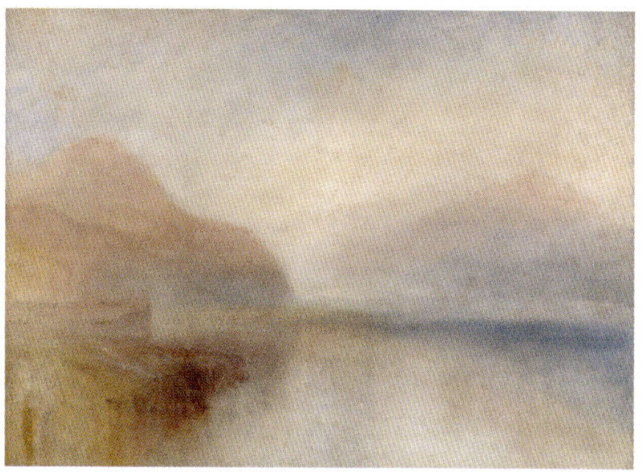

Inverary Pier, Loch Fyne: Morning, c. 1845. Yale Center for British Art, New Haven

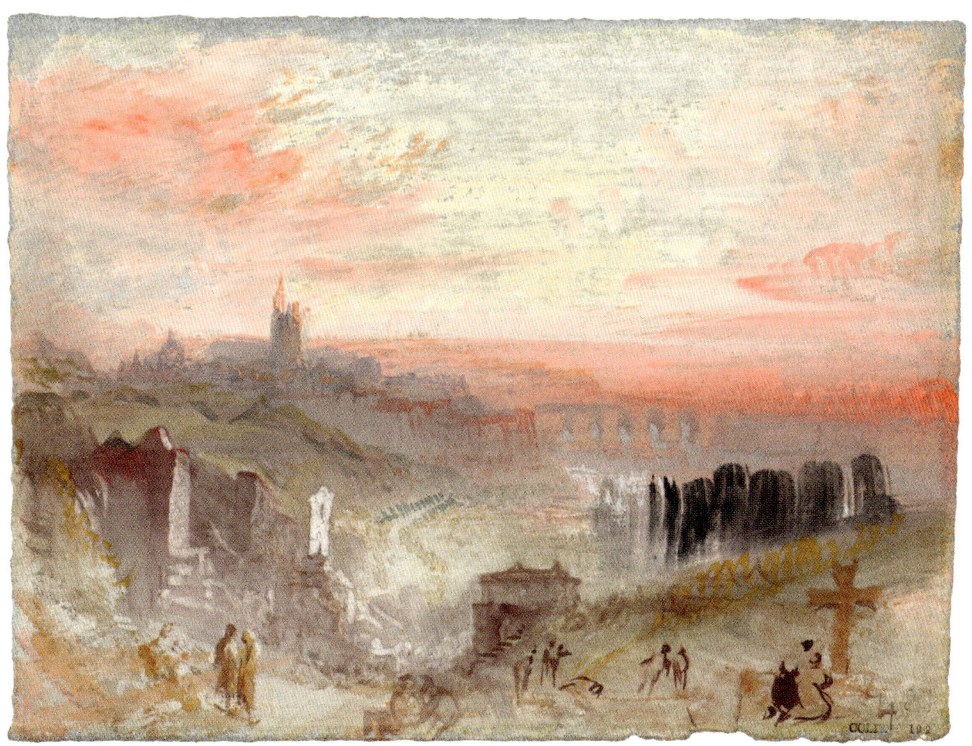

A View of Metz from the North, c. 1839. Tate, London

Further contrast could be introduced by using Indian red as a warm colour and the greener Prussian blue as a cool colour, with mixtures of mingled washes of warm and cool pigments creating a warm brown that harmonized with the purer hues. The deepest darks in such a system need either a dense application of this type of brown, or a very localized brushstroke of pure lamp black or ivory black. On a blue paper, well covered with paint, the local use of pure black, as well as warm brown, is also effective (previous page, bottom).

Creating highlights

Off-white paper of itself provides a highlight if left unpainted. Light-coloured stone in a landscape can be depicted readily by leaving large areas unpainted, as in the bridge in *Matlock* (below left). Even the unpainted reserve in a buff paper can be made to look bright and light by an artist using colour skilfully and effectively. In *High Force, Fall of the Tees, Yorkshire* (below right), the sun on the foreground

rocks is, in fact, unpainted white paper, while the waterfall was created by scraping out paint with a sharp tool.

When painting a localized bright area such as the sun or the moon, simply leaving a small unpainted area within the sky will work to dramatic effect if the surrounding colours are dark, or carefully graduated to create varied depth of colour. Applying the wash to dry paper so that it acquires a hard-edged perimeter as it dries makes the circle of light appear more intense. This circle of lightness can be preserved while the sky is worked up by stopping out, or applying gum or glue size neatly into the planned reserve of white paper with short, curling brushstrokes to prevent any subsequent enthusiastic passes of a brush for clouds, moonlight, and so on from sullying the light circle.

This was a likely process for the moon in *Alnwick Castle* (opposite). It would take a premeditated application of paint to create a more carefully planned wispy cloud scudding across

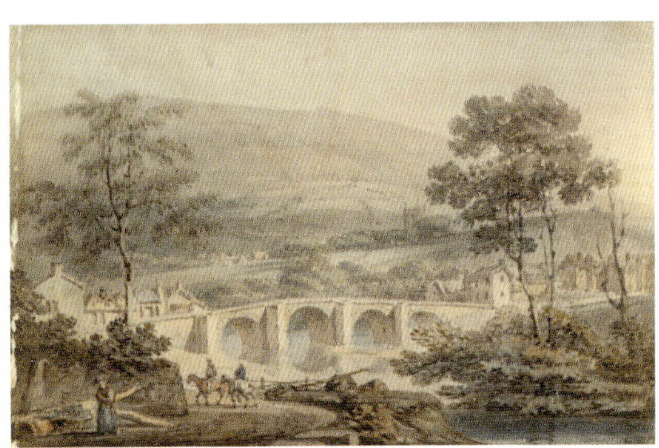

Matlock, 1794. Indianapolis Museum of Art

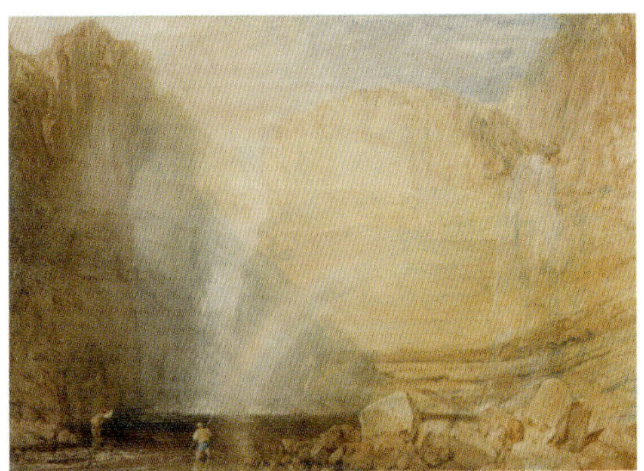

High Force, Fall of the Tees, Yorkshire, 1816.
Art Gallery of New South Wales, Sydney

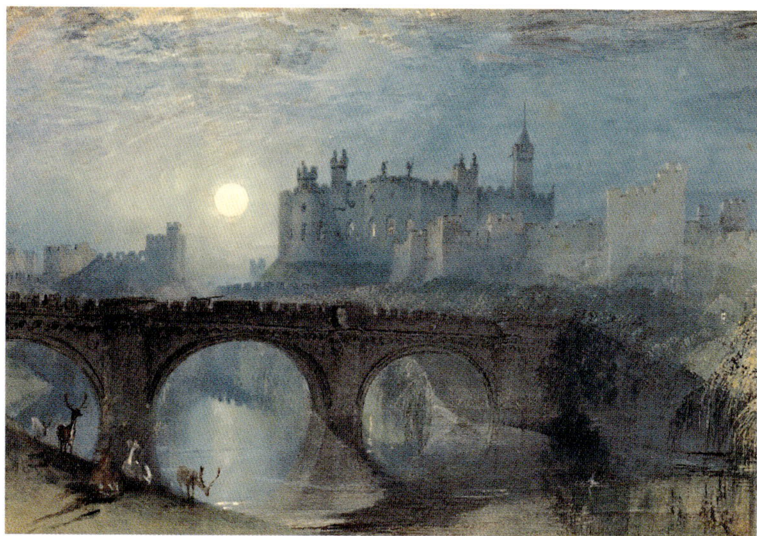

Alnwick Castle, c. 1829. Art Gallery of South Australia, Adelaide

such a moon, applied with a fine brush slowly enough to partially dissolve the stopping out, so that the paint would remain on the paper – an effect Turner did not employ for *Alnwick Castle*, though he did use it elsewhere. Sweeping over an earlier wash of colour with a brushload of clean water creates low-key and soft-edged lighter areas, especially if the coloured wash has not yet dried.

Here, the patch of reflected moonlight in the water was probably created by this means. Picking out details from dried colour with a small, wetted brush, held upright to make it into a very fine pointed tool, gives a sharper and more clearly outlined local light, as was done for the castle windows – clearly with a steady hand – which appear lit from within. This implies that these details were more premeditated than spontaneous in their execution. Such work can be done even a few days

after painting and initial drying. Choosing where to apply one deft, dark brushstroke for a distant bird that will give depth to the whole landscape would be a similarly meditative step.

Gentle abrasion of a dried coloured wash gives all the options of highlight in between the swift scratch and the planned lifting off of colour to reveal the paper. One traditional means of correcting small mistakes, or creating space for foreground detail to be applied last, was to use a piece of natural sponge, wet or dry; another was to use a piece of bread as an eraser. Professional artists who painted daily were advised to pinch out some dough from each day's loaf and retain it, which after a few days gave a range of textures, from doughy to craggy. Neither method leaves indisputable evidence of use, but both would have been effective on some of the monochrome

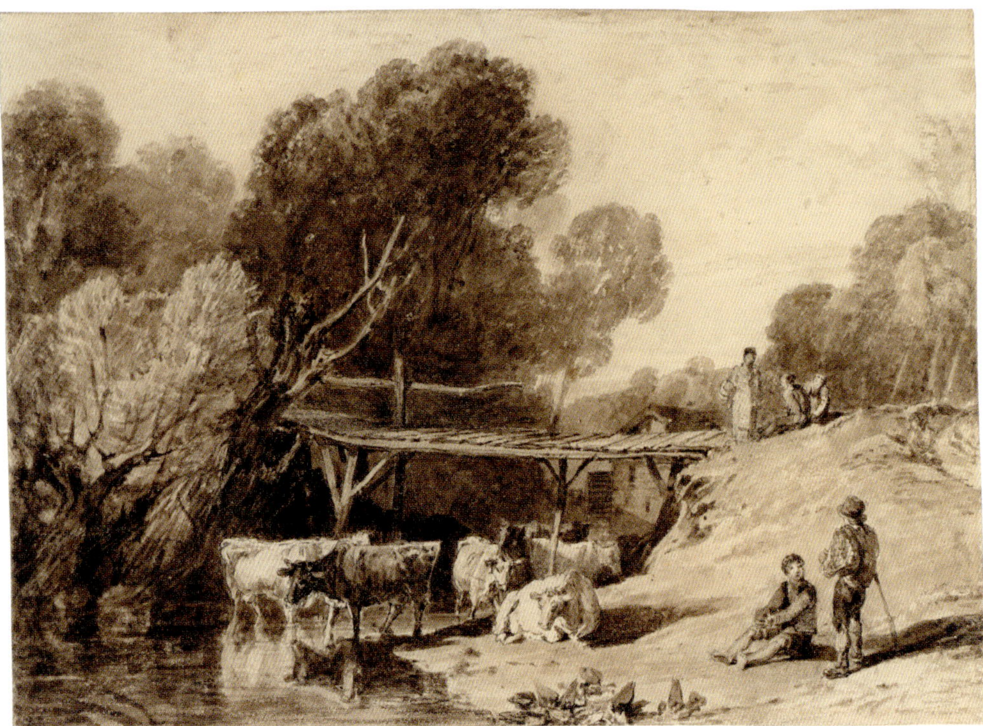

Bridge and Cows, c. 1806–7. Tate, London

watercolours painted to be engraved for the *Liber Studiorum*, notably *Bridge and Cows* (above), specifically the apron and arms of the woman in the distance (opposite, left), which are softer in outline than the washed-out reflections of the cows in the foreground (opposite, right) and the white-outlined branches overhanging the bridge.

Even at this early stage in Turner's career, a great variety of lights created by scratching out and lifting off of colour can be seen throughout the series – indeed, in these works he used more tools for scraping than he applied shades of brown, made from different pigments. Having acquired skills in engraving for this project, as noted earlier,

Turner therefore must have possessed needles, gravers and a roulette rocker (which creates parallel scratches), used alongside the wooden end of paintbrush handles and his fingernails – if, as contemporaries suggested, he kept them long and shaped for this purpose. Scratches that correspond to all of these tools are evident in many of the *Liber Studiorum* watercolours, which provide the clearest examples of use since there are no distractions from colour. Sometimes a few short, parallel scratches can be seen, which could have been made in wet paint with the roulette rocker. The highlights and rings created by the leaping fish in the foreground water of *Alnwick Castle* were scratched quite deeply, perhaps with a needle, while the softer scratches on the right bank could have been made with something blunter or broader, like a fingernail.

Fingerprints in the wet paint where Turner manipulated it, probably using all ten digits, can be seen in his watercolours from the first decade, and ever afterwards. Sometimes the dragging trail of a forefinger can be recognized, as in, for example, the mixed greenish marks in the foreground of *Kirkby Lonsdale* (ill. p. 104, bottom). Flicking with a sharp thumbnail was another process Turner was observed to use. It leaves a characteristic curved mark that is capable of replication, recognizably made by both left and right hands, suggesting a spontaneous scratch by the left hand as he painted, and possibly a more considered placement of a light by pausing to rest the brush in his other hand, before using his dominant right hand to put in a light.

Some of the most interesting marks caused by scraping out can be made with a sharp tool into very wet paint: after the brush is lifted, the scratch comes out darker than the paint. At some point during drying, the same scratch dries lighter than the surrounding paint. All of these subtractive methods must soon have become instinctive to Turner, which makes them harder to discern among the multitude of marks and paint manipulation in later and more finished works. The scratching out in *The Burning of the Houses of Parliament* (overleaf) includes this type of scratching into drying paint, and may include thumbnail scratches, as well.

Driving the colours about

Simply covering a sheet of paper with colour, and then re-wetting one of the colours to tease the paint into more detailed forms, is an effective means of developing a scene with an identifiable locality

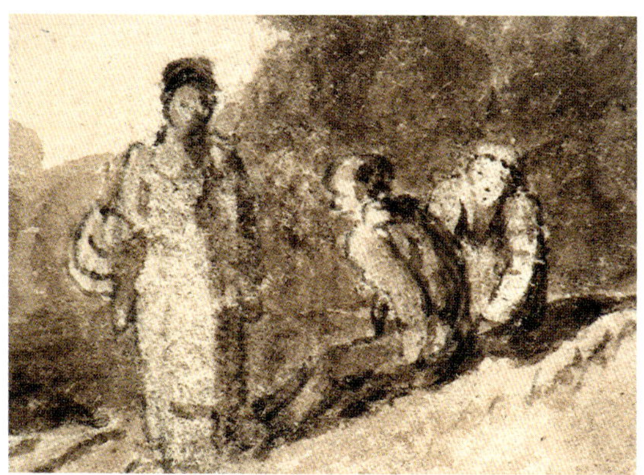

Detail from *Bridge and Cows* (opposite), showing the woman in the distance

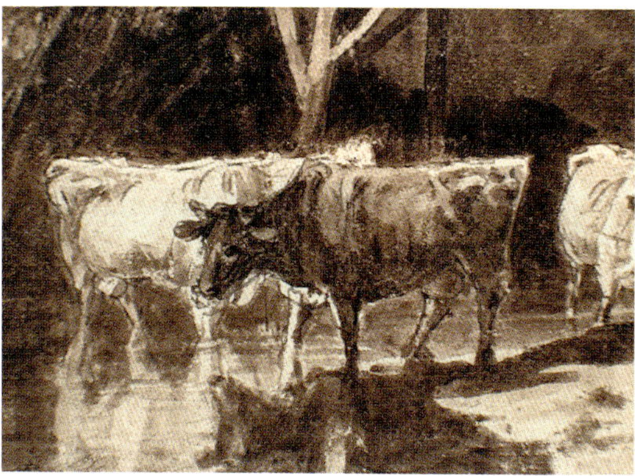

The cows in the foreground, created from a reserve of white paper, their reflections washed out with water

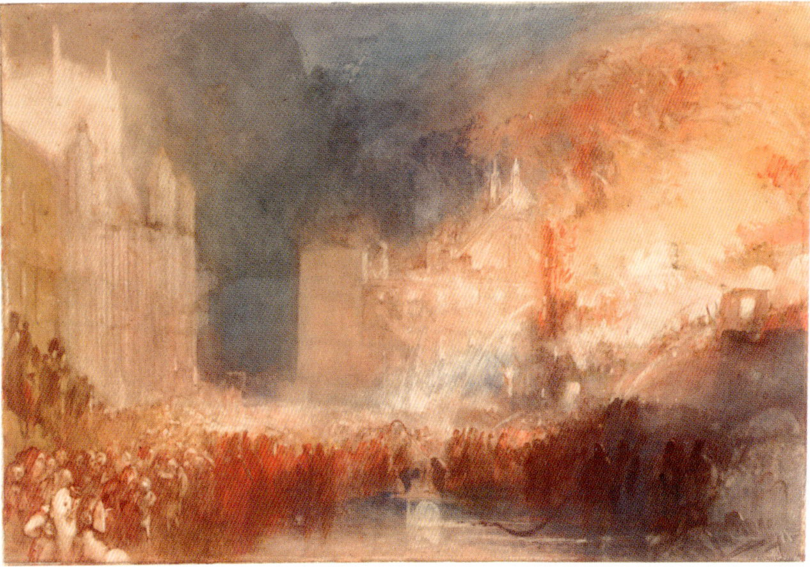

The Burning of the Houses of Parliament, c. 1834–35. Tate, London

from a colour beginning with infinite possibilities. Beneath the paint layer of *Storm Clouds over a Landscape at Sunset* (opposite, top) is a light, sketchy pencil drawing, establishing broad divisions between sea, land and sky. Turner did not follow these lines at all closely after he had soaked the paper and applied broadly horizontal washes of colour. The paint of the dark clouds was stirred around to heighten the dramatic effects already begun by the spontaneous movement of wet washes. Tilting or bending the paper would have encouraged the process (this was eminently possible, since there is no evidence to suggest the paper was taped or restrained during painting). The washes were worked with fingers and thumb, particularly where the near shore meets the water, to create further effects to be built upon (opposite, bottom).

The deep shade of chrome yellow is a very early use, though it loses impact when placed next to the deep blue-grey clouds and greenish-grey vegetation of the shoreline. The grey clouds were mixed from indigo and vermilion, while three pigments in combination made the dark greens of the distant trees on the horizon. The light areas below the dark cloud were washed out.

It is clear from examining Turner's part-developed compositions that he often worked purely in colour. This is the case for *Storm Clouds over a Landscape at Sunset*, and also for *Shields Lighthouse* (ill. p. 23), of the same date and on similar white wove paper. Dark washes of Prussian blue were stippled onto dry paper for the sky, washed over with purplish brown ochre to create greyer tones.

The lighter blue washes in Prussian blue were applied to wetter paper. Washing out was used for the moon and its reflection, leaving sufficient cleared white paper for the yellow radiance round the moon to be applied in chrome yellow, without the danger that it would overlap with a blue wash and appear green, rather than yellow. The reflection was also washed out, with a fairly large brush. Vermilion mixed with Prussian blue was used for the most crimson clouds.

While it is possible to see the individual steps Turner took to create lights in a less complex work, to control the wetness of the paper and the way a wash of paint would dry, or to apply and manipulate paint on the paper before it dried, it becomes impossible to follow his work, step by step, in a highly finished image such as *The Blue Rigi, Sunrise* (overleaf). Indeed, Turner could have applied his repertoire of methods in different orders, and still created a very similar image.

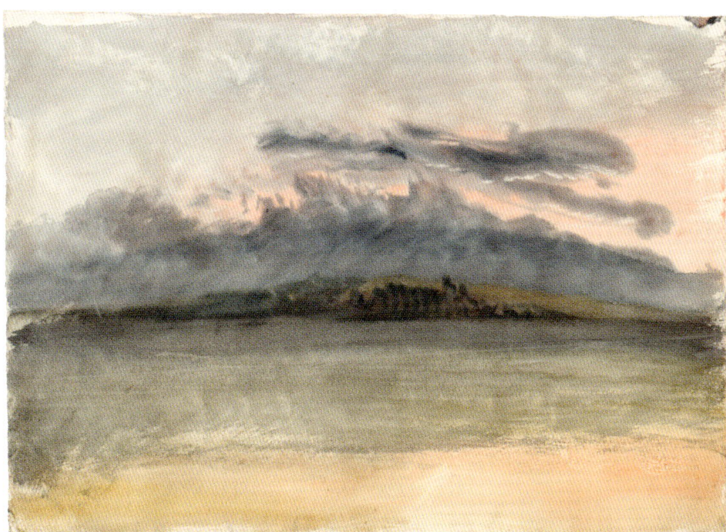

Storm Clouds over a Landscape at Sunset, c. 1823–26. Tate, London

Turner's fingerprints in the foreground and part of a Whatman watermark, viewed in reverse

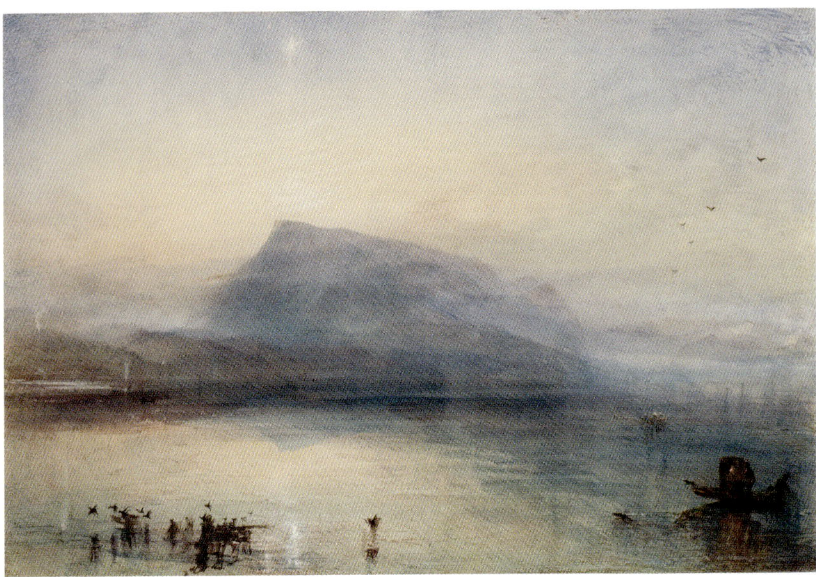

The Blue Rigi, Sunrise, 1842. Tate, London

It is impossible, even with a microscope, to deduce how many different blue pigments Turner used for this view of a mountain in the Swiss Alps, and how many other distinct colours there are elsewhere. The Rigi would appear less blue if not surrounded by the palest of yellow skies; the yellow less pale without the dark birds flying low over the black jetty in the foreground; and the width of the lake less dramatic without the birds flying high, close to the mountain. One can only marvel at the result.

Colour beginnings of the same locality – not necessarily made as studies for a finished work, but more likely done on a later trip – show different starting points for the same subject. *The Rigi and Lake Lucerne: Yellow and Rose* (opposite, top) – these have been titled by cataloguers, not by Turner himself – was begun with very wet paper and the palest of light washes for the clouds. As the paper dried, slightly more loaded washes of blue and rose were nudged around, so that they would dry as a more definite outline of the mountains. Then yellow was applied to complete the trio of primary colours. A colour beginning of a more distant view (opposite, bottom left) was taken one step further, but completed before the paper had begun to dry. Turner began another view with drier paper and denser brushloads of the same blue (opposite, bottom right), but mixed in yellow to the red, working quickly before the paper dried further. Any of these could have been the first steps in the making of the finished watercolour, which includes rubbing and wiping – even scratching, but not with as sharp a tool as a needle or a fingernail – as well as fine brushwork and delicate manipulation of wet paint on partly wet paper.

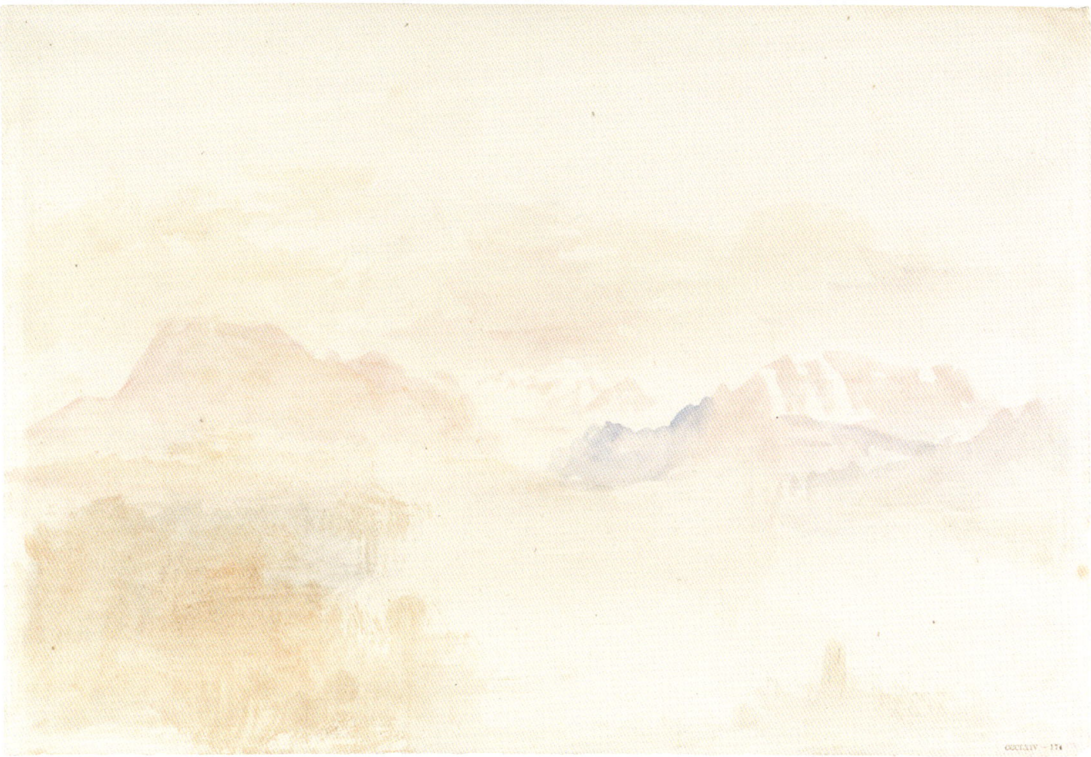

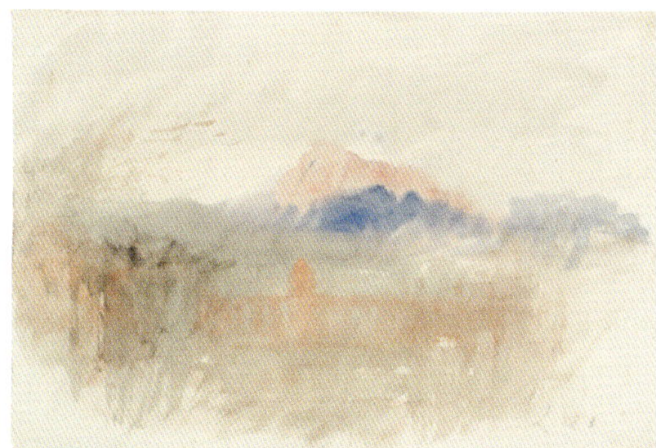

The Rigi and Lake Lucerne: Yellow and Rose, c. 1844. Tate, London

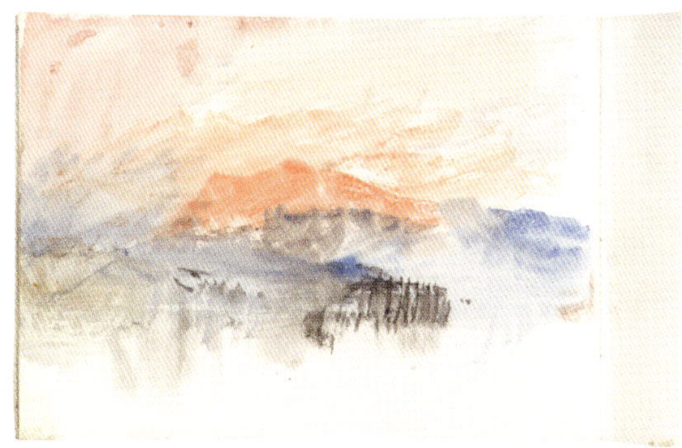

The Kapellbrücke at Lucerne, with the Blue and Rose Rigi in the Distance, c. 1844. Tate, London

The Red and Blue Rigi, 1844. Tate, London

These three colour beginnings of the Rigi would have taken less than a minute each. The finished watercolour might have been done all in one painting session, so over no more than the daylight hours in one day, but might not have been done outdoors, or even in Switzerland, whereas the colour beginnings were possibly done in situ, but more probably indoors after a day of intensive looking and active walking.

That this is possible can be illustrated by an anecdote from a trustworthy source, recounting the painting of *A First Rate Taking in Stores* (below) between breakfast and lunch (a period between roughly 9 or 10am and 3pm in the 1830s or '40s) for the son of Turner's friend, Walter Fawkes. The challenge was to depict the huge scale of such a ship, on a sheet of paper of normal size, and he met it admirably by including the small supply boat dwarfed by the huge battleship. The process of making this highly detailed and accurate watercolour was described by a family member:

He began by pouring wet paint onto the paper till it was saturated, he tore, he scratched, he scrubbed at it in a kind of frenzy and the whole thing was chaos – but gradually and as if by magic the lovely ship, with all its exquisite minutiae, came into being and by luncheon time the drawing was taken down in triumph.[21]

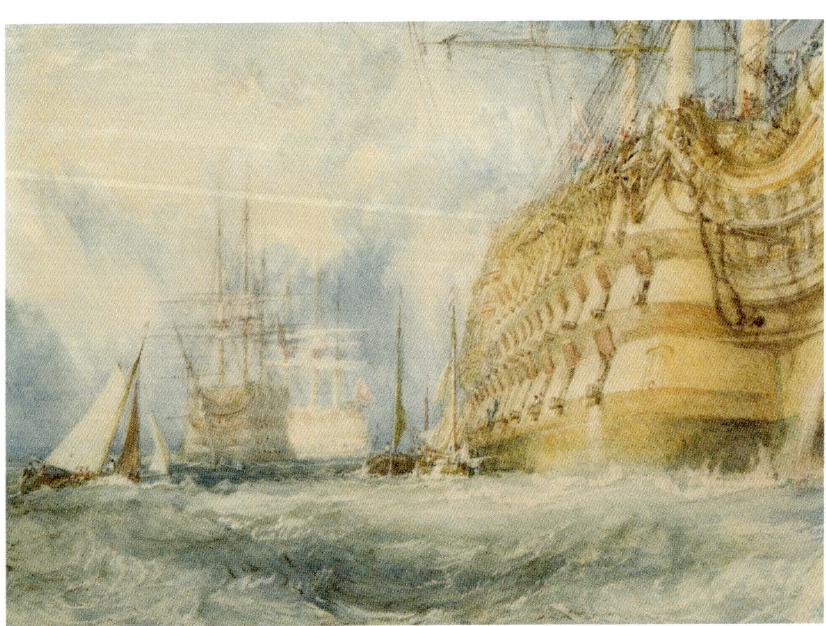

A First Rate Taking in Stores, 1818. Cecil Higgins Art Gallery, Bedford

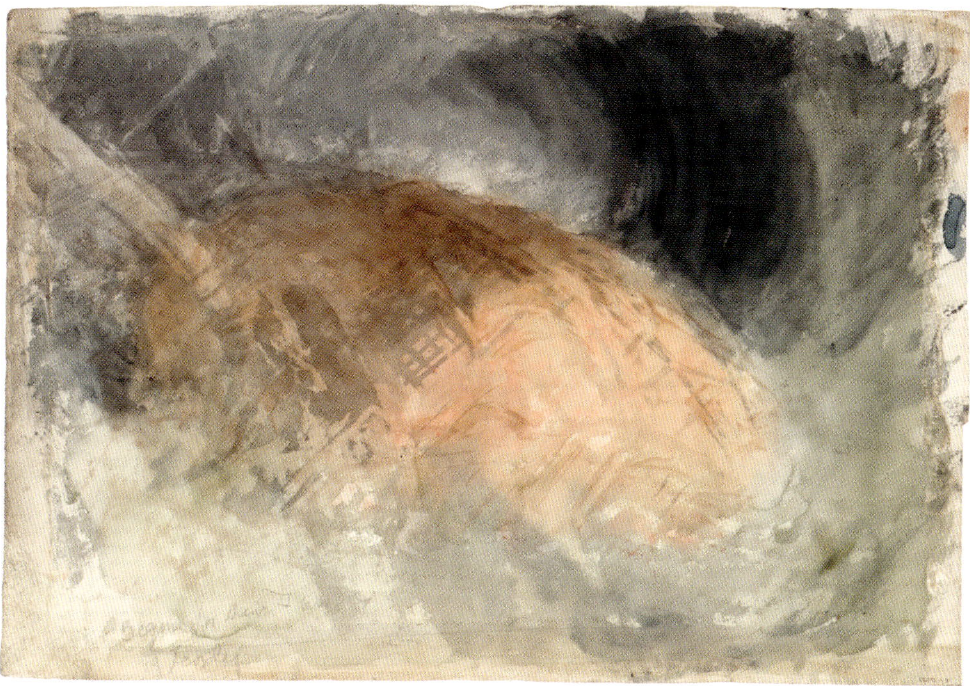

Study for 'The Loss of an East Indiaman', c. 1818. Tate, London

The number of pigments is likely quite limited, including a yellow ochre shade for the ship, applied at many different densities, one blue for the sea and another for the water, perhaps combined with the same yellow, and telling areas of probably just one red for the clothing of the tiny men aboard both vessels, applied as a lighter wash for the opened gun-ports. One can imagine that the initial 'chaos' might have resembled the colour beginning for *Study for 'The Loss of an East Indiaman'* (above), which shows the badly listing hull in a maelstrom of waves and scudding dark clouds, most of the paper covered, but not all of the brushstrokes yet making sense to anyone other than Turner himself. This, too, has a limited tonal range that includes vermilion and red lake mixed in for the threatening grey clouds, as well as indigo. It is a rare untrimmed example, showing how the artist made use of the margins for colour trials as he mixed his paints.

TWO

MAKING OIL PAINT DO EVERYTHING TURNER WANTED: MODIFIED PAINT MEDIA

Painting as cookery

Oil-based paint is far more plastic and tactile than watercolour, and many critics over the decades have described the paintings Turner exhibited each year in terms of food, albeit disparagingly. They were referring both to his wide range of surface colours, and to the varied texture of his paint surfaces, especially when writing in the 1830s and '40s. His old friend Henry Trimmer, inspecting Turner's studio after his death, described the painting materials he saw:

The palette – at least that in use, for he possessed two large and splendid ones – was a homely piece of square wood, with a hole for the thumb. Grinding colours on a slab was not his practice, and his dry colours were rubbed on the palette with cold-drawn oil. The colours were mixed daily, and he was very particular as to the operation ... His brushes were of the humblest description, mostly some large round hog's tools, and some flat. He was said to use very short handles, which might have been the case with his watercolours; but I observed one very long-handled brush ... according to his housekeeper, he used the long brush exclusively for the rigging of ships, etc. However, there were a great many long-haired sables, which could not have been all employed for rigging. She also said that he used camel's hair [a cheaper type of brush, made from squirrel] for his oil pictures ... and some Chinese brushes ... there was a jar of wax melted with rose madder and also with blue ... it might have been for watercolours ... a bottle of spirit varnish and a preparation of tar, tubes of megilp, old bladders of raw umber and other dark earths, all Newman's, from whom might be learnt what colours he used ... [22]

The comparison with a kitchen, the tools to hand, the preparations for the next meal with some anticipation of leftovers to be used at a later date, is irresistible. It was a well-stocked kitchen by the standards of any professional artist of the era, to judge by the number of different materials, mostly coloured pigments, in the Turner Bequest. Turner's travelling paintbox alone includes over seventy visually distinct materials (ill. p. 113), and that might not include everything he was using in his last years. The evidence that it is incomplete lies in the absence of white paints and pigments. Perhaps the executors thought this was less interesting to preserve, despite Ruskin's eulogizing on several occasions over Turner's nuanced use of many different shades of white: 'He gives a dash of pure white for his highest lights; but all the other whites are pearled down with grey or gold.'[23]

Some examples of what Ruskin was describing can be seen in *George IV's Departure from the 'Royal George', 1822* (overleaf), and in *Waves Breaking against the Wind* (ill. p. 69) and

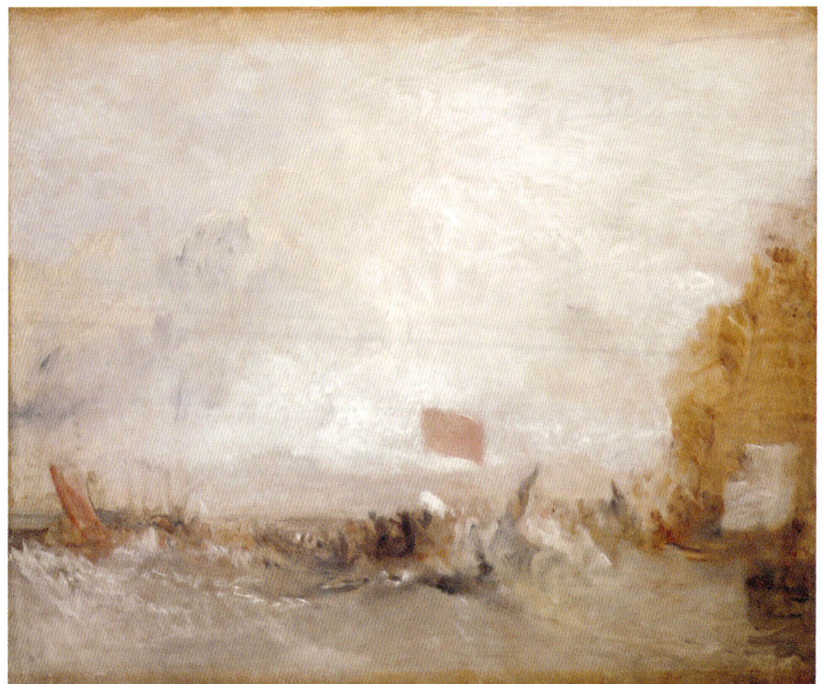

George IV's Departure from the 'Royal George', 1822, c. 1822. Tate, London

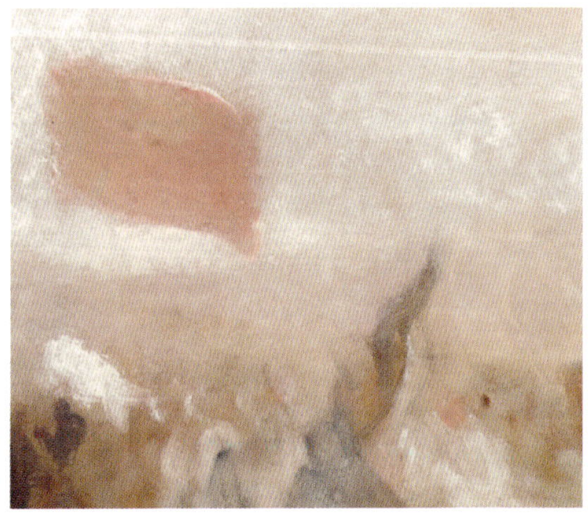

Detail showing unmodified lead white-based paint

Detail showing paint made from lead white and a megilp

A River Seen from a Hill (ill. p. 81). Turner's white pigment for oil painting was lead white (basic lead carbonate), but varying levels of purity and particle sizes could be obtained from different colourmen. For most of his life, he used the very traditional stack process lead white, which had a wide range of particle sizes and probably a lot of 'bite' under the brush, a desirable property when painting impasto. It was free of extenders and probably expensive. Turner was reported by his first biographer to use 'silver white', just such a product.[24]

Working out what colours Turner used begs another kitchen analogy: the herbs and spices to hand on any given day. Most of the favourites are probably present if a guest strolls into the kitchen, but a few are only represented on the shopping list (the equivalent being Trimmer's account, and the very few other descriptions of Turner at work) or in the food being prepared (meaning that we should study Turner's last paintings, too – the ones that might have used up some of his colours). Cooks work creatively, constantly experimenting and tweaking recipes to see if the result will be even better, just as Turner must have done. This is not to say that plain ingredients and a simple recipe cannot give good results: we see that they can in the paintings abandoned at an early stage.

Artists choose types of paint that do what they want them to do, and that can be used expressively, without having to fight with the medium. Earlier 19th-century painting materials must have been far less uniform, since they were handmade products, and therefore more varied than those sold today,

in terms of handling, drying time and appearance when just dry, and after a few weeks when fully dried. Many artists cooked up a variety of paint types that worked for them, and had been doing so at least since the time of Turner's birth. They did this by adding medium modifiers, either purchased in liquid or gel form, or by mixing, heating and using genuine kitchen and household ingredients like egg or animal glue.

Reynolds had begun the fashion, and remained one of the more adventurous users of lusciously thick and impasted paints, which he contrasted with intensely coloured thin glazes and deep glossy shadows applied on top. A generation of artists followed his example and became experimental cooks. By the time Turner chose to paint in oil, it was becoming clear that much of Reynolds's paint was darkening, cracking to reveal the different colours beneath, and falling off the canvas in lumps.

But no one knew for certain which recipes or methods of preparation or application were durable, as well as looking wonderful. Turner committed himself to 'cooking with paint', and he was not alone. Since he was nearly always painting when not travelling, he ended up using a range of well-tried recipes for paint mediums that allowed him to work spontaneously and creatively,[25] without the inspiration-killing need to pause while one brushstroke dried before proceeding with the next.

Preparing the ground[26]

In Turner's era, linen canvas was prepared for oil painting by sizing it thoroughly with animal

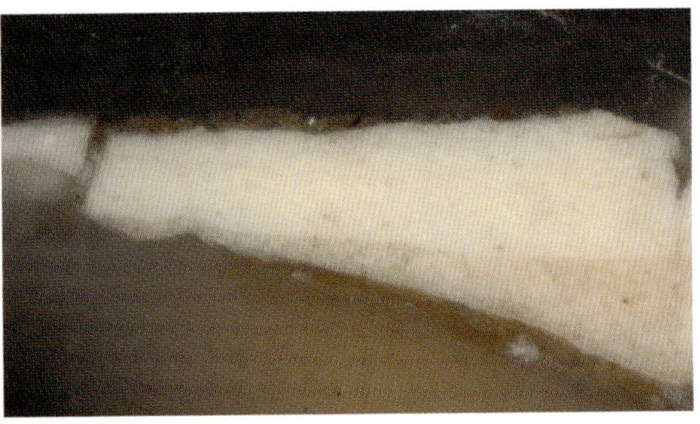

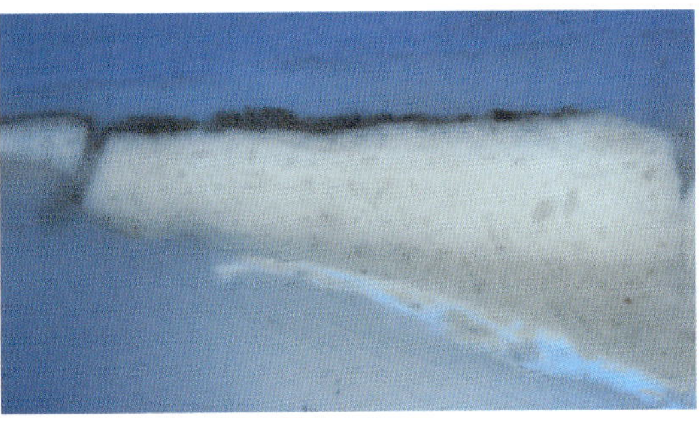

Cross-sections from *Venice, the Piazzetta with the Ceremony of the Doge Marrying the Sea* (full work ill. p. 143), with thin brown paint and two layers of white priming (left), and seen in ultraviolet light (right), revealing a thick glue size beneath the priming

glue, which the colourman did to large pieces of newly woven canvas, tacked out onto vertical frames under tension, and with the fixing edges consequently left unprimed. Without sizing, the oil from the paint would soak in and cause the canvas to darken and grow brittle decades sooner than it ordinarily would in a polluted urban environment like London. A ground or priming was also usually applied by the colourman, often as several thin layers, rubbed down between applications to give a smooth surface.

Canvas could be purchased by the roll after the priming had dried, or was stretched and tacked onto a wooden stretcher (with expandable corners, for adjusting canvas tension) or strainer (with fixed corners). These were made in a series of standard dimensions favoured from the 18th century, which ranged from small portrait formats for just that purpose, to wider landscape formats that used the full width of the loom for the height. Very large canvases had to be stitched together from two pieces, before being stretched and then primed, which concealed the join.

Large stretchers have cross-members to brace and stiffen them, placed diagonally across the corners in the later 18th century, and set horizontally and vertically from early in the following century. Even if the wood on the canvas side is well bevelled and smoothed, the marks of the first stretcher appear in the paint as tell-tale cracks, decades later. Cheaper or homemade stretchers are not as bevelled, and leave more obvious patterns.

Oil-based primings were typical. In the 19th century, a layer of chalk with lead white in unmodified linseed oil, followed by a second layer of lead white with less chalk in the same oil, and a small amount of brown ochre to make a warmer off-white than a pure white, was the most common type in Britain. This partly conceals the texture of the woven fabric, and gives it a pleasing 'tooth' for painting. The priming was made from stiff paint without excessive amounts of medium, intended to absorb some oil from the paint, which would be more medium-rich, especially if it included a medium modifier. Rubbing-down by the colourman likely increased the absorbency.

Colours darker than off-white would have been achieved by the colourman or the artist by adding another layer. Turner very rarely did this. He certainly preferred white to off-white primings with very little added coloured pigment, when one compares his primings to those used by others, a typical example being shown in a cross-section from *Venice, the Piazzetta with the Ceremony of the Doge Marrying the Sea* (opposite). A seascape in calm weather, like *The Junction of the Thames and the Medway* (below), requires a white ground for the sky to be rendered so brilliantly, while a landscape in overcast weather, such as *Dolbadarn Castle, North Wales* (ill. p. 14), does not. It is only occasional early canvases that have an added coloured ground, generally reddish but never blue, such as *Morning amongst the Coniston Fells, Cumberland* (overleaf), whose rather thick paint disguises its colour.

Turner had a marked preference for absorbent primings.[27] This was practical for an artist who worked fast and to whom colour was supremely important: the first brushstrokes are rapidly absorbed and dry fast, revealing final colour sooner, thus becoming ready for further paint. Quite a number of his canvases up to the 1820s and beyond have an alternative absorbent ground, a single layer of pure lead white and whole egg, as do some panels and non-standard supports that could be repurposed materials.

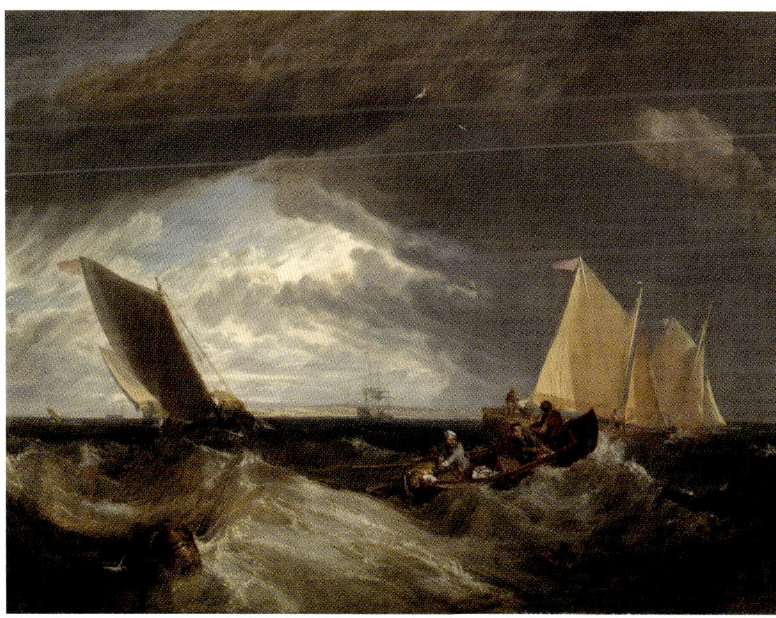

The Junction of the Thames and the Medway, 1807.
National Gallery of Art, Washington, DC

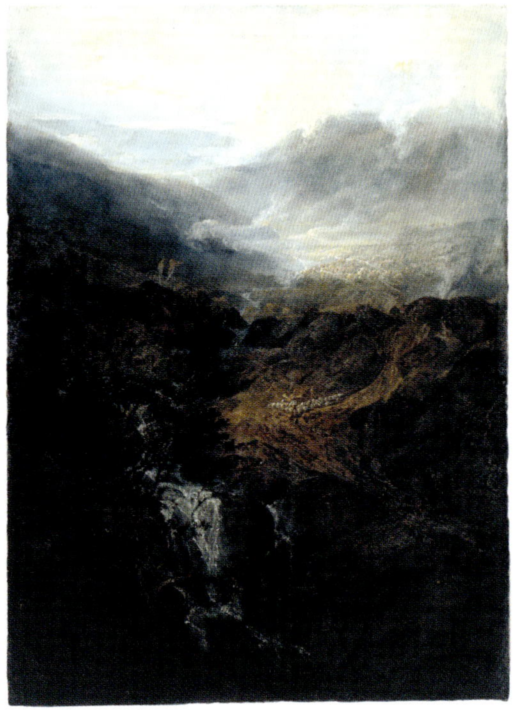

Morning amongst the Coniston Fells, Cumberland,
exhibited 1798. Tate, London

This, and the period of use while Turner's father was alive, but only for a few years after, suggest that they were made at home by William. Some such primings have sweeping brushstrokes suggestive of arm movement, a feature less often seen in the rubbed-down and more uniform commercial products. Reconstructions of this simple recipe gave a very white priming that is more absorbent than the commercial ones, with a good tooth. It was ideal for Turner's painting process.

After William's death in 1829, Turner had to source his own supports. For stretched canvases, he used the colourman Brown in High Holborn regularly, as well as Sherborn in Oxford Street, and Roberson & Miller in Long Acre. All of them stamped the reverse of the canvas with the company name at intervals, at the priming stage; like water-marks, the stamps can be seen on some canvases (opposite), in varied places. These canvases often had standard dimensions of 36 × 48 in., 24 × 36 in., and 31 × 31 in. or 34 × 34 in. (91 × 122 cm, 61 × 91 cm, and 79 × 79 or 86 × 86 cm, respectively).

The larger sizes, in landscape format, were possible for a short man to carry around his studio unaided, as Turner then had to do, and have the advantage of fitting into standard frames if he chose to change the display in his gallery. All have very pale off-white grounds and are pretty absorbent, with a double priming made of lead white and chalk in linseed oil. On a few occasions, Turner purchased panel supports from Davy in Newman Street; these still bear labels that state 'absorbent ground'. All of these suppliers continued to trade in the district where Turner had grown up.

Accustomed as he already was to working on standard-sized papers that were fractions of regular-sized sheets, Turner could instinctively keep his developing composition within his chosen support – unlike artists who built up a landscape in a more analytical way from sketches, only to find the composition running off an edge. When this happened, they unpicked the canvas from the stretcher to enlarge it, something Turner never did.

The third dimension: adding texture

Hand-grinding paint on a stone slab is laborious and slow work, which most artists delegated to colourmen or to assistants. As much pigment

Stamp for Sherborn, on the reverse of
Steamer and Lightship (full work ill. p. 98)

Stamp for Brown, on the reverse of
A River Seen from a Hill (full work ill. p. 81)

as possible was combined with the oil, and the grinding required physical effort, with a large heavy stone muller propelled with two hands and all of one's weight behind it. Some colours took up more oil, with lamp black requiring ten times as much as lead white did, but the process was always to grind and grind, until no more dry pigment could be combined with the paint. It is possible that Turner's father ground some paint at home, when his son had sourced an exciting new pigment that was supplied as a dry powder. The paintings cannot furnish any evidence on this matter.

In Turner's day, ready-ground paint would have been supplied in a keg or a barrel for larger quantities and regularly used colours such as white, or wrapped in pigs' bladders (the small brown balls seen in the upper compartments of his travelling paintbox; ill. p. 113). Such paint could be used straight away, but it dragged somewhat on the canvas, and always held the brushmarks. If it began to dry out because the bladder had been opened, it might only be possible to put it on in small dabs.

In general, professionally hand-ground oil paint would have been less runny than oil paint from modern tubes. It must have felt like set honey, or even set honey that had been chilled until solid, when it was used. This, of course, was perfect for depicting sea spray whipped by wind, but less good for soft clouds. Turpentine, or oil of turpentine – a similar but more viscous material, whose presence may be indicated by very white ultraviolet fluorescence in the hazy clouds of *Steamer and Lightship* (overleaf) – could be mixed into the pure oil paint on the palette to give a more workable medium that would go on smoothly and more thinly.

Adding more thinner would eventually give a runny paint that would become uncontrollable, flowing down the canvas on the easel. Adding a lot of turpentine resulted in a matte appearance once the thinner evaporated, or even little beads of paint with gaps between, which could not cover the surface. Some of Turner's contemporaries saw this effect in seascapes such as *Stormy Sea with Dolphins* (ill. p. 51, left), in which the masts and rigging or distant waves are seen through a violent storm (see p. 51, right), and suggested that he

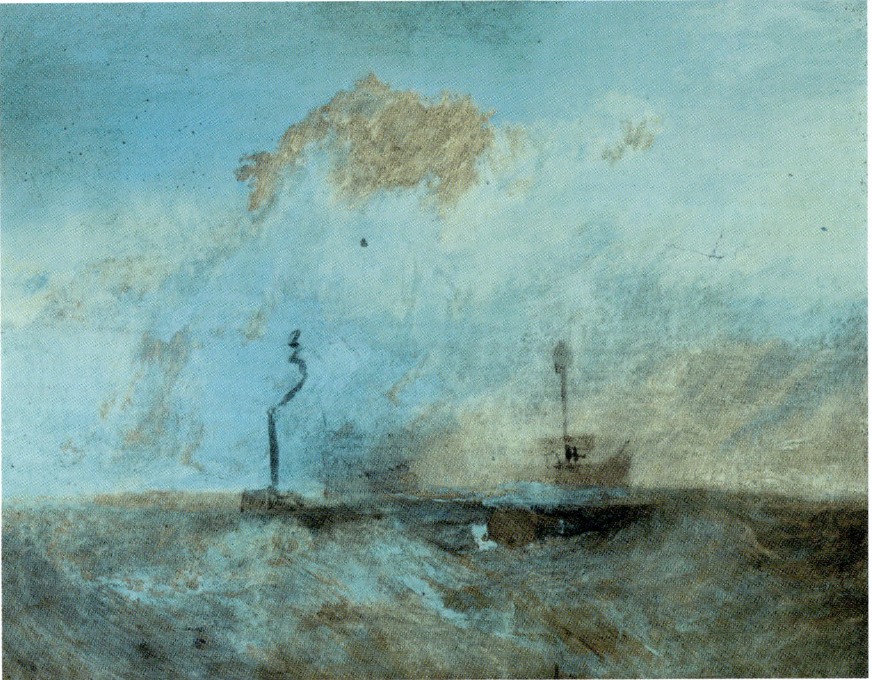

Steamer and Lightship; a study for 'The Fighting Temeraire', seen in ultraviolet light, the moderately bright fluorescence in the sky suggests thinning with oil of turpentine, while the brighter streaks in the sea suggest the addition of resin (full work ill. p. 98)

used watercolour medium for these last stages of painting. This, however, seems unlikely. Adding so much thinner that the dried paint would form a broken line of little spots was another of Turner's premeditated methods, and one that occurs only in appropriate places, such as water seen through mist and spray. He employed it pretty regularly, and almost without conscious planning.

Even paint made from pure lead white and a simple oil (like linseed or poppy) would not dry quickly to a tough surface, ready to take more paint. An artist who returned to a painting the following day risked picking up the previous day's

paint and disturbing work he would rather have retained. Instead, paints could be ground in heat-treated oil, which was thicker and more yellow, and dried faster. This gave a glossy effect, even after thinning with turpentine. A lead-based drier (a compound like lead oxide, also known as litharge, or lead acetate) could be ground up with the paint and oil, introduced as a liquid medium modifier added to the basic paint on the palette and stirred in with the brush, or sprinkled onto the painting after brushing out. Professional housepainters used lead oxide, because paint applied in cold weather would otherwise be tacky for days, and applying

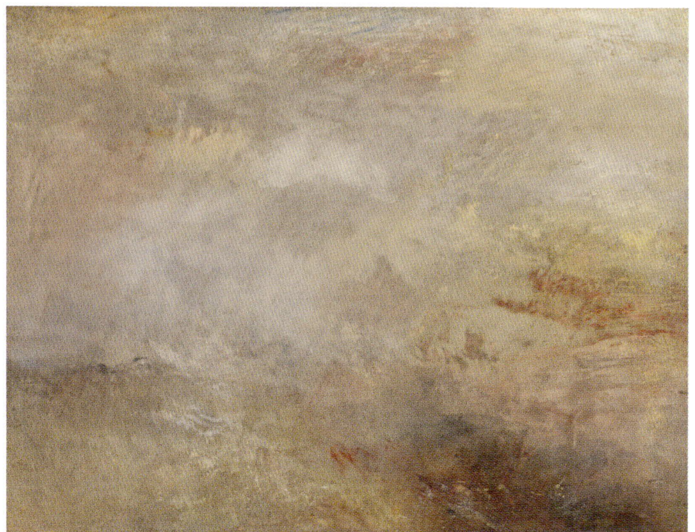

Stormy Sea with Dolphins, c. 1835–40. Tate, London

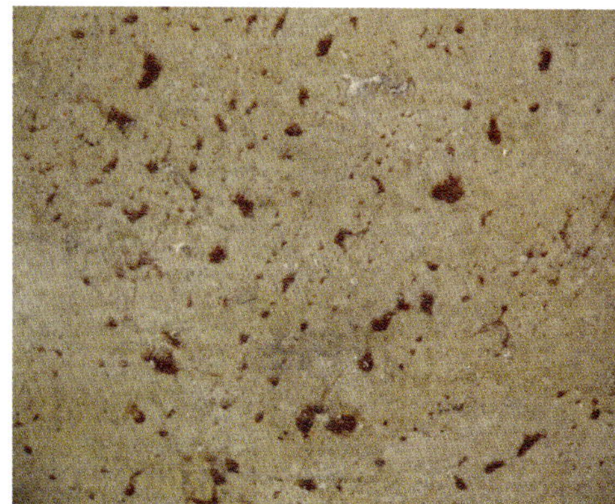

Overthinned paint

several coats would be too time-consuming. This was an additive that could make white paint look slightly yellow, but some artists, including Reynolds, did use it.[28] Others tended to use lead acetate, or an oil prepared with lead acetate, if they wanted faster drying times, because the strewing method was seen as leading to spotty paint in the long term. Turner chose lead acetate, usually incorporated into the paint recipe, but was at times accused of strewing it.[29]

Adding a medium to modify the paint would open up new and wonderful possibilities: it could provide a thinner and more workable paint that would not run down the canvas and form drips, or slump when the brush was lifted. This desirable quality was called 'body' in the 19th century, while such paint is now called 'thixotropic'. We are accustomed today to thixotropic paint, as

it behaves like good-quality housepaint by staying where it is placed, without dripping, while the brushmarks level out naturally as it dries to give a smooth finish. It can be brushed thickly to hide the colour beneath, or very thinly to cover an uneven patch, without pulling apart into little islands of paint with low-lying gaps in between.

A minor addition of varnish made from a natural resin, such as mastic dissolved in turpentine (usually bought as a varnish, the preparation on a domestic fire being not without risk), would improve things, and add a little body to the paint (see opposite and p. 98). Too much varnish, like too much turpentine, made the paint runny. The addition of a small amount of glue size, or even some egg (yolk or a beaten whole egg), could confer body on oil paint to a surprising degree when only a tiny amount was added – likely as little as just a drop, since 1 per cent by weight added can make an astonishing difference to the handling of the paint. This would give paint that would hold impasto when the brush was flicked off, and it is known that John Constable (1776–1837) used this method.[30] It is not so clear that Turner did.[31] Detailed analyses of the paints from his first decade of oil painting suggests that Turner used some odd ingredients on occasion, as he sought to 'cook' the perfect paint medium. Perhaps he was experimenting with different types of drier, or with oil from different colourmen, who had prepared it with driers so that the paint could go on thickly without running before it dried.

By the 1820s, and probably earlier, Turner had found a material that did what he wanted, and the modifiers – from analysis and the crack patterns they now show on the surface – seem to be more similar and consistent. The material that turned stiff, sticky oil paint into desirable thixotropic paint, which could be brushed out like a glaze and hold soft impasto peaks that would dry without brushmarks, was called megilp, and it could be bought ready-made from a colourman.

Henry Trimmer's description of Turner's studio after his death (see p. 43) mentioned 'tubes of megilp'. There were many recipes published in the 18th and 19th centuries, which called for mixing different proportions of an oil made with a lead-based drier, and a solution of mastic varnish in turpentine.[32] There were probably a number of products available, but very few colourmen's records survive to confirm this. Other varnishes, such as copal, could be added to the mix, but were more commonly added after Turner's time.

At its simplest, a megilp could be created in the middle of a painting session, with the artist simply taking a brushload of mastic varnish, or dripping some from a bottle, onto a blob of paint prepared with an oil that already included a lead-based drier. This leads to paints with wildly varying proportions being used in a single painting, and to different degrees of tackiness and dust trapping, yellowing, wrinkling and solubility during conservation treatments.

Turner did not know this, of course, but the variability of his paint from one spot to the next, so worrisome to conservators today, is a powerful argument that he mixed the megilp in with his brush in the heat of the moment – in keeping with the few snatched glimpses we have of him painting busily. The combination produced a paint with a different chemical composition and different flow properties, so that it is possible to analyse paint samples for exactly this material, though not to find out its proportion in the paint.[33]

Megilp has another advantage: adding lots of it gives twice as much paint as before, just as intensely coloured, and still glossy when dry, whereas simply thinning paint leads to a paler, more matte surface colour.[34] This miraculous multiplying is possibly the biggest incitement to use megilp, apart from the way it transforms stiff oil paint into a thixotropic material, offering an experience akin to painting with mayonnaise, rather than set honey. Paint with added megilp is touch-dry sooner than thinned oil paint, an additional advantage when an exhibition was looming, or work was being done at the exhibition itself, among bustling artists and dust in the air.

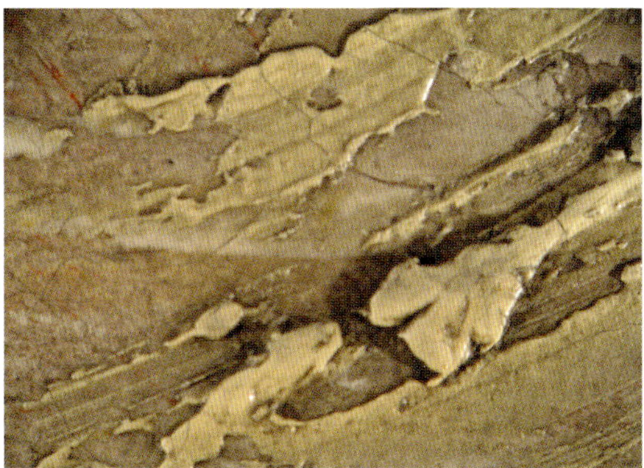

Wax-based impasto in *Stormy Sea with Dolphins* (full work ill. p. 51)

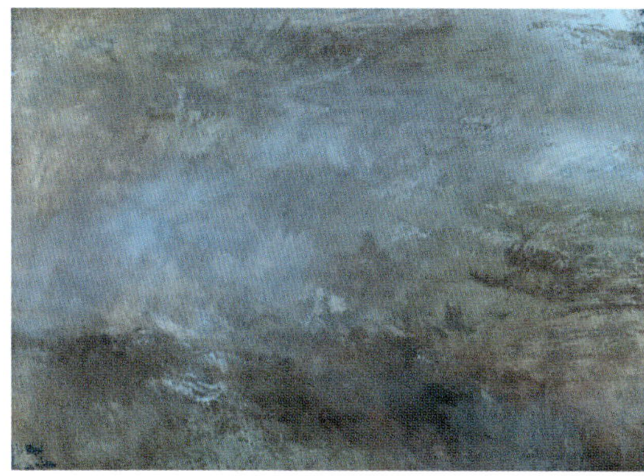

Seen in ultraviolet light, showing the bright-white yet cloudy fluorescence of wax-based paint media in the white-capped waves, and at the top-right corner

Turner's megilps included lead acetate and not lead oxide, when they have been analysed to this level of detail in well-preserved paintings, in white impasted areas.[35] This variety that yellowed less was the more obvious choice of megilp for an artist who used a lot of white paint, pale yellow and pale blue for skies, and who sought to create glossy shadows and small details with varied gloss. Even this recipe would have looked a bit yellow when mixed into the paint.

There seems to be a limit to the height of impasto that can be achieved with megilp. It is probably about two millimetres, and the outer edges of such a mountainous island of megilp slump down a little to the level of the surrounding paint. Even thicker impasto capable of forming islands with cliff-like edges is achievable with wax-based medium modifiers added to oil paint. Recipes using beeswax, turpentine, occasionally water and many other ingredients were discussed and used by Reynolds and his contemporaries. They could be stirred into

paint on the palette, much as megilp could be.[36] Paint with added wax-based medium modifier tends to dry more matte than paint with megilp added. If very little colour is added to such paint, it has some gloss, but a slightly cloudy surface, as well as a craggy appearance (above, left and right).

The wax can be discovered in Turner's paint by chemical analysis or by heating tests, and therefore it was sometimes discovered too late by 19th-century restorers when they used excessive heat in treatments designed to preserve his paintings. Where it survives in less severely treated works, such paints occur as high impasted areas with slightly flat tops, often white, rather than mixed with colours. Turner used such paint for heavily textured white clouds, choppy seas with a lot of white water, and distant shores with cliffs. The wax used was beeswax, to judge by paint analysis and measurements of its melting point of 60–61° C (140–142° F). Sometimes it was unrefined beeswax, which melts at about 57° C (135° F).[37]

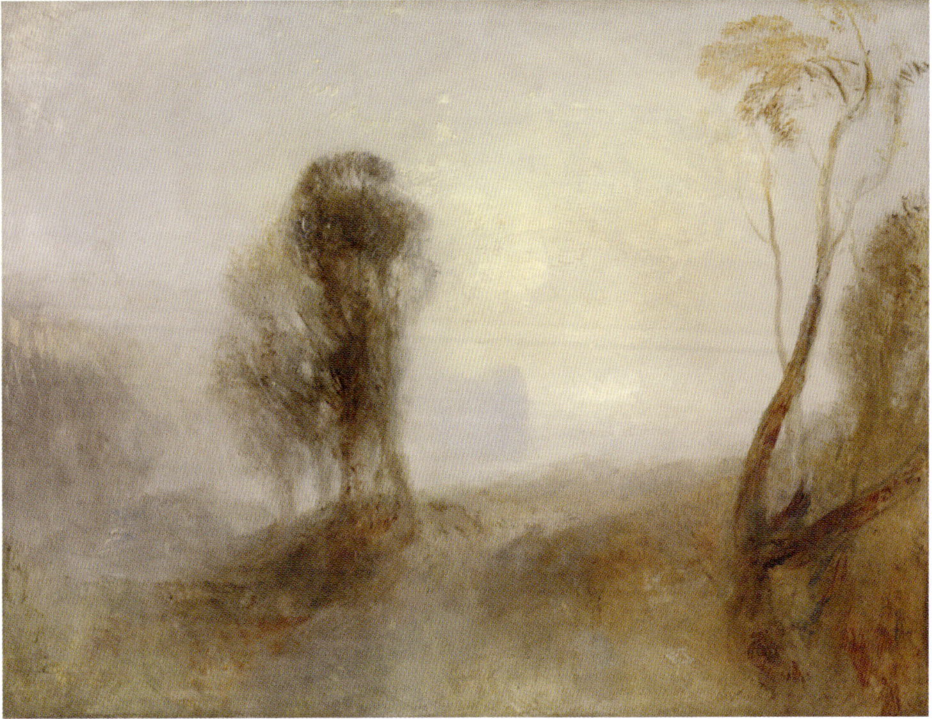

Sunrise, a Castle on a Bay: 'Solitude', c. 1840–45. Tate, London

In the few late oils known not to have had heat treatments, such as lining to a support canvas, a then common wax with a far lower melting point (about 45° C, or 113° F) has been discovered: spermaceti wax, made from whales, used extensively for domestic candles (less expensive than beeswax candles, a luxury product). Both types of wax were obvious products to be sold by colourmen in bottles of liquid wax-based medium, which could be added to paint like megilp. They have been found in the paintings of the 1830s and '40s, after William Turner's death in 1829, so it seems probable that Turner purchased the wax ready-made, though the ingredients to make both types were probably available in his own house.

Tools for applying paint

Artists' brushes were made from high-quality animal fur, and were quite small in scale by modern standards. Those for watercolour painting were often made by fitting and gluing a bunch of hairs into the quill of a feather, creating round brushes that were limited to a few millimetres wide, even for the biggest feathers available, from geese or swans. Brushes for oil painting were mostly made as round brushes in Turner's time, with the hairs contained in a metal ferrule. This type of brush head could be flattened, and both types could be trimmed. Large brushes for oil painting were sold as a quarter or a half-inch in diameter (6 or 12 mm) and since the hairs were only a little longer, this is the widest mark they could make, even if used sideways, as Turner sometimes did. On large canvases, brushmarks up to 50 mm (2 in.) wide can be seen, implying that he also used other brushes made for decorators or varnishers. Brushes with long, soft hairs were good for a free-flowing paint with megilp or a wax-based medium added, while short and stiff bristles made from hog's hair were better for stiff, pure oil paint. These came with wooden handles of varied lengths.

Clearly, other larger brushes were made for those who needed them (housepainters, for example), but in the early 19th century it was highly unusual for a professional artist to adopt such artisan tools. The acceptable exception would have been wide, soft-haired brushes for varnishing – though even this was considered a mundane, uncreative task, more usually outsourced to a colourman and his assistants. The descriptions of Turner at work imply that he used quill brushes made for watercolour paint or artisan use at the finishing stage of his oils: they were perfect for fine details (see 'Turner's performance art'; pp. 79–91), and could be bought with interchangeable heads for the wooden brush handle,[38] since oil paint would spoil them for work in other media.

It is also clear that Turner smeared and dabbed on paint with a palette knife. Sometimes such dabs were dotted over a large sky, and he would come

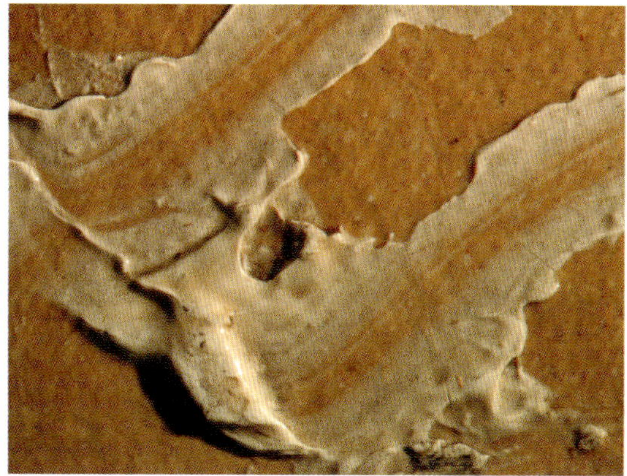

Paint applied with a knife, but not brushed out in the sky

back to tease out these spots of colour with a brush, sometimes leaving a few of the knife-applied blobs alone because he was concentrating on other areas. *Sunrise, a Castle on a Bay: 'Solitude'* (opposite) shows such areas as applied (above) and brushed out (overleaf, top left and right). Flat, flexible palette knives with a blade 15 mm (a little more than half an inch) or so across, and triangular ones shaped more like a tiny trowel, were available. Turner used both, to judge by the paint he failed to brush out. Some of the triangular blades were quite small, among the tiniest that were advertised.

To achieve broad effects appropriate to the scale of a large canvas, 2 m (6 ft 6 in.) wide or more, a larger tool was required: Turner must have used rags. Many of the surreptitiously sketched images of the artist at work (overleaf, bottom) show his pockets bulging with rags, and holding a palette that has two integral containers for liquid medium modifier, while two more glass bottles for medium are placed behind him.

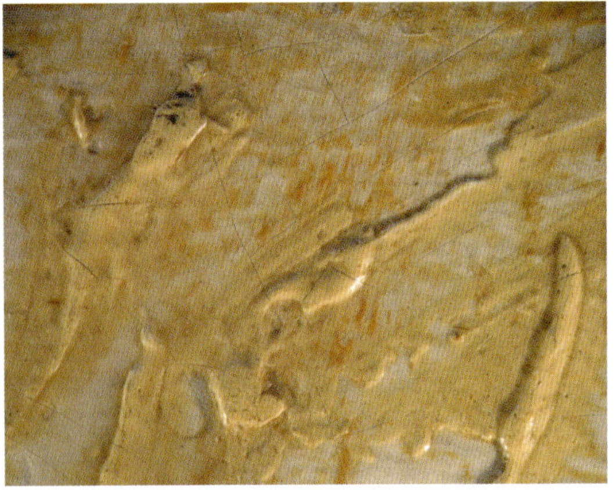

Paint applied with a knife, partly brushed out in the sky

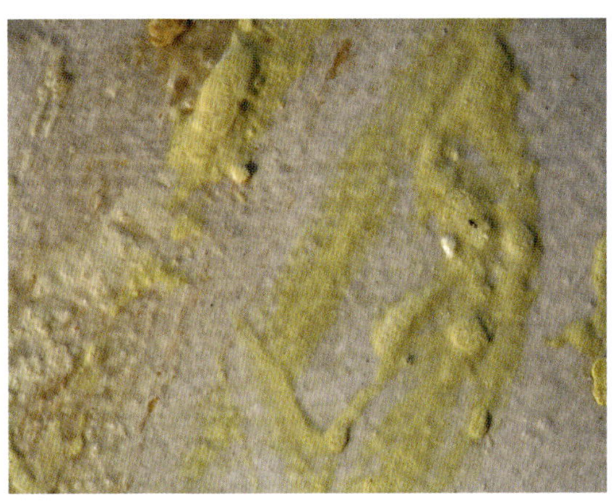

Megilped paint in the sky

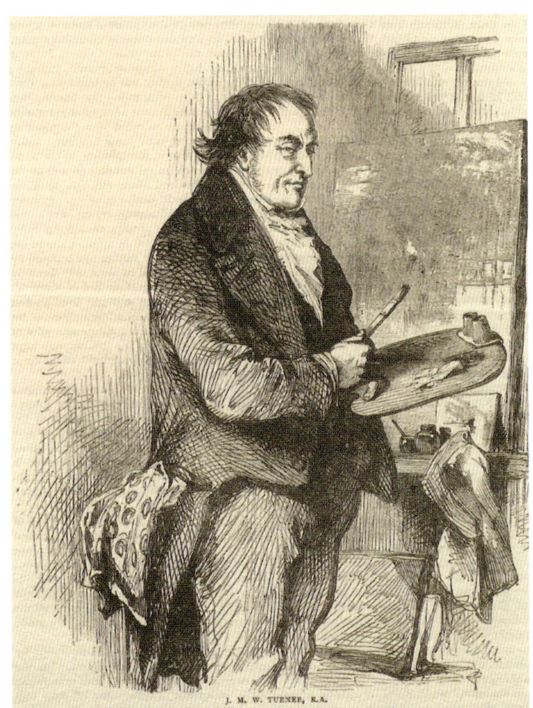

after Sir John Gilbert, *Joseph Mallord William Turner*, 1846.
National Portrait Gallery, London

The lovely veils of broken colour in *Solitude* that lie beneath much of the impasto and dabs of paint with medium modifier could be created easily with a good turpentine-soaked rag that had been passed over the surface often enough to pick up many colours (opposite, top). This gives a very thin paint layer, in contrast to the thick ones for the impasto. Cross-sections (opposite, middle and bottom rows) reveal a bewildering variety of thin and thick layers in modified paint media, reflecting Turner's very localized application and removal of paint with both brush and rag.

It is also clear from close looking that Turner moved the paint about with his fingers on occasion, adding or subtracting material as the moment required and leaving his fingerprints behind, or scratching into the paint. The end of a wooden brush handle gives a straight scratch. There are curved scratches, as well, which are consistent with descriptions of Turner using his thumbnail. As expected for

Pale paint at left edge, worked over many times with a rag, beneath pale yellow paint applied with a palette knife

the right-handed artist that he was, who mainly brushed up from left to right, the curved strokes, in most cases, were made in oil paint with his right hand. This suggests that he paused and transferred the brush from that hand before making a deliberate scratch.

A further dimension: adding transparency

It is clear that adding megilp to some paints and cloudy-looking wax-based materials to others introduced wider possibilities for varying the gloss of paint than would thinning it down to an ever-more matte appearance. Deep golden shadows could be created by simply applying pure megilp,

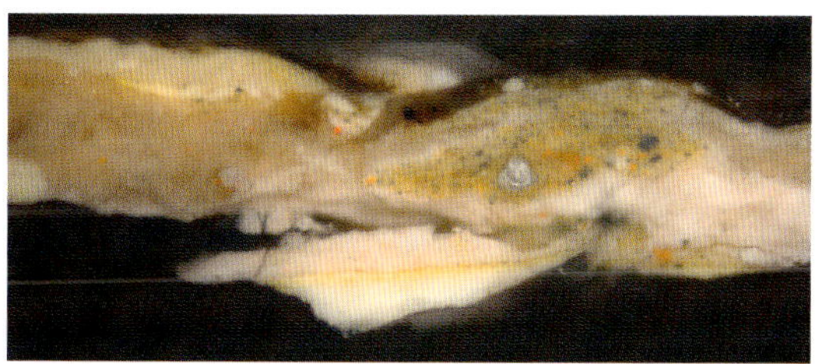

Cross-section from the left edge, showing several thin wiped-off layers between thicker applications of paint

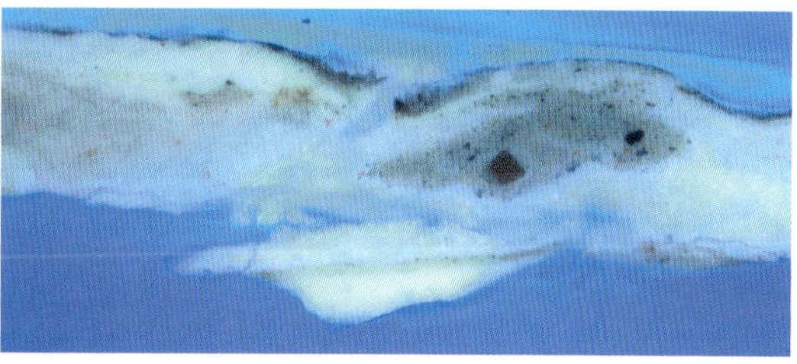

Varied fluorescence of the same section in ultraviolet light shows that Turner used wax-based and resin-based medium modifiers

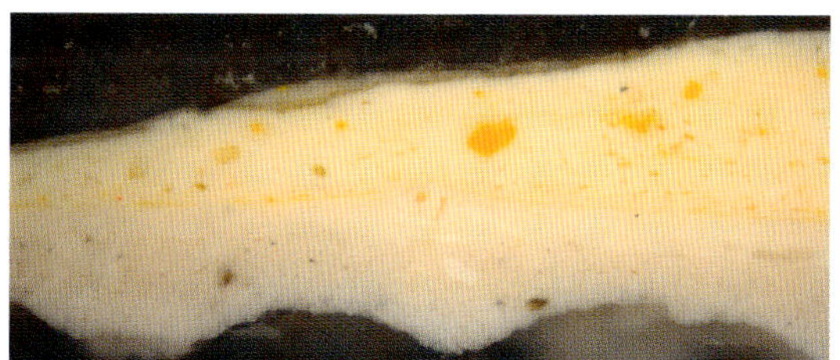

Cross-section for the sky left of centre, showing thick applications of pale paint

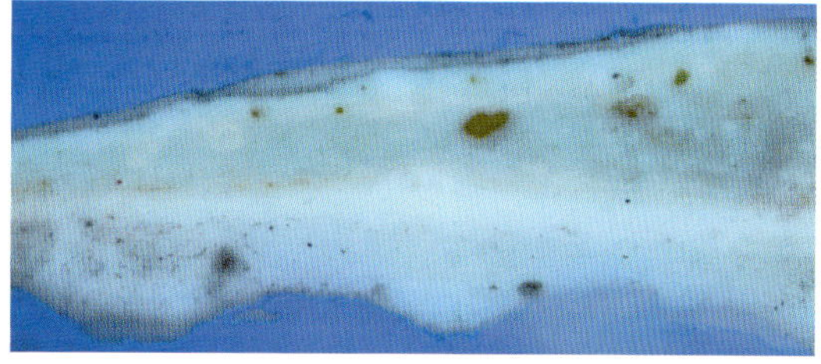

The same cross-section in ultraviolet light, indicating resin in the thin pale upper layer and wax-based paint in the thicker yellow layer

unmixed with paint, either in a thick glassy layer or as a thin glaze. Such materials offer far more variety than the addition of a localized gum wash to watercolour. Megilp was therefore a very versatile material to use in the final stages of a painting. Indeed, it was the perfect material to use when time was running out. It was also ideal for depicting wet sand in seascapes that included a shore, and for the watery footing of the eponymous wreckers, scavenging for whatever the waves wash in to them (below).

Other glossy materials could be obtained, based on bitumen, also known as asphaltum, a natural material found oozing out of the ground in some Middle Eastern countries. This was prepared by the colourman, and numerous recipes have survived, some using genuine asphalt and some employing newer substitute materials that were deplored even in Turner's day. Bitumen was literally 'cooked' at a high temperature, usually for hours, to prepare this medium modifier, and is very difficult to identify chemically.[39] Whether Turner used it is unproven.

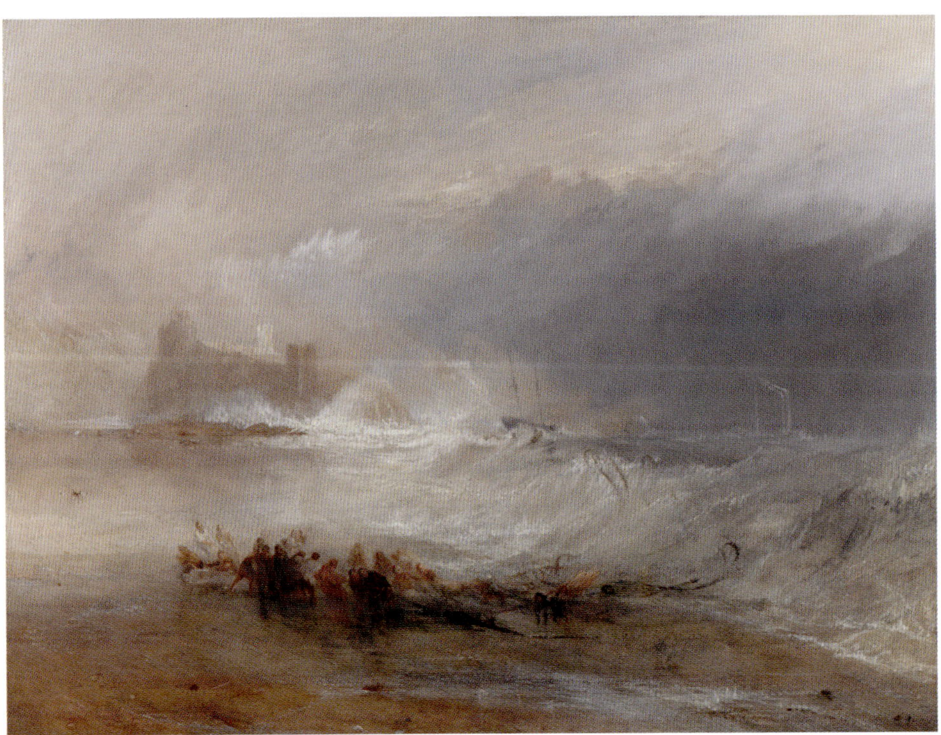

Wreckers – Coast of Northumberland, with a Steam-Boat Assisting a Ship off Shore, 1833–34. Yale Center for British Art, New Haven

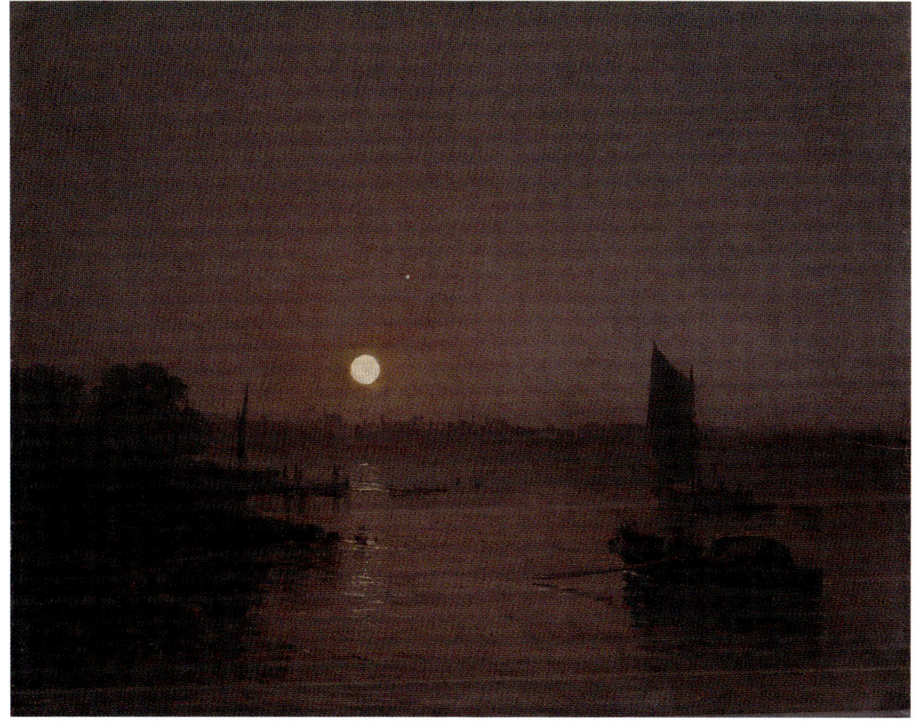

Moonlight, a Study at Millbank, exhibited 1797. Tate, London

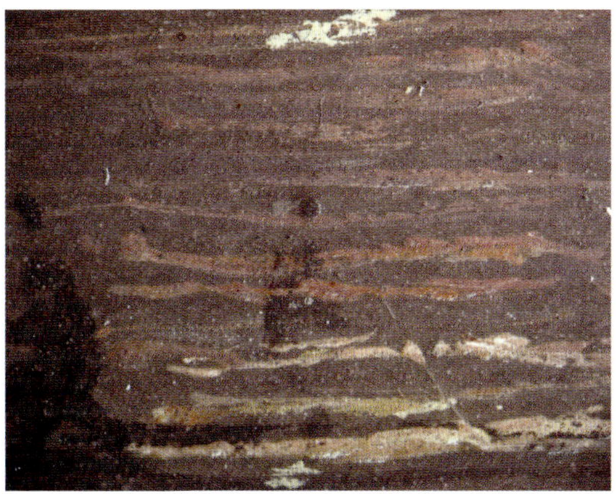

Micrograph showing the reflected moonlight

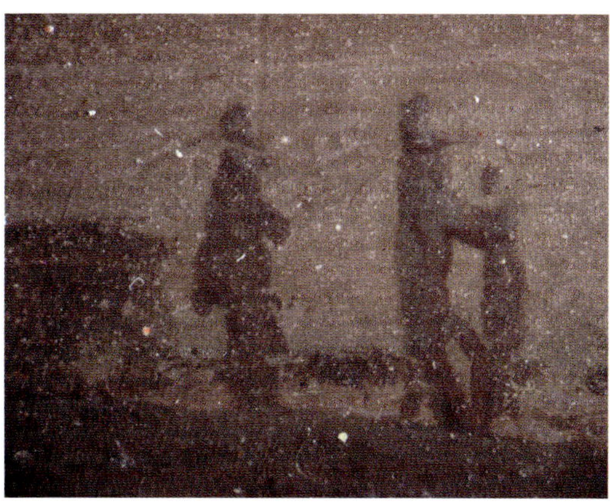

Micrograph showing the men on the shore

His contemporaries sometimes wrote that he did, inferring from the cracks in his paint that he used a material that made their paintings crack, as well. The analytical evidence is against this idea, however. The deep and glossy shadows in the foreground of Turner's Italianate landscapes could have been achieved readily with megilp, which darkens as it ages and causes the shadows to deepen. The range of surface cracks seen in the deep shadows is consistent with both megilp and bitumen, and would follow from his known use of lead acetate driers. The glossy depths of his rough seas could have been achieved with thin applications of wax-based paint with rather little colour added, glazed over with megilp to make them look even deeper and more watery.

The key to the wondrous colour and depth of Turner's paint, so changeable from one brush-stroke to the next, is his fearless application of different paint formulations, one over the other. This is an excellent strategy for producing an exciting and varied surface, but a dangerous one if the surface is to survive unchanged, as each layer dries in its own way and in its own time, sometimes contracting earlier layers into fine wrinkles, or repelling later ones that were still soft, making them contract into islands of paint.

A feast of medium modifiers

In his very early years, Turner occasionally used plain and simple paint to good effect, as can be seen in one of his earliest oils, *Moonlight, a Study at Millbank* (previous page, top). For this atypically small work, he used very small brushes, as though working at the scale of a watercolour.

The reflected moon in the water is depicted with fine bars of orange and yellow, the paint fairly stiff, but applied in such delicate lines that it looks ethereal (previous page, bottom left). The details on the shore, only discernible at all because the moonlight is so bright, were applied with highly thinned paint (previous page, bottom right).

A very good example of the use of many types of modified paint media is *The Opening of the Wallhalla, 1842* (opposite), exhibited in 1843 and sent by Turner to the Congress of European Art exhibition in Munich two years later.[40] The imaginary scene was inspired by a real event and by his travel experiences in Germany along the Rhine. There is a wealth of thickly textured paint on the bank in the foreground, crowded with people (opposite, bottom left), while on the hillside the Walhalla itself (this, not Turner's, being the correct spelling) stands out as a thick, white crust of paint, as does the church (opposite, bottom middle), both dazzling against the bright morning light. Some of these thick impasted areas include the spermaceti wax mentioned earlier (see p. 54).

The sky is thickly painted, too, covering nearly half of the surface (roughly a square metre). Some areas have a fine mesh of drying cracks, others do not. This reflects the amount of turpentine Turner added to keep the area up to the hillside and middle ground workable (opposite, bottom right), as it was painted last of all, using large amounts of the pale chrome yellow and cobalt blue he often used for morning light. The mist, still dispersing in the middle ground, is made from a number of very thin layers of wax-based paint in pale pink and blue tones, incorporating three

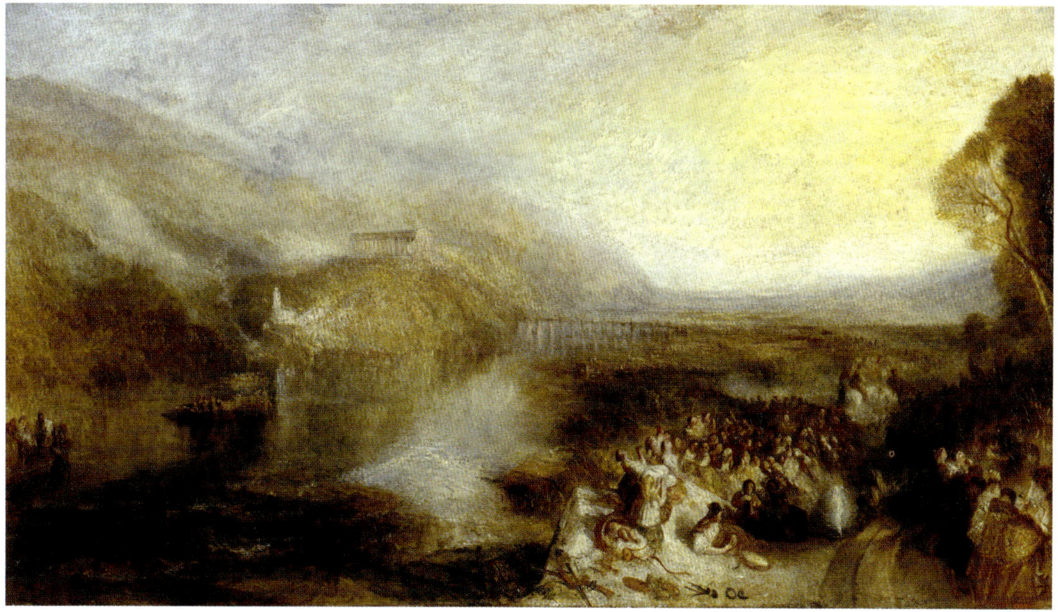

The Opening of the Wallhalla, 1842, exhibited 1843. Tate, London

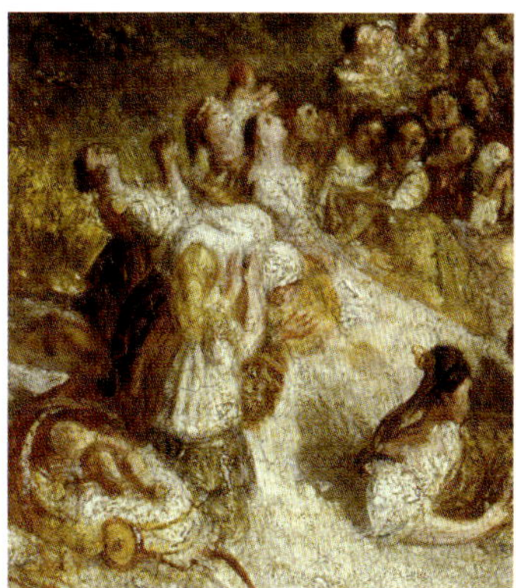

Some of the figures in the immediate foreground

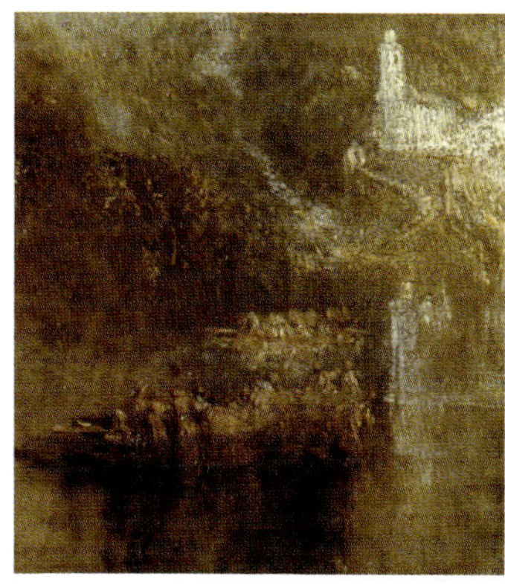

The church and its reflection in still water

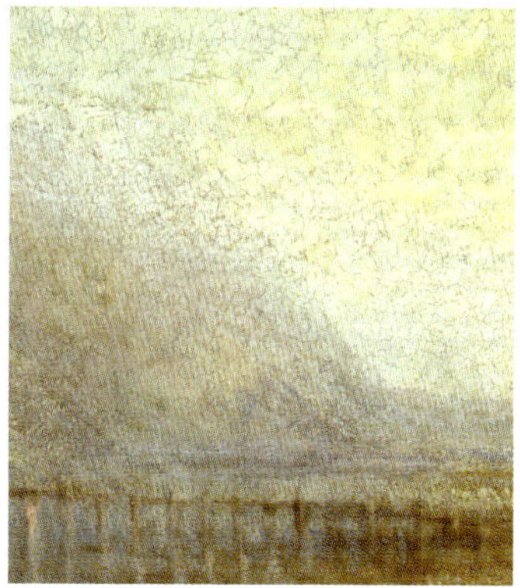

The sky, middle group and bridge

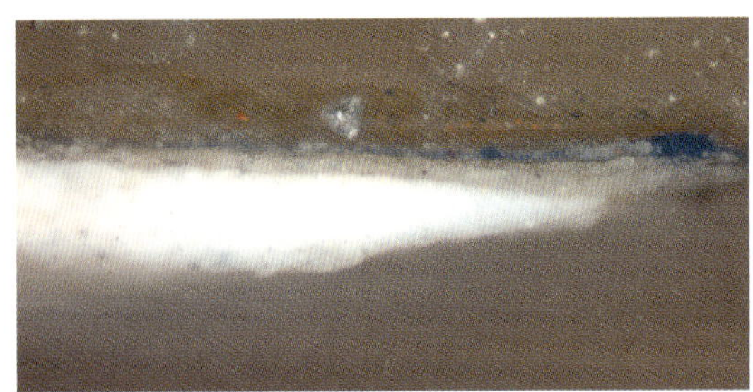

Cross-section through the still water, in visible light

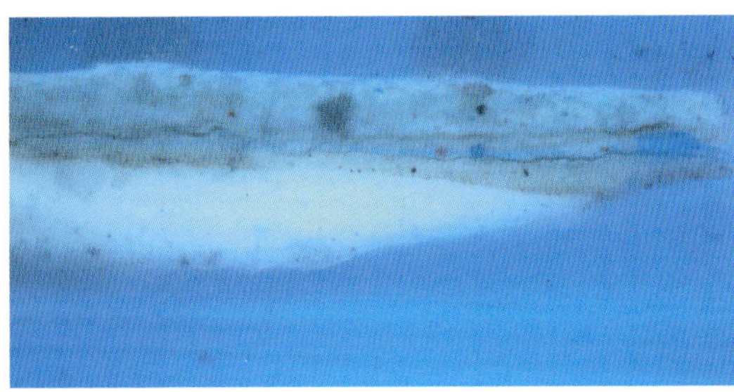

The same cross-section in ultraviolet light

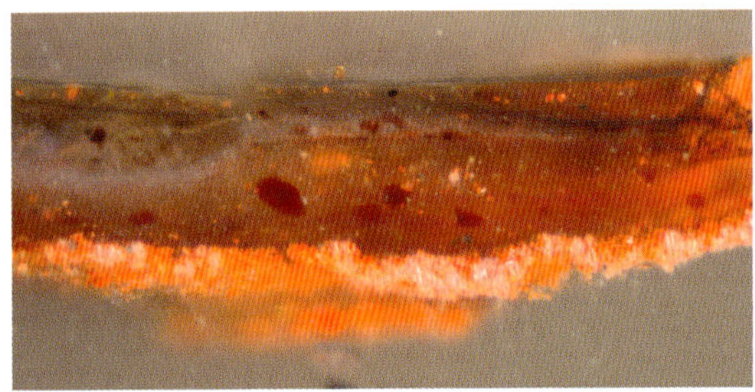

Cross-section from the red costume of a figure in the foreground

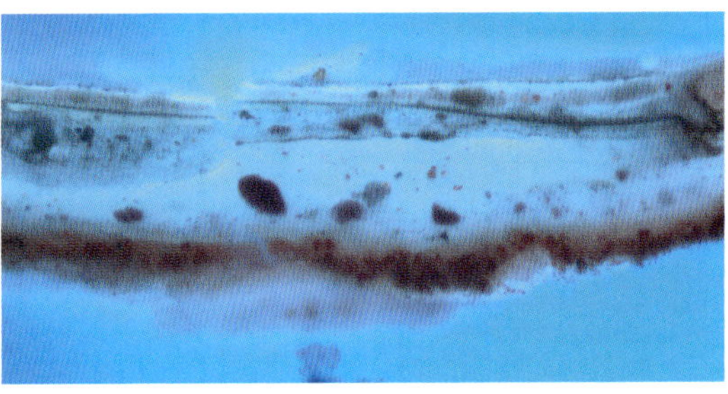

The same cross-section in ultraviolet light

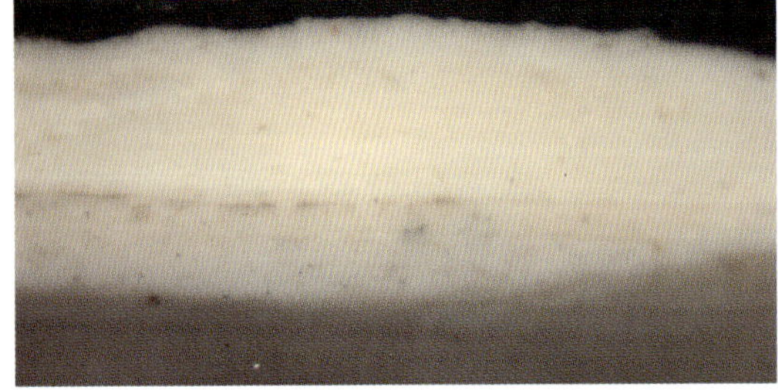

Cross-section from the pair of trees at the right edge

The same cross-section in ultraviolet light

distinct red lakes and natural blue ultramarine. The deeper brown shadows in the still water were also painted using wax-based paint made with beeswax, but with earth colours, and the brighter mars orange predominating instead. Brighter pigments were carried over into the thin layers with a brush that had probably dripped turpentine onto the palette many times. Such layers add 'nothing, yet everything', when four or more are touched over the one spot (opposite, top row).

The wealth of people and objects in the foreground, including their symbolic wreaths and musical instruments, was created with fewer, localized applications of vermilion (opposite, middle row), deep chrome yellow, chrome orange, emerald green, viridian and Prussian blue, applied with a fine brush in lead acetate-based megilp. Many of these areas have fine-scale cracking, so that a tiny flake from the topmost layers can be removed and set as cross-sections. The paint thickness is considerable for the white waxy impasto, even for the leaves at the right edge (opposite, bottom row), but elsewhere (the water and mist) the same material is thin and applied in multiple layers that hardly register as a colour. Wax-based paint lies over megilp and vice versa, with localized wrinkling between the layers.

Ruskin's observation that every spot on the surface differed from the next is apt:

It is the most difficult, the most rare thing, to find in [Turner's] works a definite space, however small, of unconnected colour; that is, either of a blue which has nothing to connect it with the warmth, or of a warm colour, which had nothing to connect it with the greys of the whole … Intimately associated with the toning down and connection of colours actually used, is his inimitable power of varying and blending them, so as never to give a quarter of an inch of canvas without a change in it.[41]

It is possible to see the variety of modified paint present in a detailed oil painting in ultraviolet light, provided that there is no sequence of later varnishes on top to dull the effect. *Stormy Sea with Dolphins* (ill. p. 51), unlike the *Wallhalla*, was not developed into a finished painting with a title and a publicly presented meaning. The depths of its storm-blown water look cloudy and less bright than other areas in ultraviolet light, an indicator of wax-based paint that has been applied thinly. The brightly rendered flecks of high impasto for flying foam over the sea include beeswax and an added resin, such as rosin, in addition to oil, as do little yellow areas of high impasto in the fast-moving clouds. The oil itself is heat-bodied, which confers gloss, and includes either walnut or poppyseed oil, both of which were thought to yellow more slowly than linseed oil (Turner's usual choice), and a good one for such pale paint, which would have been ground in these oils by the colourman.

Bringing it all together

To recall the advantages of contrasting texture and gloss offered by oil paint, it is instructive to contrast a beautiful and highly finished watercolour that necessarily lacks these extra dimensions. *Oberwesel* (overleaf, top) in watercolour and

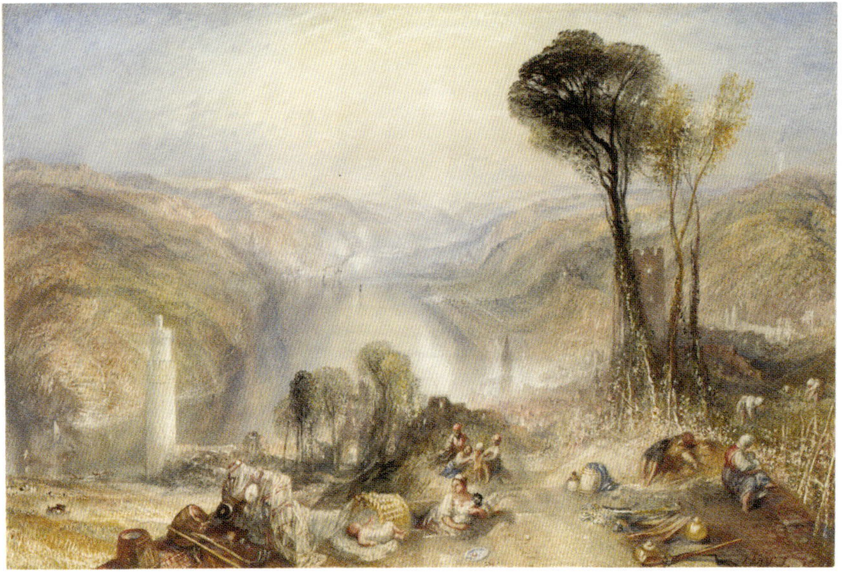

Oberwesel, 1840. National Gallery of Art, Washington, DC

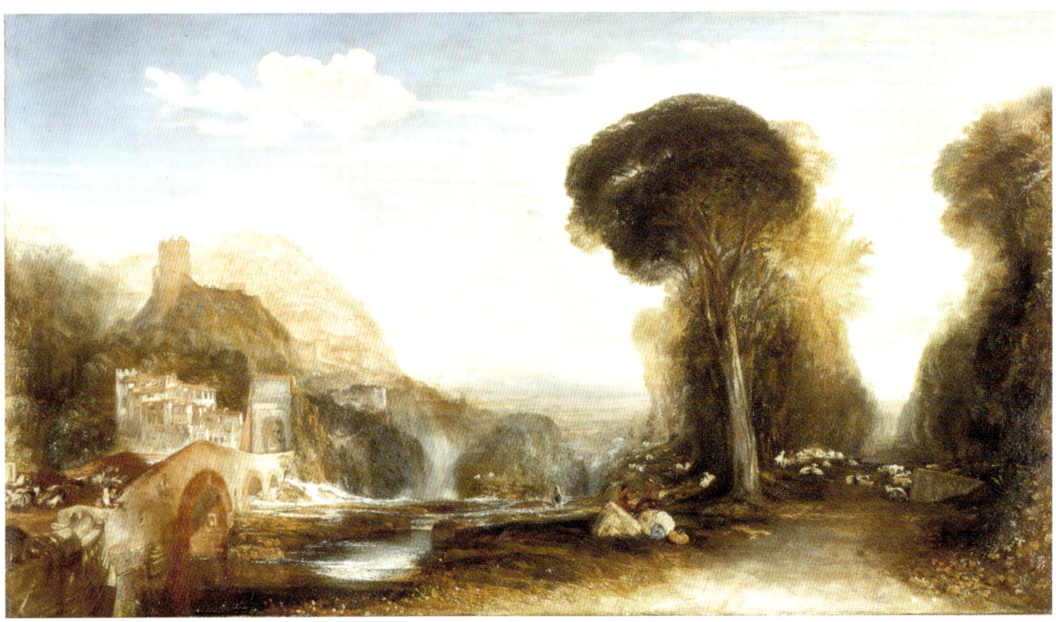

Palestrina – Composition, 1828 (exhibited 1830). Tate, London

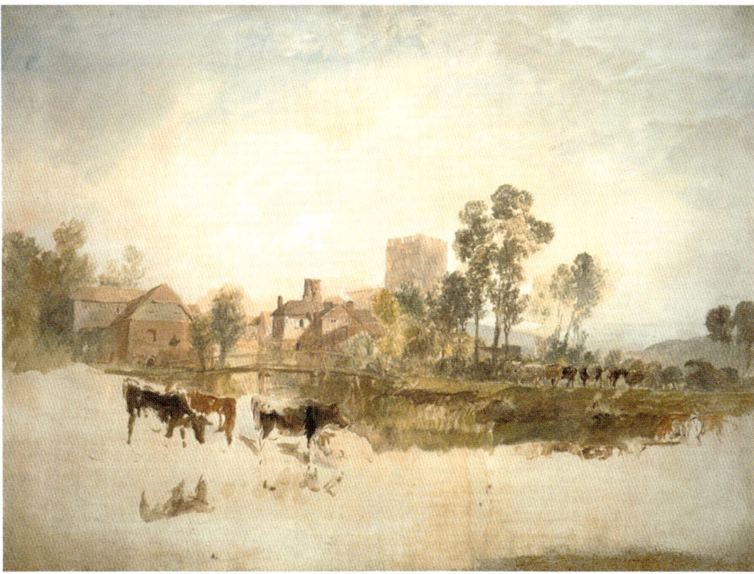

Goring Mill and Church, c. 1806–7. Tate, London

Palestrina (opposite, bottom) in oil have common features – a calm scene in soft, bright afternoon light, and the predominant use of primary colours, with many other colours used tellingly but to a very limited extent – and both are archetypal Italianate landscapes by Turner. Scratching out to reveal the paper and the very considerable use of unpainted paper for the tower and central area are pretty convincing substitutes for impasted white paint in the oil. But images of such complexity always carry more power when the colours can be saturated by varnishing and the shadows strengthened by glazing.

Canvases in the Turner Bequest, developed to different degrees, demonstrate exactly how the artist painted in oil. The following six canvases – *Goring Mill and Church*; *Rocky*

Bay with Figures; *Sunset*; *Sketch for 'Ulysses Deriding Polyphemus'*; *Ulysses Deriding Polyphemus – Homer's Odyssey*; and *Waves Breaking against the Wind* – were titled and dated by 20th-century cataloguers, since Turner himself did not exhibit them and never added titles to such unfinished works. Yet any viewer can understand the subject and mood of each one. Some of the earlier stages in this sequence could, if viewed as a small illustration, easily be mistaken for a watercolour, rather than an oil on canvas, so similar was Turner's approach in both media.

Goring Mill and Church (above) is close to the stage described for Turner's watercolours as a 'colour beginning'. The scene – a wooded river bank next to a mill building, with three cows grazing in front – is established near the centre

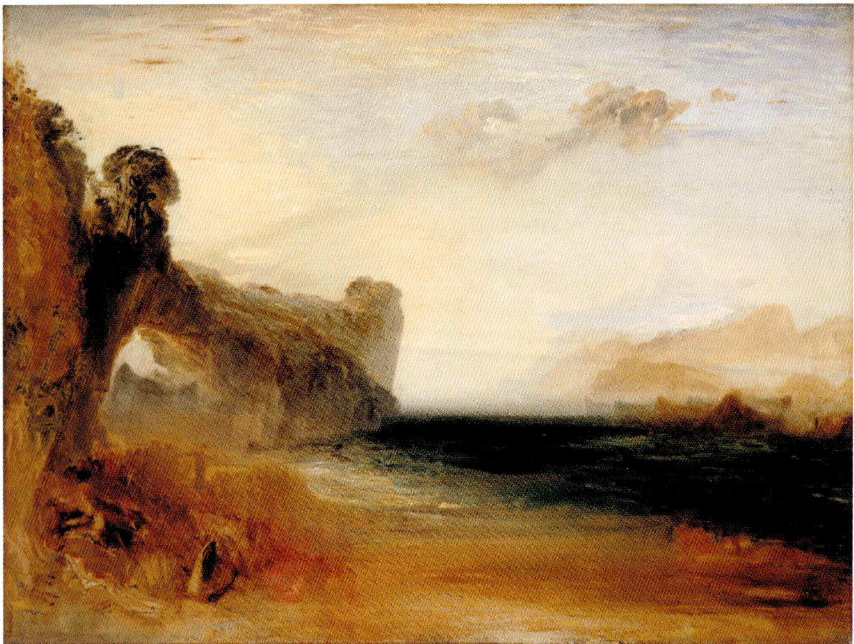

Rocky Bay with Figures, c. 1827–30. Tate, London

of the canvas. The paint is almost transparent, owing to the highly thinned washes of oil paint in a warm yellowish brown. There is a light wash of blue paint at the upper left, indicating that the weather is calm. Half of the canvas, with its off-white priming, has no, or virtually no, paint present. The section at the upper right – in reality, unpainted – already reads as pale clouds. Most of the foreground is blank, except for the reflections of the cattle and the near bank at the right: clearly, this is the river, and equally clearly, the water is moving, since the reflections are so broken up. The trees on the farther bank are a greener, cooler brown than the rest of the sketch, and are likely the last brushstrokes that Turner applied.

The contrasting warm yellow and cool blue washes of *Rocky Bay with Figures* (above) are taken further, their intensity strengthened until, in some parts of the canvas, the paint appears more opaque than transparent. The same intensity could have been achieved with watercolour on off-white paper by using the same colours. Again, the shore in the foreground is predominantly yellow, but now the canvas is covered with paint in a high key, and the mood feels less English and more suggestive of the Mediterranean. Figures seem to be present on the shore, but it is impossible to count them. The pale blue of the sky depicts calm and bright weather, and some golden clouds have been introduced as further contrast. In the foreground, the first brown

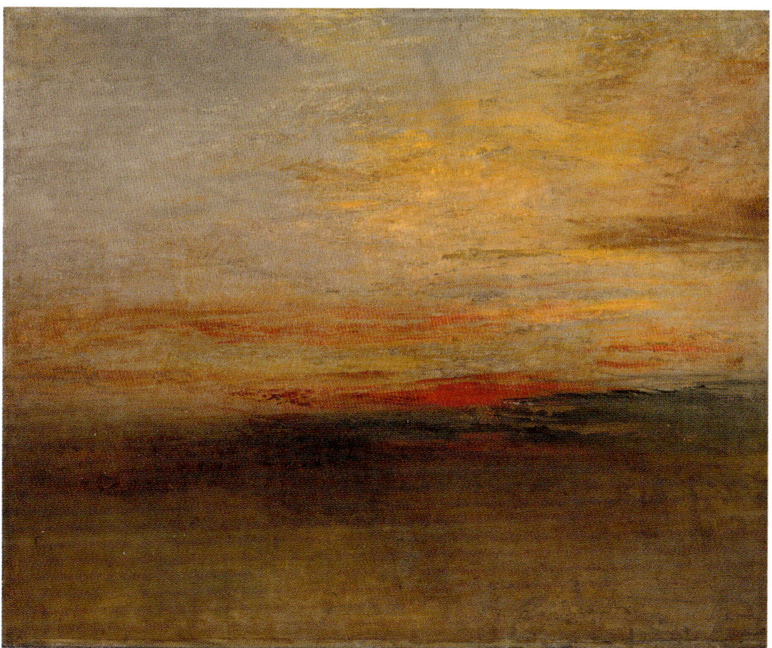

Sunset, c. 1830–35. Tate, London

wash for the shore has been strengthened with a warm bright red, a lot of golden yellow and warm darks. The oil paint has been applied in most places as a pure colour, but some opaque white has been introduced to create clouds, rather than merely suggesting them with bare priming.

Sunset (above) has more opaque paint with added white pigment, and more areas of red than *Rocky Bay with Figures*, giving it a wider tonal range. It is at a similar stage, and its subject is likewise unclear. Because of its theme – the setting sun – warm colours predominate, yet the blue paint plays a key part in the balance of the whole. The entire canvas is well covered with paint, but it is likely that Turner has not yet added

any medium modifiers. This canvas could have been developed into many different narratives, if he had chosen to do so. This is possibly the work referred to by the younger Trimmer: 'There is a red sunset, simply the sky ... the finest sky, to my mind, ever put on canvas.'[42]

Sketch for 'Ulysses Deriding Polyphemus' (overleaf, top) has a lower key than *Rocky Bay with Figures*, yet shows a further stage of development. Sufficient white opaque paint has been introduced into the sky to make it clear that the subject – Ulysses blinding the giant Polyphemus in order to make his escape – is far more dramatic and violent. The subject is only recognizable because Turner developed it further on another

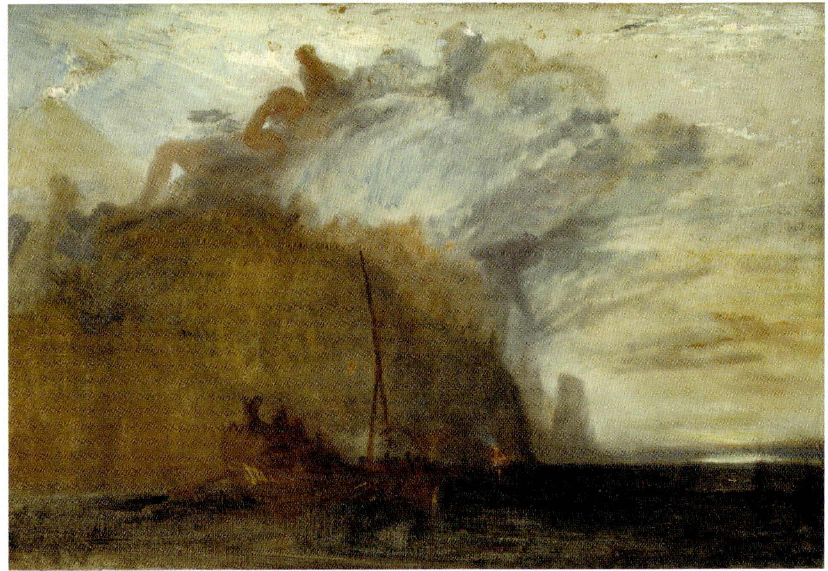

Sketch for 'Ulysses Deriding Polyphemus', c. 1827–28. Tate, London

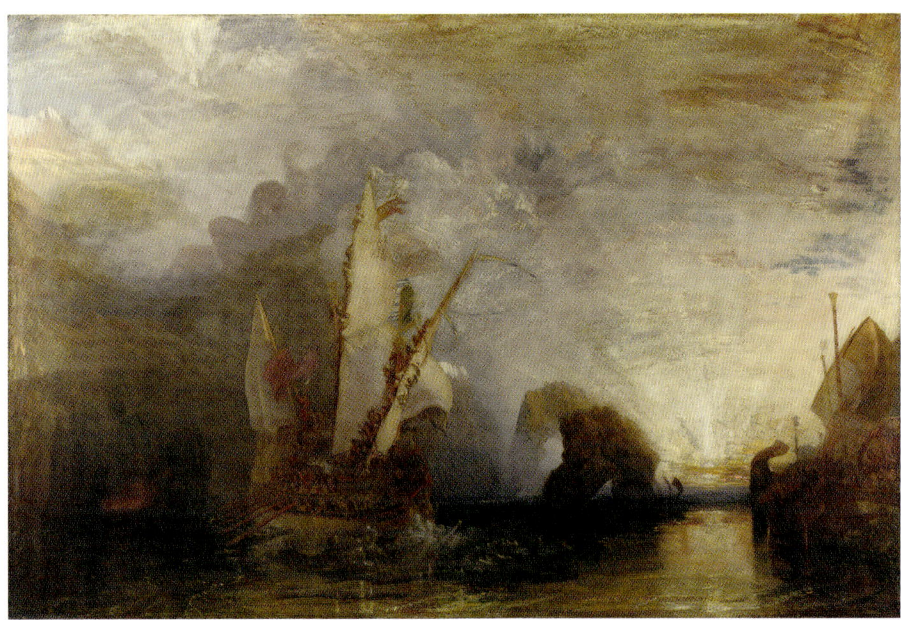

Ulysses Deriding Polyphemus – Homer's Odyssey, 1829. National Gallery, London

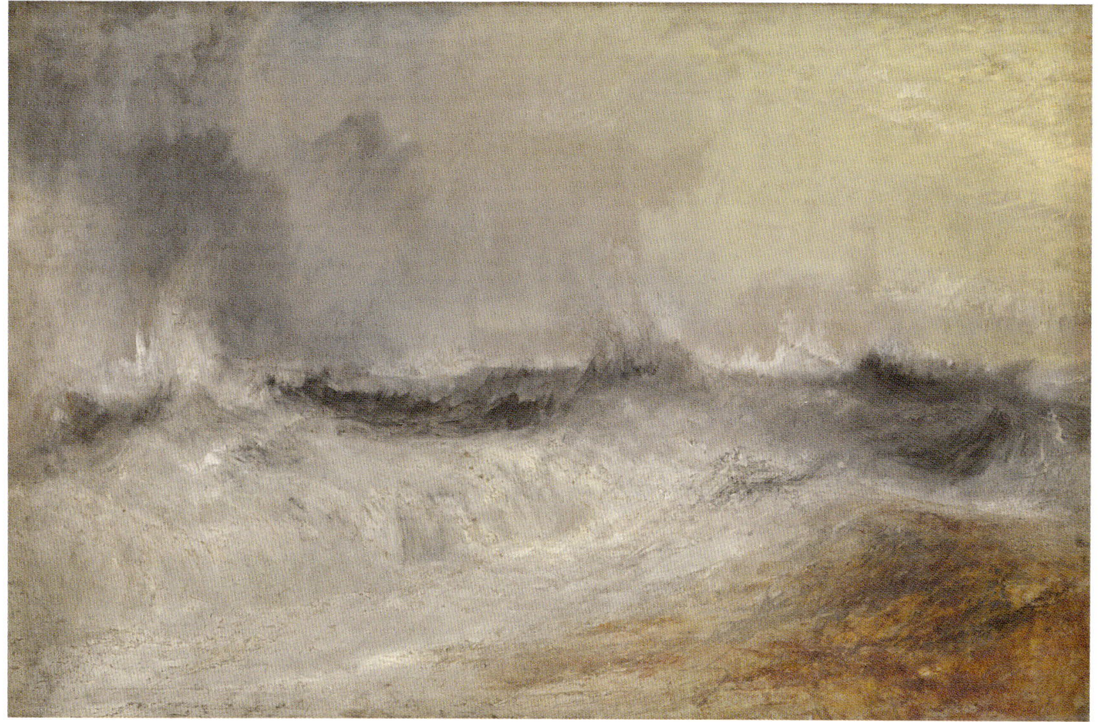

Waves Breaking against the Wind, c. 1840. Tate, London

canvas (opposite, bottom). By introducing the figure and the ship, he created a narrative but limited his options for the composition, except by the drastic action of wiping over the whole canvas with a turpentine-soaked rag and taking it back to a stage more akin to *Rocky Bay with Figures*. The tonal range has begun to diverge from what is achievable in watercolour by most artists working at the time, yet the paint is still thinly applied and no medium modifier has been used.

Waves Breaking against the Wind (above) is at a still later stage of development, yet the time of day and the narrative are not so easy to pin down.

Plenty of opaque white paint has been used for the flying spray, and the yellow paint of the sky on the right applied thickly with a palette knife, then brushed out. This paint is bodied. There is far more texture, especially for the breaking wave at the centre (overleaf, top), which must include many successive brushstrokes, and some contrast of glossy paint for the wet shore in the foreground (overleaf, middle), with the more matte paint for the sky, which fills half the canvas. The shoreline has been rapidly yet extensively worked, mostly in warm colours, strengthened with darks. Viewed closely, a wide range of colours is present here.

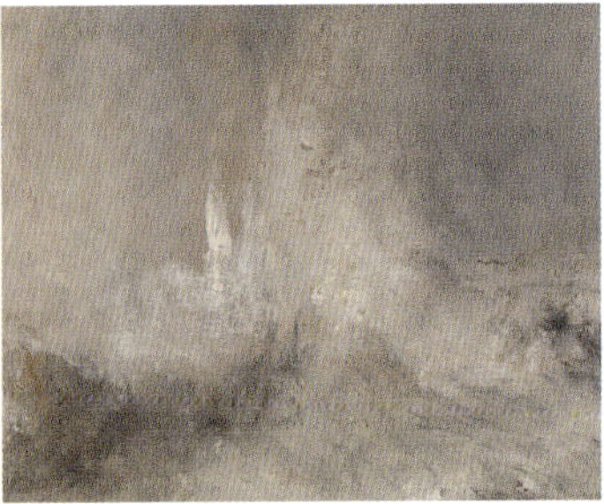

The wave in *Waves Breaking against the Wind* (full work ill. p. 69)

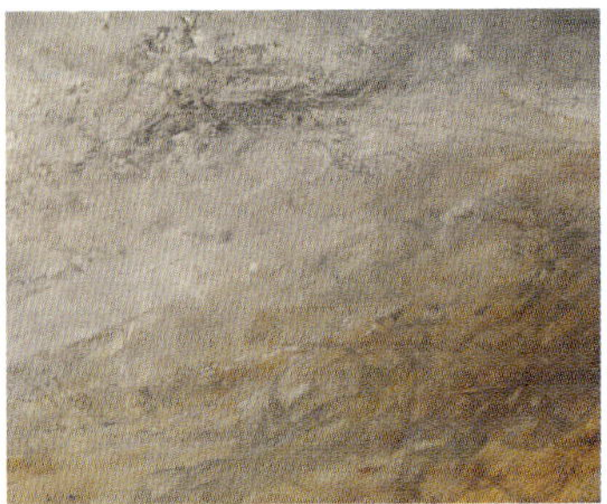

Detail of the shore

The sky, still pink where it was protected by the frame

There is a predominance of warm yellows and cool blues in the composition, and apparently no reds. This, however, is deceptive, since colour has been lost from a red lake in the sky (bottom left), which extends from the upper right of the canvas to the centre. Large pigment particles of a salmon-coloured red lake can be seen with a microscope right across this area of sunset, as thin washes applied to the yellow, but small and medium-sized particles only survive at the right edge, where they were protected from light. This might have suggested that the worst of the squall was over as the sun was setting.

The New Moon; or, 'I've lost My Boat, You shan't have Your Hoop' (opposite) has a coastal town in the background that makes the country, and even the location, recognizable – it is the south coast of England. The paint for the town, though it is distant, is highly impasted and craggy (ill. p. 72; top), and would have been made most easily by using a wax-based medium modifier. The balance of warm and cool tones dominates the composition, with the contrasts between them repeated at ever-finer levels of detail. The wet sand was achieved with thin applications of medium-rich paint, probably using megilp, with localized opaque paint on top for contrast – in the reflection of the white dog (ill. p. 72; bottom), for example, and the incoming waves. The dark dog has an ill-defined reflection, as it would have had in real life.

The whole composition is much more refined than the preceding sketches, and Turner gave this painting a title, albeit an obscure one. An X-radiograph (ill. p. 73) renders the lead white-based

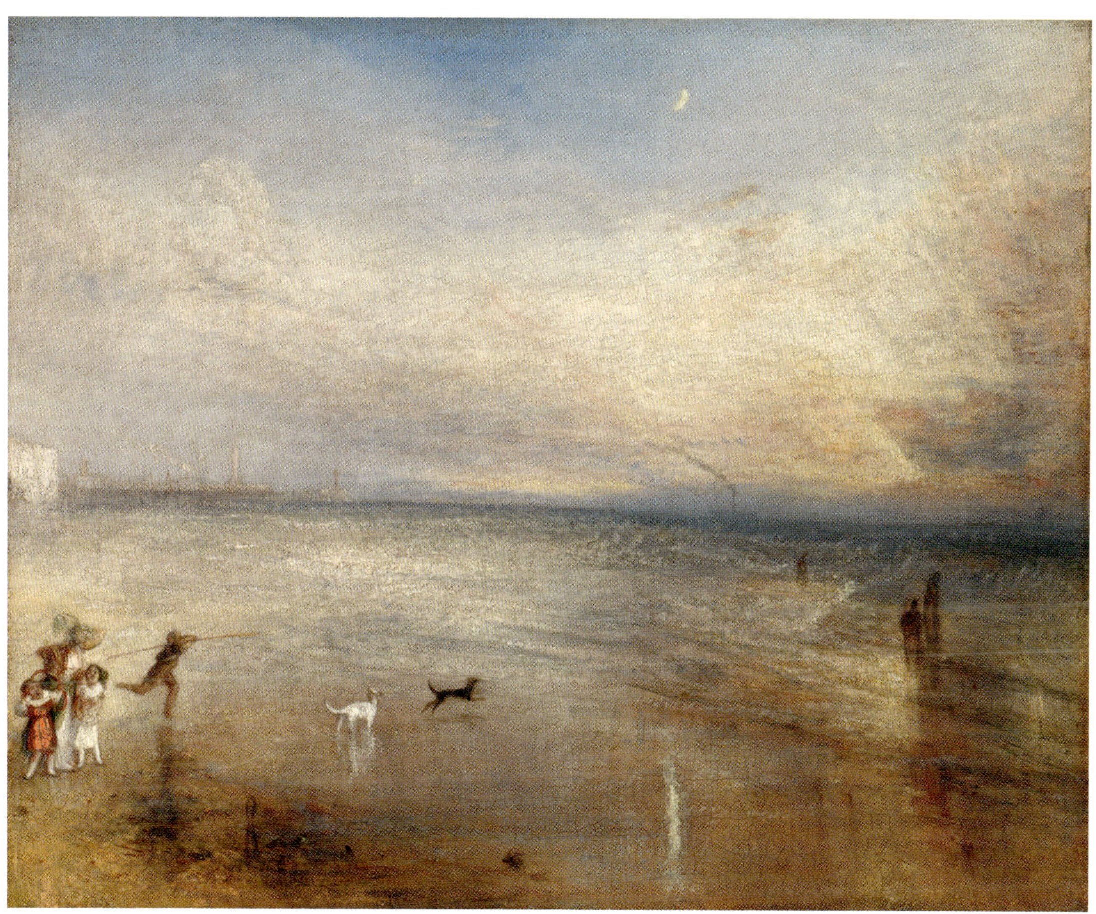

The New Moon; or, 'I've lost My Boat, You shan't have Your Hoop', exhibited 1840. Tate, London

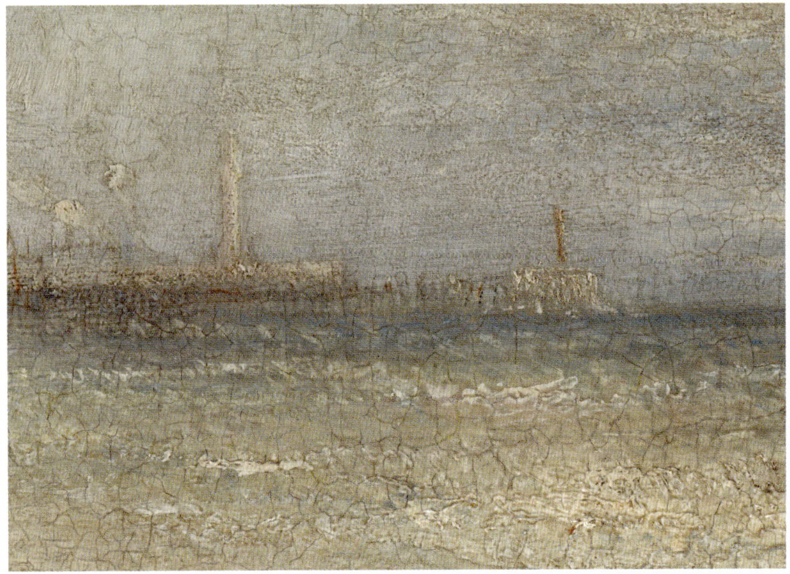

Detail from *The New Moon*, showing the town (full work ill. p. 71)

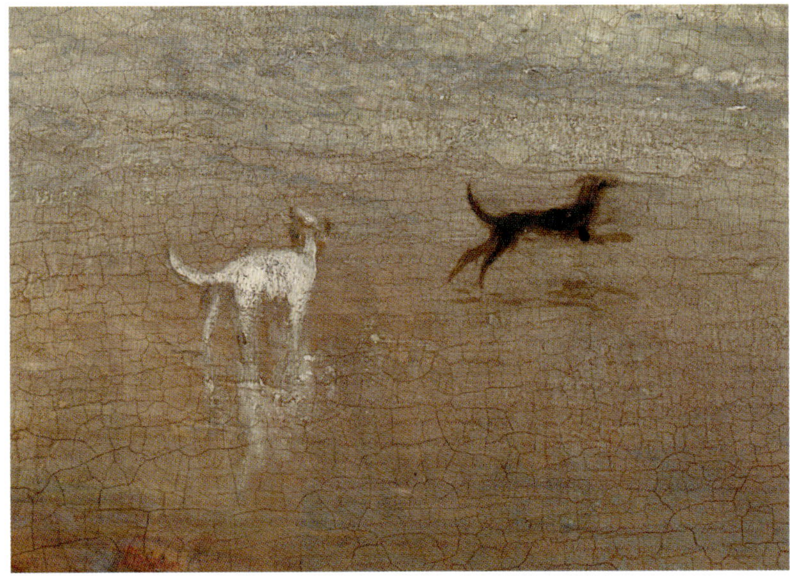

The dogs and their reflections on the beach

impasto for the sky, the distant town and each wave clearly (but not the medium-rich coloured glazes made from megilp that lie on top), as though we could see the composition at an earlier stage of its development. The more finished the oil, the more processes Turner used. At the later stages, he could have created the image by different sequences of paint application, and by different combinations of removing and adding paint. He had planned to give expression to an idea to the best of his ability, but not precisely how to do it: creative instinct must have taken over. Turner himself would have been unable to explain how he had got to that point, even had he been gifted with the mastery of words of a poet, as well as the skill of a painter.

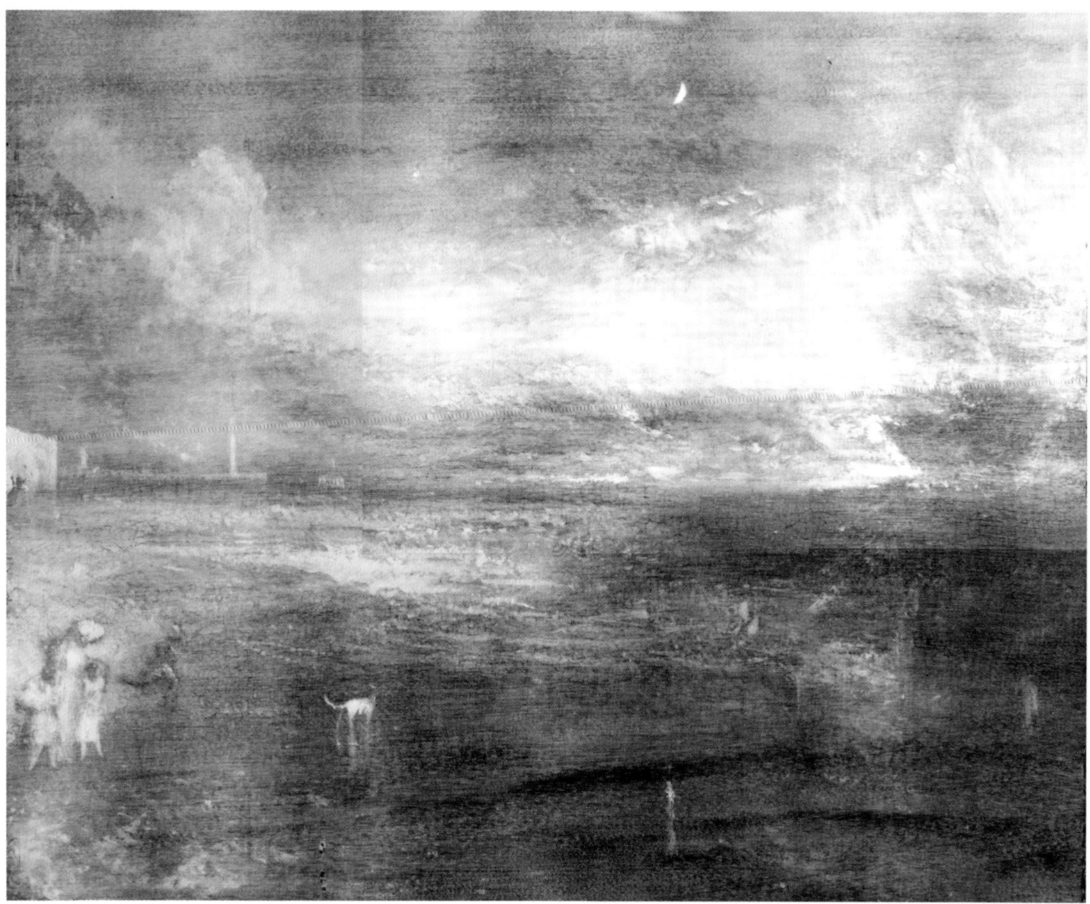

An X-radiograph renders the impasted white paint more clearly, as bright white

THREE

FINISHED PAINTINGS AND THE 'VARNISHING DAYS'

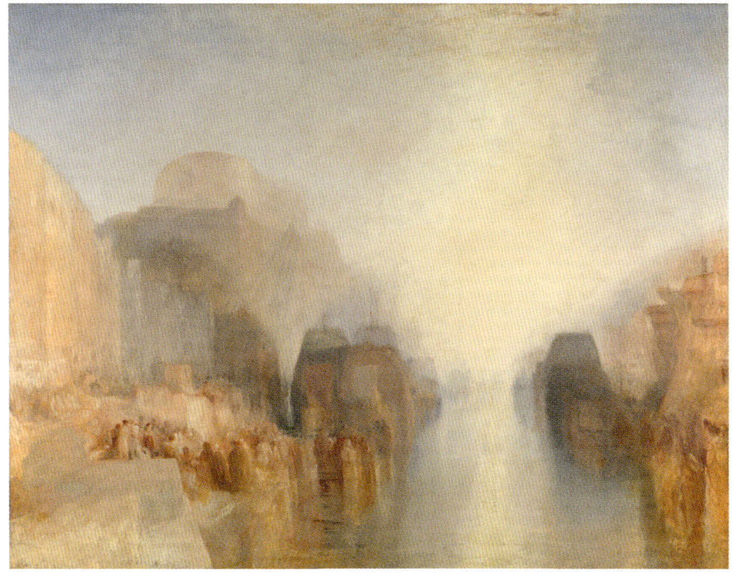

The Harbour of Brest: The Quayside and Château, c. 1826–28. Tate, London

What did 'finish' mean in Turner's time?

A group of three paintings of French ports from c. 1826–28 perfectly illustrate the difference between an unfinished work of great beauty to modern eyes – such as *The Harbour of Brest: The Quayside and Château* (above) – and finished paintings like *Harbour of Dieppe: Changement de Domicile* (overleaf, top) and *Cologne, the Arrival of a Packet-Boat: Evening* (overleaf, bottom left), which were more acceptable to Turner's contemporaries and predecessors.[43]

Turner's increasing commitment from his thirties onwards to experimentation with new materials and ever more complex ways of applying paint ran counter to much of the expectations of his contemporaries. Today, his most highly regarded works are often the ones that even he would not have dared to exhibit: barely begun compositions, or those laid aside while the subject could still have been taken in many different directions. But what made a painting 'finished'? Balance and harmony, a well thought-out composition and the realistic portrayal of an idealized human form all contributed to the idea of finish. The landscape, also idealized, might have a foreground with realistically portrayed plants and flowers, a middle ground with buildings that evoked the classical past, and a distant view seen through a bluish haze, as in *Modern Rome – Campo Vaccino* (overleaf, bottom right), in which the unheeding peasants and their goats are contrasted with the ruins of imperial Rome.

Reynolds clothed the figures in his history paintings in timeless classical costumes, rather than

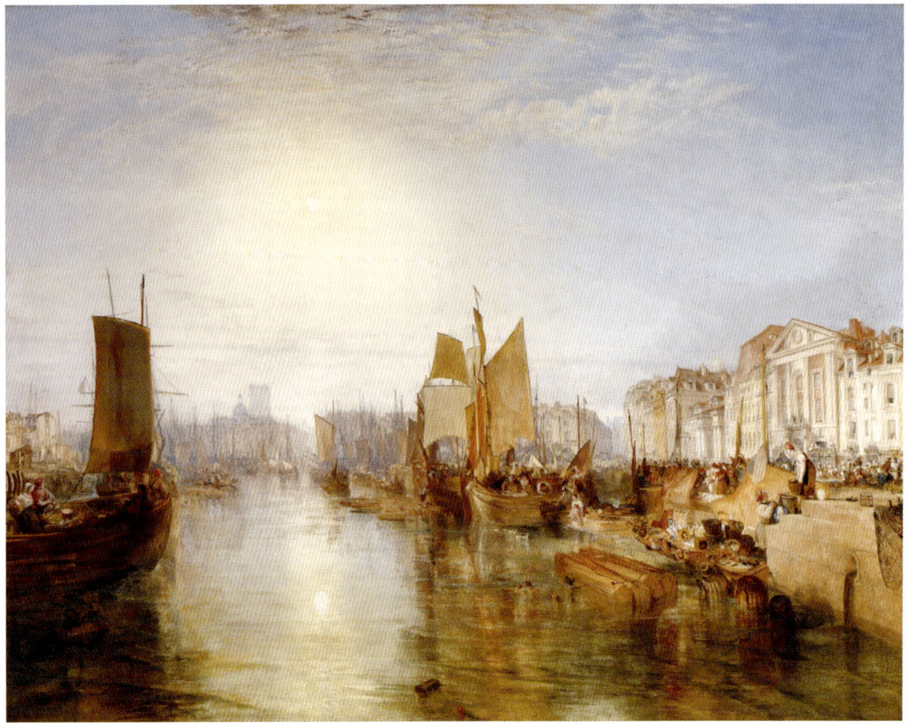

Harbour of Dieppe: Changement de Domicile, exhibited 1825. The Frick Collection, New York

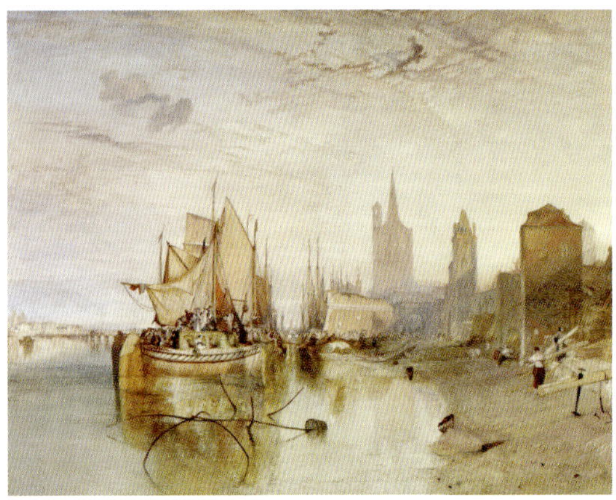

Cologne, the Arrival of a Packet-Boat: Evening, 1826.
The Frick Collection, New York

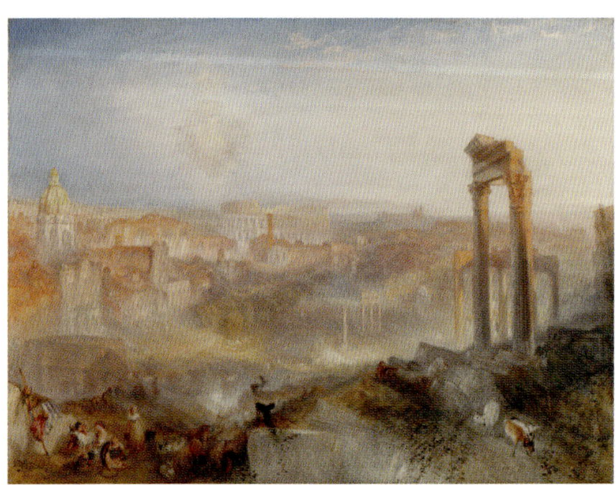

Modern Rome – Campo Vaccino, 1839.
J. Paul Getty Museum, Los Angeles

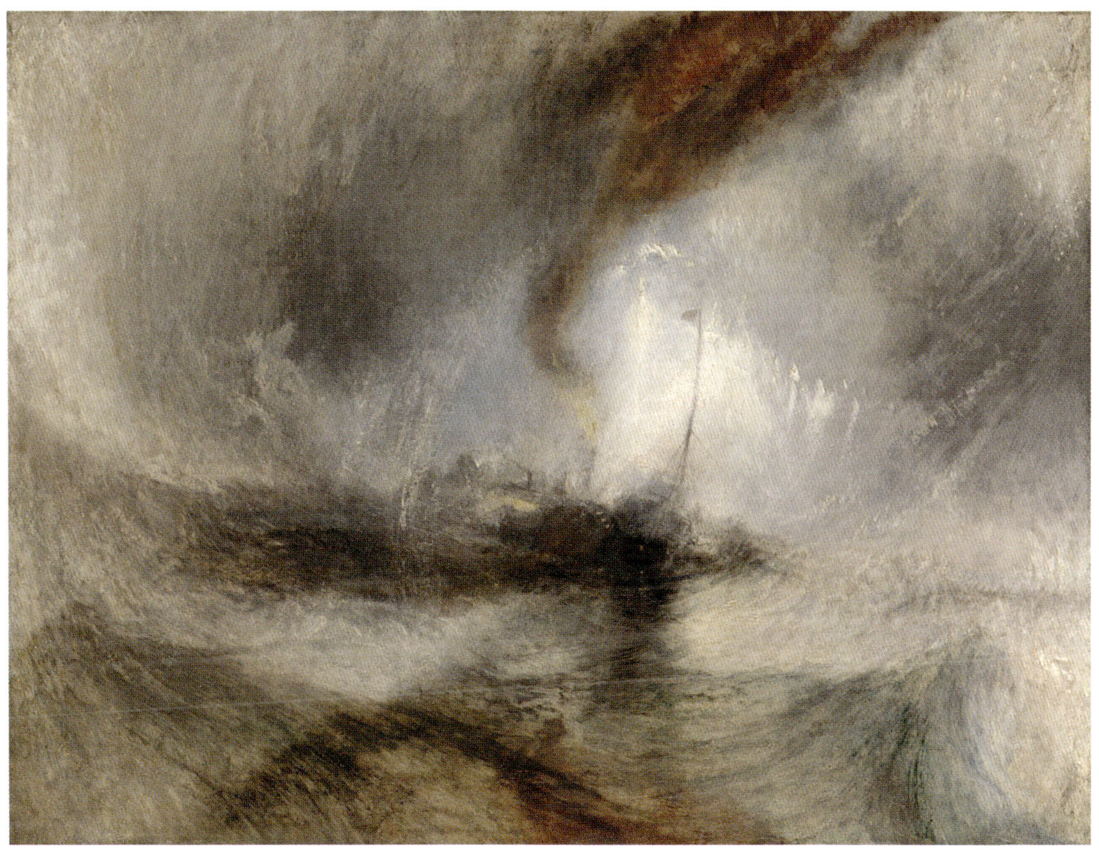

Snow Storm – Steam-boat off a Harbour's Mouth, exhibited 1842. Tate, London

contemporary dress, which would appear dated, and even laughable, in a few decades, fatally undermining the intended uplifting effect on the viewer. Raw nature could be improved upon by depicting the natural world as it might have been in ideal weather and growing conditions, while trees and well-known buildings could be moved around to form pleasingly balanced compositions, thereby portraying a more universal truth, not degraded and spoilt by discordant reality.

Realism was often seen as 'mere realism', but this is what Turner excelled at when painting stormy seas and violent weather, making the viewer feel like a participant in an experience lived by the artist. The viewer of a finished painting would perhaps expect a less participatory experience, but would still be expected to empathize with the situation of the figures portrayed. *Snow Storm – Steam-boat off a Harbour's Mouth* (previous page) is the perfect example of a highly accomplished painting that emphatically does not have finish.

The best example of a finished work is perhaps *The Fighting Temeraire* (ill. p. 149), a painting that can make some claim to being one of the nation's favourite works of art. During the Second World War, it was kept in London to inspire a war-weary populace, but there are few still alive today who can recall being cheered by it. This composition shows Turner at his best: it is technically complex, very beautiful, and yet not realistic. The contrast between the pale ship and the dark tug towing it indicates which vessel to empathize with, while the glorious sunset (painted not in the west, but in the east, as the *Temeraire* was coming up the

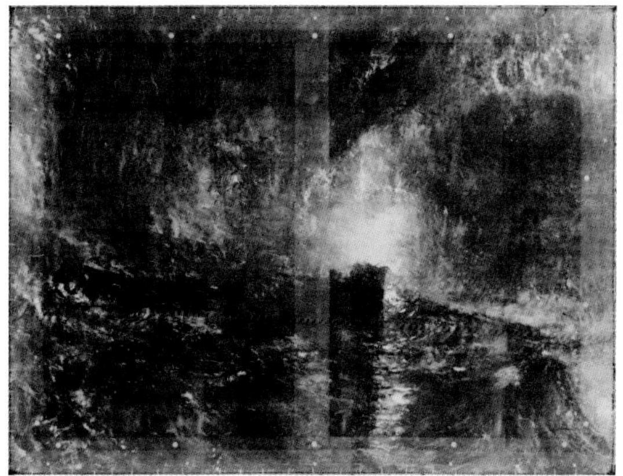

X-radiograph of *Snow Storm – Steam-boat off a Harbour's Mouth* (full work ill. p. 77)

Thames) unmistakably signals a valedictory mood. It embodies the artistic skills that arise from a lifetime's experience, as well as constant practice of one's profession.

Close examination of this very well-preserved work not only is rewarding, but also reveals examples of a huge number of Turner's habitual techniques and materials, skilfully brought together in an image that conveys pride in the past, with an acknowledgment that progress is part of life and that all things decay. The full title of the painting is *The Fighting Temeraire tugged to her last berth to be broken up, 1838*, and the narrative would have been very clear to coeval viewers, for this was a ship that had taken part in the Battle of Trafalgar, and had therefore helped to preserve British sovereignty.

Snow Storm has no such universality. It depicts a snowstorm, not a subject of enduring or national interest, and it draws in the viewer, rather than inducing sober reflection. Contemporary critics described it variously

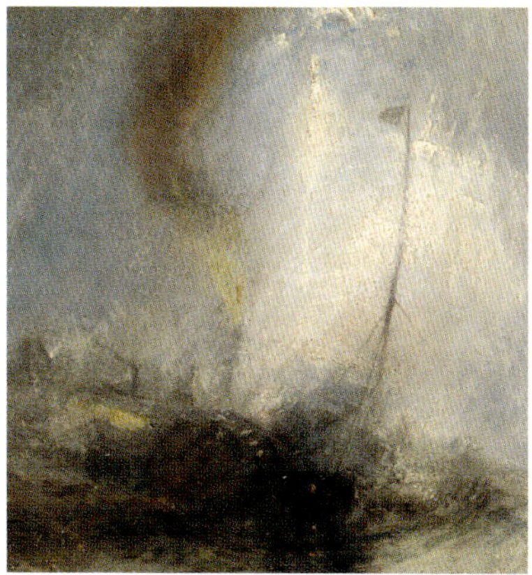

Detail of the steamship

Dark steam and pale snow and clouds at
the top right

as 'soapsuds and whitewash' (an anonymous reviewer) or 'one of the grandest sea-pieces ever painted' (Ruskin),[44] but even the lengthy and descriptive title conferred by Turner himself (*Snow Storm – Steam-boat off a Harbour's Mouth making Signals in Shallow Water, and going by the Lead. The Author was in this Storm on the Night the Ariel left Harwich*) cannot impose the

necessary gravitas. The subject is perhaps too close to a lived or imagined experience for the contemplative, reflective thoughts that a finished painting was meant to induce in viewers.

It does enable the viewer today, however, to imagine painting like Turner. The X-radiograph (opposite) shows how he painted the waves with broad sweeps of his arm across the canvas. The finishing creates a vortex shape that blurs the underlying structure of the composition, the ship having been applied over the seascape (left, top), with the snow virtually encircling it (left, bottom). Finish in an oil painting was a concept that outlived Turner by many decades. One thing that artists and connoisseurs did not expect to see was an artist finishing a painting as they watched, rather like a modern-day performance artist.

Turner's performance art

The annual exhibitions at the Royal Academy and the British Institution created not only a great deal of pressure on the artists, but also some practical problems. Large paintings had to be transported from studios, in London or further afield, and then conveyed safely indoors. For much of Turner's life, the Royal Academy exhibition room was on the second floor at Somerset House in the Strand,[45] and was – as it is today – approached by a long, curved cantilevered staircase, just wide enough for two people to climb, side by side. Paintings were hung edge to edge, as far as their differing sizes permitted, with the topmost tier tilted out and down. Each one was fitted into a frame of standard design, reused each year for the exhibition.

A ledge, slightly above eye level and known as 'the line', gave some support to large and heavy works, with added battens on the walls for hanging. The best place for one's painting was 'above the line', because visitors could always look up and have a clear sightline when it was too crowded to see across the room, as numerous images suggest it often was. Royal Academicians, including Turner himself, selected which paintings to hang from those submitted by members, and where. Bitter rivalries were never far below the surface, often erupting into altercations and incidents that have become legendary.[46]

Damage to paintings completed to such a critical deadline in professional terms, and sent to such a challenging venue, were frequent. Both institutions soon instituted 'varnishing days', which enabled artists to repair damage sustained during the transport or hanging of their work (the original purpose of the days), or to modify colours or even the overall tonality, once they saw the competition hanging all around, and the colours that had been used to decorate and furnish the room.[47] The number of days allowed for this ranged from three to five over different years. Overall varnishing took place, as well, if needed, since some artists might have cut it too fine to varnish before delivery.

Varnish should only be applied to well-dried paint and many artists in the 19th century thought that paint should dry for some years before it received the first varnish. It is more probable that the paint was still drying on many of Turner's pictures while the works were being selected and hung. This meant that some areas of the paint

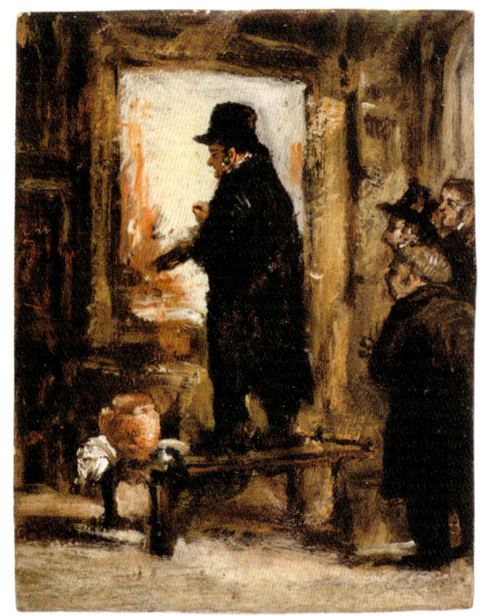

Charles West Cope, *J.M.W. Turner*, c. 1828. National Portrait Gallery, London

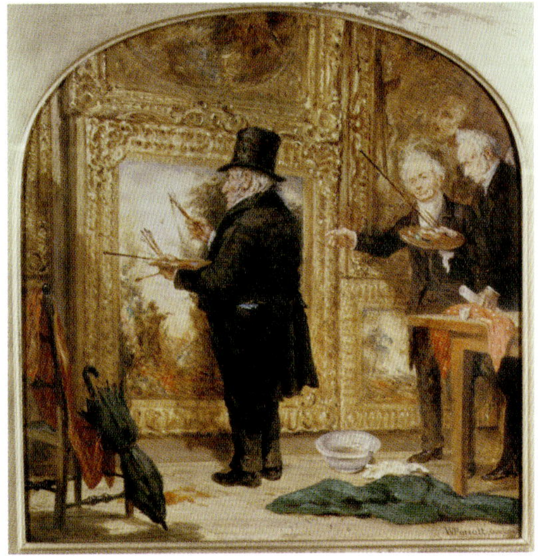

William Parrott, *Turner on Varnishing Day*, c. 1840. Collection of the Guild of St George, Sheffield

might 'sink' and look less glossy than others: local revarnishing was genuinely necessary to counteract this, and was probably more common than applying a coat of varnish all over, which is what the term 'varnishing' implies today.

Turner soon did far more than this. In the words of his contemporaries, he added all his 'finish' during the varnishing days. Some observers captured him in paint, working from memory or hasty sketches before Turner caught them in the act. Charles West Cope (1811–1890) and William Parrott (1813–1869) both sketched him working at the British Institution (opposite), each depicting a painting of moderate dimensions, hung within reach from the floor (Turner was short, and in Cope's sketch, he is standing on a low bench). Sir John Gilbert (1817–1897) also sketched Turner at work at the Royal Academy (ill. p. 56). Ruskin wrote:

His oil pictures were laid roughly with ground colours, and painted into with such rapid skill, that the artists who used to

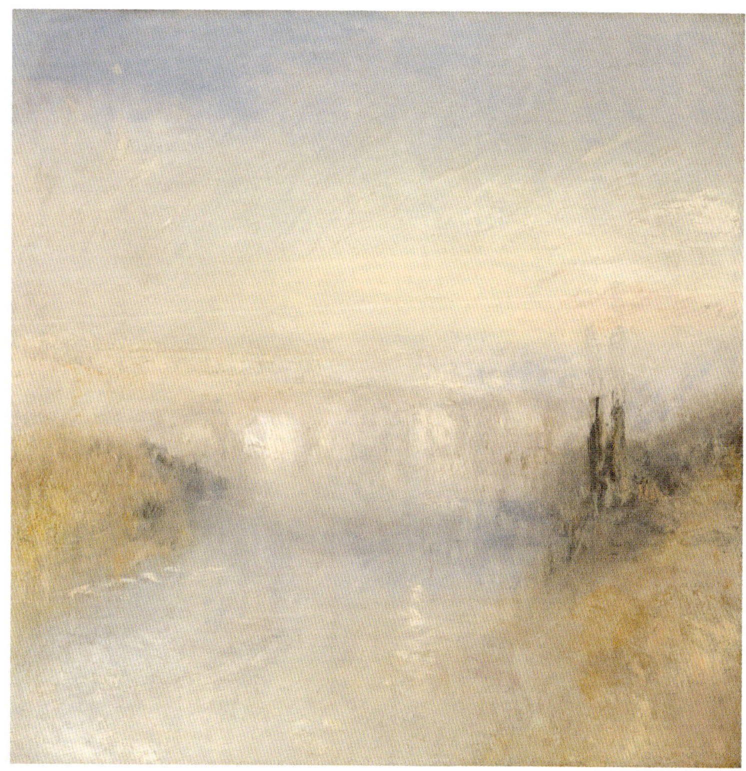

A River Seen from a Hill, c. 1840–45. Tate, London

see his finishing at the Academy sometimes suspected him of having the picture finished underneath the colours he showed, and removing, instead of adding, as they watched.[48]

Ruskin also quoted the memories of the brother of the artist Charles Robert Leslie (1794–1859), from 1832 and written fifty years later:

… on Varnishing Days … Turner stood working on these, to my eyes, nearly blank white canvases in their old Academy frames. There were always a number of mysterious little gallipots and cups of colour ranged upon drawing stools in front of his pictures … he used short brushes, some of them like the writers used by house decorators, working with thin colour over the white ground, and using the brush end on … he came, they said, at six in the morning, and worked standing all day, and his brushes were few, looked old, and that among them were some of those common little soft brushes in white quill used by house-painters for painting letters etc, with. His colours were mostly in powder, and he mixed them with turpentine, sometimes, with size, and water, and perhaps even with stale beer, as the grainers do their umber when using it upon an oil ground, binding it in with varnish afterwards …[49]

A canvas that would have seemed 'nearly blank' to 19th-century observers likely resembled *A River Seen from a Hill* (previous page), which was not exhibited in Turner's lifetime and was not even recognized as a painting until the mid-20th century.[50] The painter Edward Villiers Rippingille (*c.* 1790–1859) wrote of Turner during one of the varnishing days:

… before I came, having set-to at the earliest hour allowed … the picture when sent in was a mere dab of several colours, and 'without form and void' like chaos before the creation. The managers knew that a picture would be sent there, and would not have hesitated, knowing to whom it belonged, to have received and hung up a bare canvas, than which this was but little better … Turner, for the three hours I was there … it had been the same since he began in the morning … never ceased to work … A small box of colours, a few very small brushes, and a vial or two were at his feet, very inconveniently placed …[51]

Some of these descriptions are at variance with the paintings we know today, in terms of their surface colour or materials analysis of the topmost layers, so it is more prudent to consider that Turner immersed himself in a composition that looked something like *Snow Storm*, while applying small-scale additions more akin to soapsuds than overall whitewash.[52] There is a great deal of evidence that he must have used very fine brushes for the work done during the varnishing days, but no evidence whatever for the suggestion of using beer or glue size in the manner of graining.

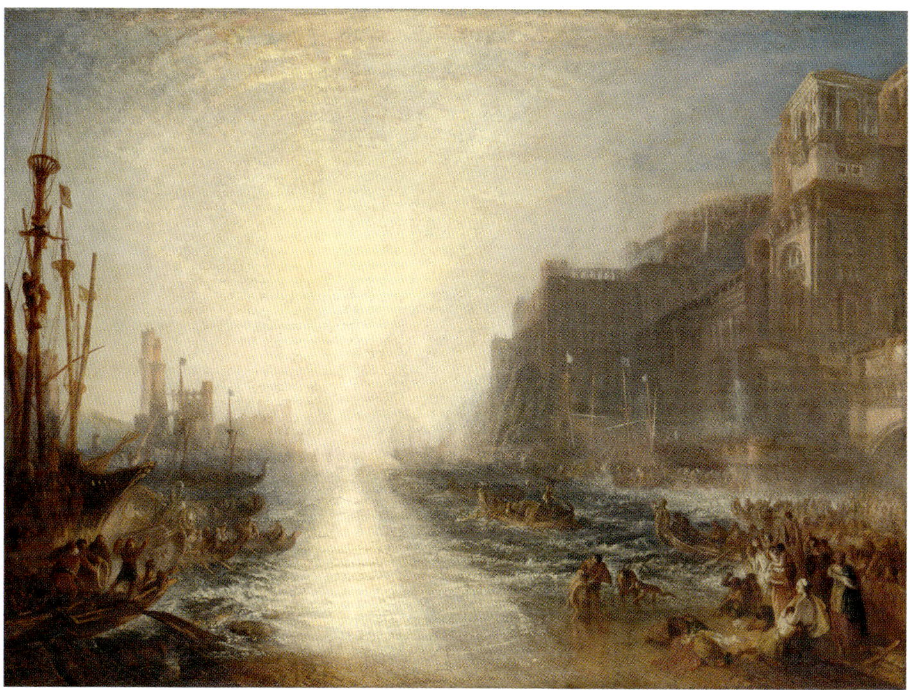

Regulus, 1828 (reworked 1837). Tate, London

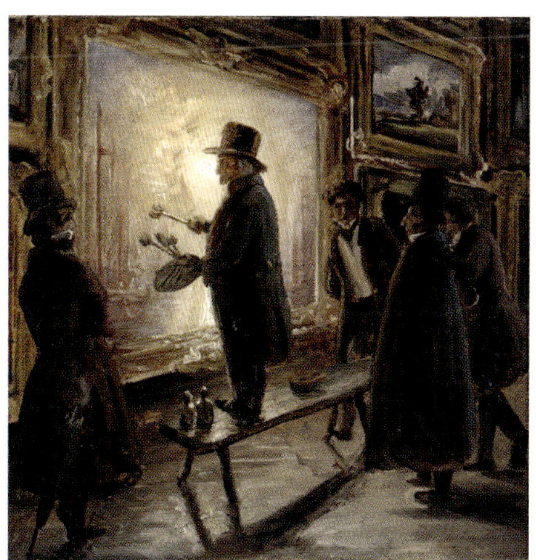

Thomas Fearnley, *Turner Varnishing*, 1837.
Private collection

All of the anecdotes have the common feature of respect from younger or lesser artists, stories that might have grown as they were retold over the decades, and a general sense that no one dared talk to Turner while he was fully engaged in the painting process, nor observed what kind of paint he was using because they dared not get too close.

It has been possible to study the surface and surprisingly accident-prone history of one such painting, *Regulus* (above). Turner completed and exhibited it in his own studio while in Rome during his second trip to Italy in 1828, had it shipped back too late for exhibition the following year, then repaired after it was damaged in his studio, reworked it to conceal the extent of the repair,

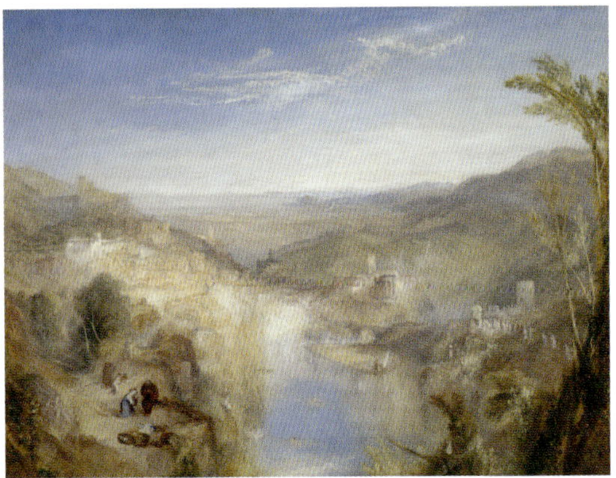

Modern Italy: The Pifferari, 1838. Kelvingrove Art Gallery and Museum, Glasgow

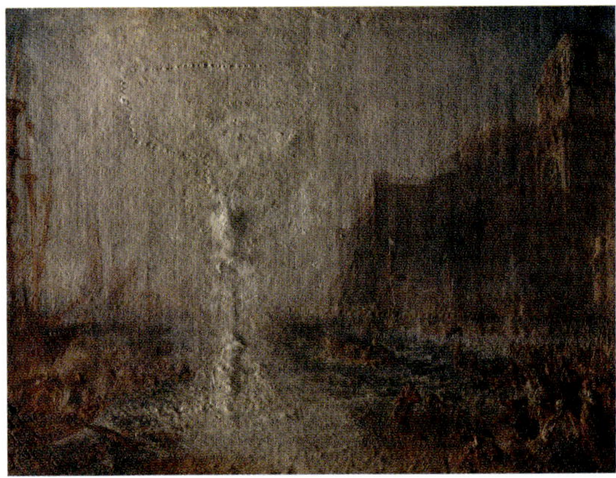

Regulus, viewed in raking light from the left. The repaired tear looks like a reversed question-mark

and finally finished it on the walls of the Royal Academy in 1837.[53] He was shown at work on this very painting by the Norwegian artist Thomas Fearnley (previous page, bottom). The prominent and numerous masts at the left, and Fearnley's known dates of travel from Norway where he worked, match it to *Regulus*. Cope's painting could also be of Turner at work on *Regulus*, but he got one detail wrong, the painting actually being in landscape format, rather than square, as he depicted it.

Firstly, it is necessary to understand the damage that the painting sustained after it returned safely from Italy, as letters confirm – at least, it is necessary to know how much repair work had to be done, even if we cannot know why it toppled onto something (a wooden chair-back or the corner of a picture frame are likely candidates) and sustained a large, curved tear in the sky. The canvas had to be lined – that is to say, adhered to another one in order to secure the tear, which had already

been stitched back together. Turner then reworked the image over the varnish applied in Rome from a tranquil Claudian seaport with a bright blue sky – rather like that in *Modern Italy: The Pifferari* (above left) – by adding thick yellow paint for the sinking sun, the rays of which seem almost linear. He also added the sun's extensive yellow reflection in the water, and glancing reflections off the forest of masts, the projections of the buildings on the right and the incoming waves. He covered his tracks so well that it is impossible to tell how much of a setting sun there had been when the painting was shown in Rome with the same title. In raking light, it can be seen how the sun stands out from the thick yellow paint (above right).

The paint is extraordinarily thick, even by Turner's standards, in terms of his use of megilp and wax-based media. The bright bluish appearance in ultraviolet light of the whole sky and the reflection on the water (opposite, top left) indicates that most of this yellow paint was wax-based,

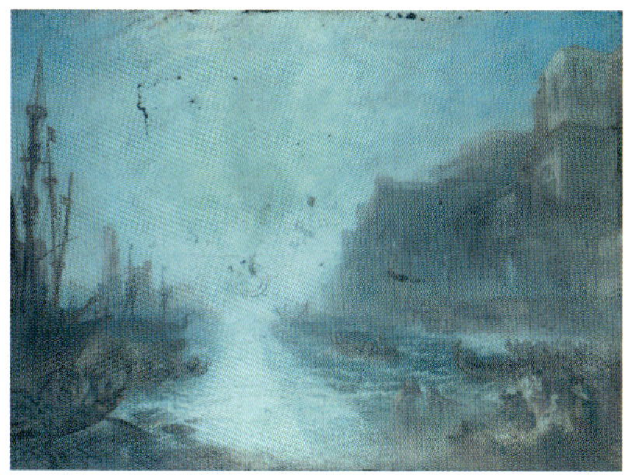

Regulus, viewed in ultraviolet light

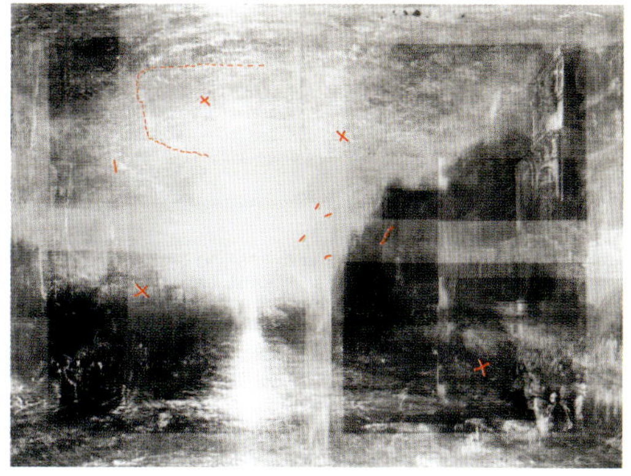

X-radiograph showing the tear sustained in the 1830s
and damage caused by a knife attack in the 1860s

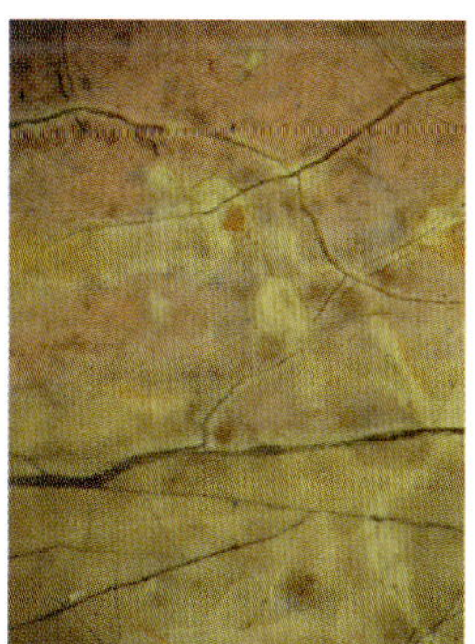

Micrograph of the sky
above the repaired tear,
showing the pink glazes
applied on the varnishing
days, which have run over
earlier ageing cracks in
the paint Turner used
after the repair

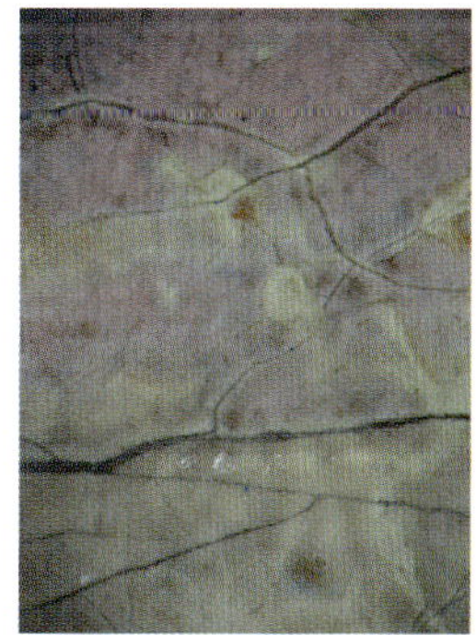

The same area in ultraviolet
light, indicating that these
glazes were made with
madder lake

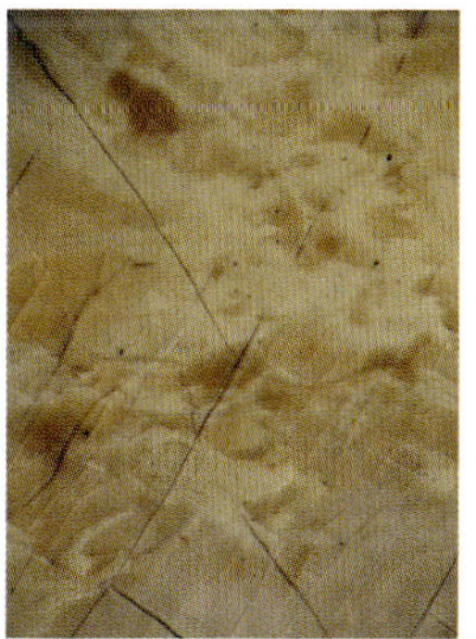

Micrograph showing the
outer edge of the yellow
sky Turner applied to the
repaired area, running
over the blue sky painted
in Rome

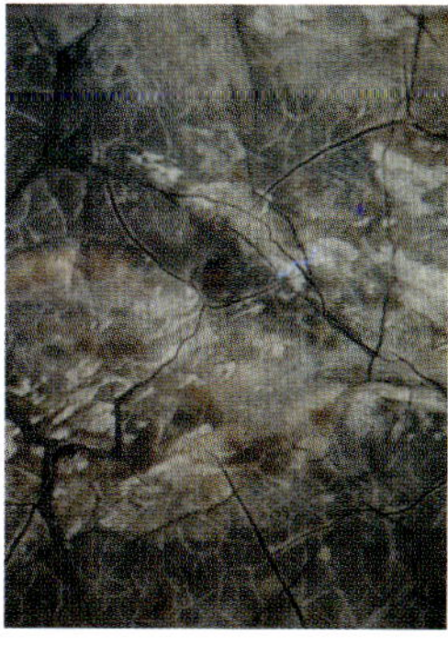

Micrograph in ultraviolet
light, showing small-scale
white impasto applied on
the varnishing days over
the yellow reflections added
when Turner worked over
the repair

necessary to build up the thickness and conceal the tear. No other medium modifier could have created such bodied paint needed to cover the stitching and the resulting deformation in the canvas. The X-radiograph (previous page, top right), which renders all of the lead white mixed with the lead-based chrome yellow, also shows this, because where the image is most white and bright, the paint is physically thickest. The curve of the tear and some later damages are marked on the X-radiograph. This unusual level of reworking could not all have been done in situ at the British Institution, since it includes several layers of paint on top of the varnished surface of what had been an exhibited painting. It would not have been possible to apply them all in the same few days.

What Turner did do in a recognizable third campaign of painting, which could easily have been accomplished over a few days, was to intensify the sunlight by adding very localized

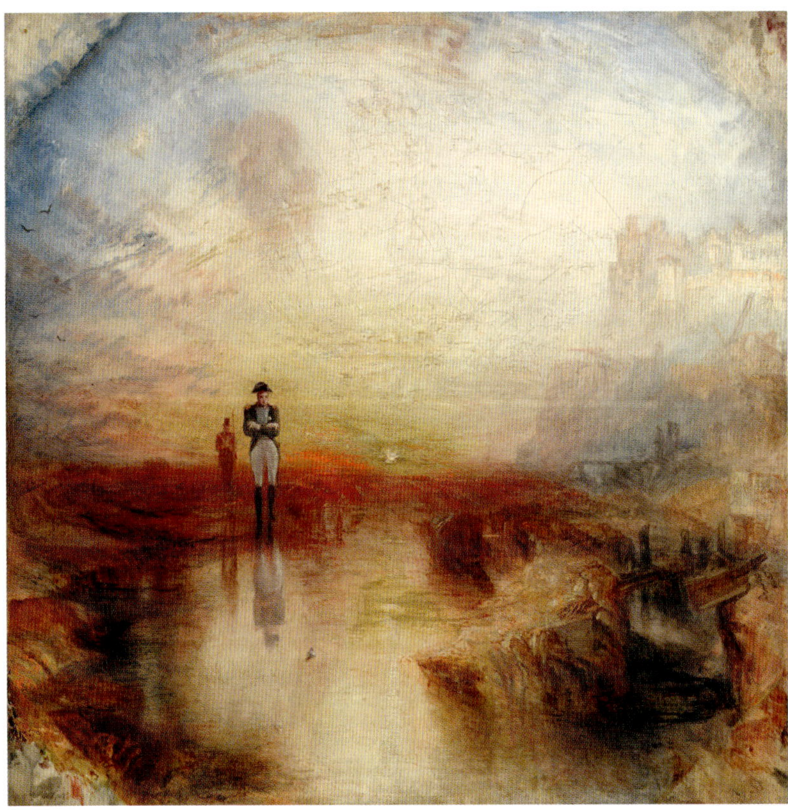

War. The Exile and the Rock Limpet, exhibited 1842. Tate, London

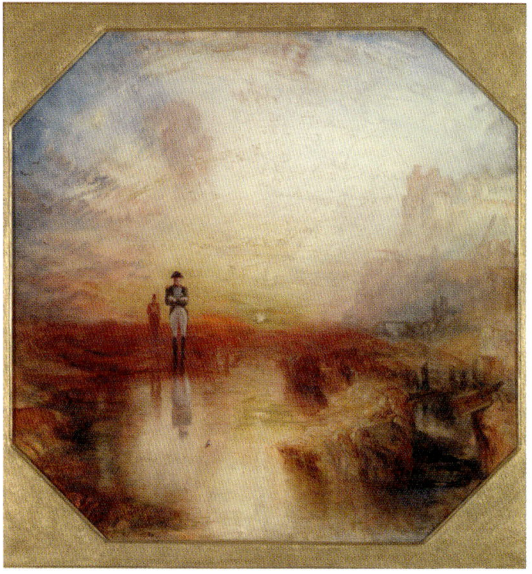

Shown with a modern gilded mat covering the corners.
The whole is then framed for display.

The protected top-right corner, not painted on the
varnishing days

transparent glazes, predominantly pink, at the top edge (p. 85, bottom left) in a curved line high above the sun, and blue ones in the water, over the extra dashes of yellow impasto, which had been applied for reflections on the crests of the waves when he disguised the repair (p. 85, bottom right). These gave life and variety to the more yellow reflections that were by now well dried, but had not been varnished, as is clear from cross-sections. Later cracking and cupping of the paint in the sea, comprising many thin layers in a variety of mixed media, now conceal how lively the water must have looked. It is easier to appreciate Turner's work in the upper sky. The slightly yellow patches seen in the ultraviolet image show the limited extent of this finishing.

In 1842, Turner exhibited a number of paintings at the Royal Academy in a new format: square canvases of identical size, slightly smaller at just under 80 cm (31 in.) each side than the rectangular canvases he had purchased and exhibited fairly often.[54] These came from the colourman Brown of High Holborn, just like the regular formats did, and have the same off-white priming. This format lent itself to framing with a circular or octagonal gilded mat within the frame,[55] creating a symmetric composition that could readily be painted to depict a vortex of light or swirl of movement, even more dramatic than the sweeping, curved brushstrokes seen in *Snow Storm – Steam-boat off a Harbour's Mouth* (ill. p. 77), shown in the same year.

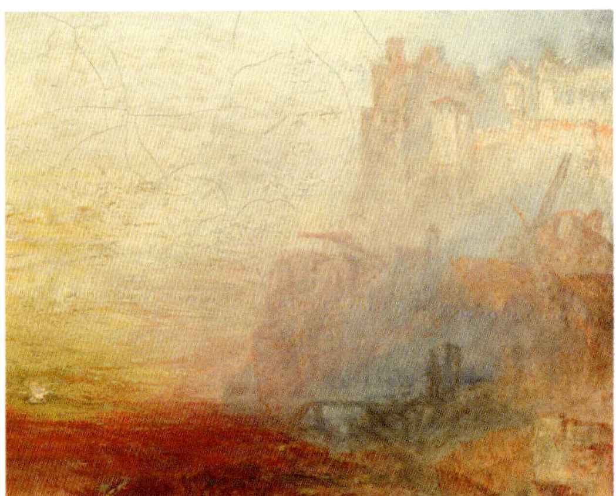

Detail showing the Italianate town at the right

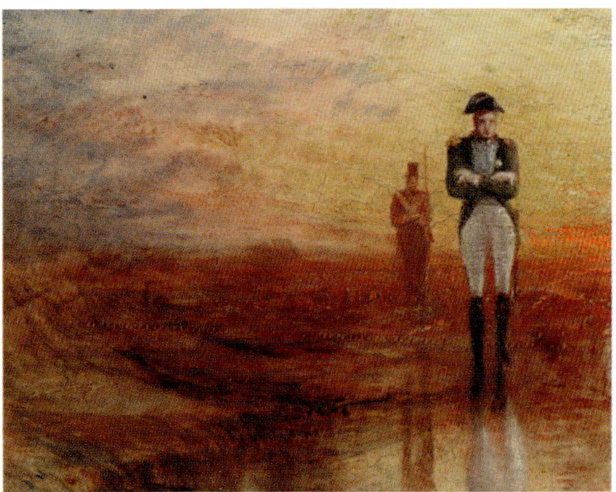

Detail of the central figures

One of the group is *War. The Exile and the Rock Limpet* (ill. p. 86), also shown with a modern gilded mat (previous page, above left). At first, Turner worked on the whole canvas, including the four corners, as he did for most of the square canvases, using much thinned oil paint. Quite quickly, however, he decided that the image would be circular. He did not pause to mark off the corners in pencil, but instead they became useful spots for trying out colours (previous page, above right). Later still, he settled on an octagonal mat instead, as he continued to paint in his studio. There is no paint running down the edges at this point, so the assumption that the canvas was on a sloping easel of the kind he sketched in his studio at Petworth (ill. p. 119) and was portrayed using (ill. p. 56) cannot be verified.

The composition developed in clear, bright blue contrasted with warm pink, and the peaceful scene included an Italianate hill town (above left) that would later be situated on the island of Elba, where Napoleon was exiled. What was in the middle of the canvas is partly lost to view beneath the later paint, and cannot be explored successfully with technical imaging, but there was a figure in similar colours where Napoleon now stands. From the edges, the painting looks like a pretty finished and exhibitable composition. This must be what went to the Royal Academy, framed with an octagonal mat, to be completed during the varnishing days.

The finishing that created the blood-red sunset and brooding figure of Napoleon was all done in the frame, since the paint does not extend beneath the outermost 10 mm (less than half an inch) covered by the mat, at any edge. The paint was runny, and flowed unevenly under the diagonals of the mat, towards the corners. The whole sunset and its reflection, both hinting at Napoleon's gloomy contemplation, was added over the sunny landscape, mostly using megilp and opaque pigments such as red vermilion and a mid-toned chrome yellow, with a much paler shade for the sun sinking below the horizon. The sky of the more pastoral scene was left alone, but the sentry and

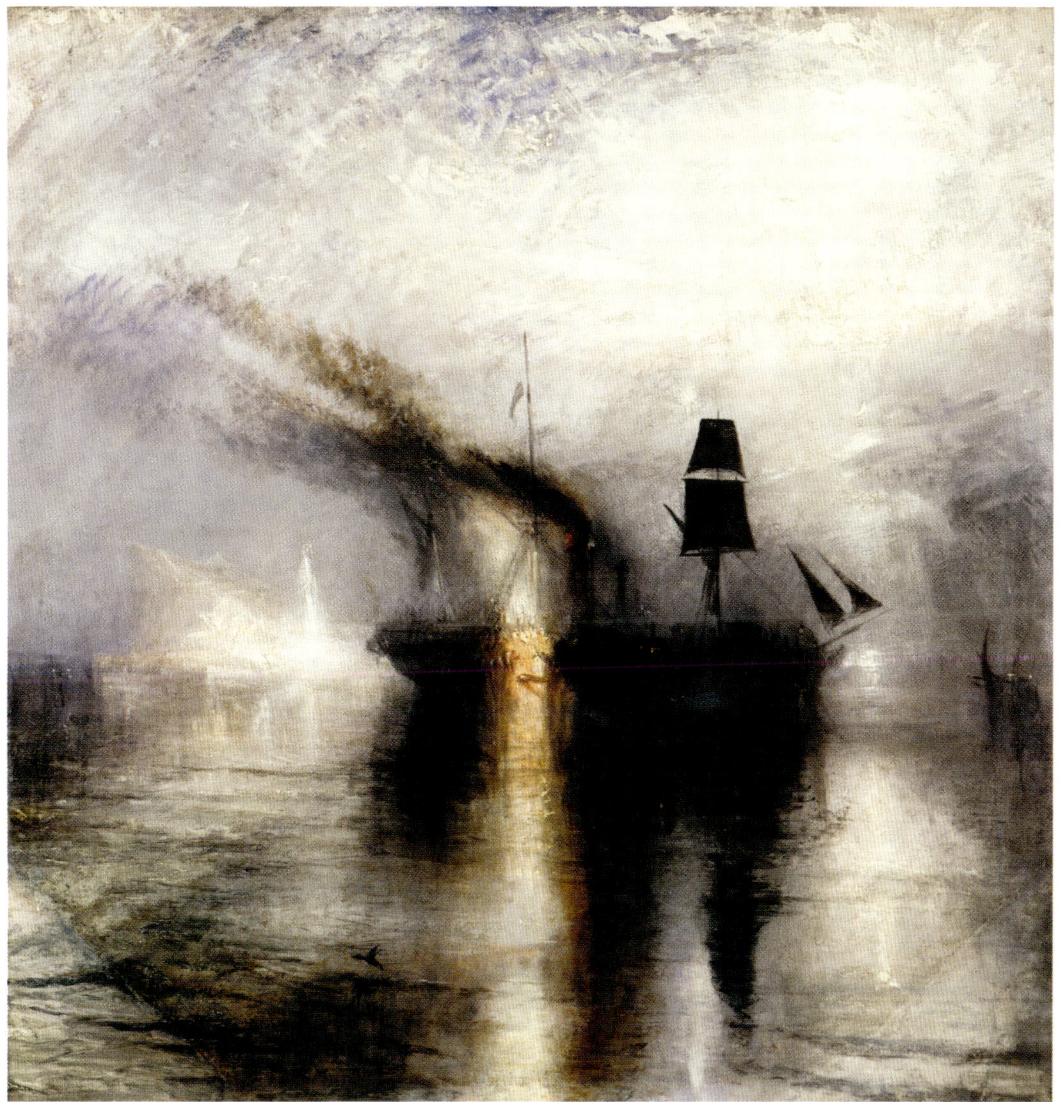

Peace – Burial at Sea, exhibited 1842. Tate, London

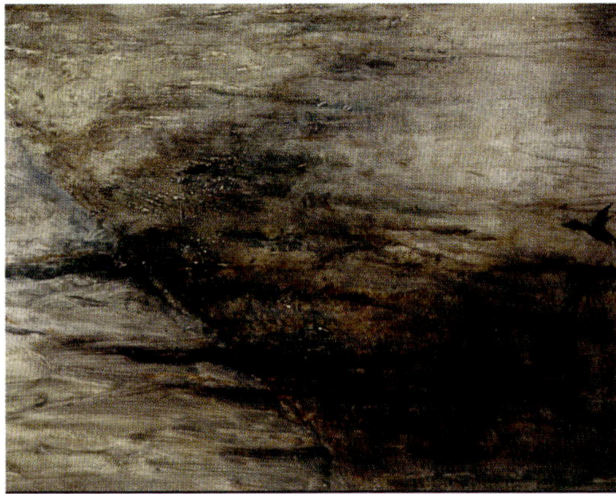

The lower-left corner of *Peace – Burial at Sea* (full work ill. p. 89)

The top-left corner, shown from the centre of the composition

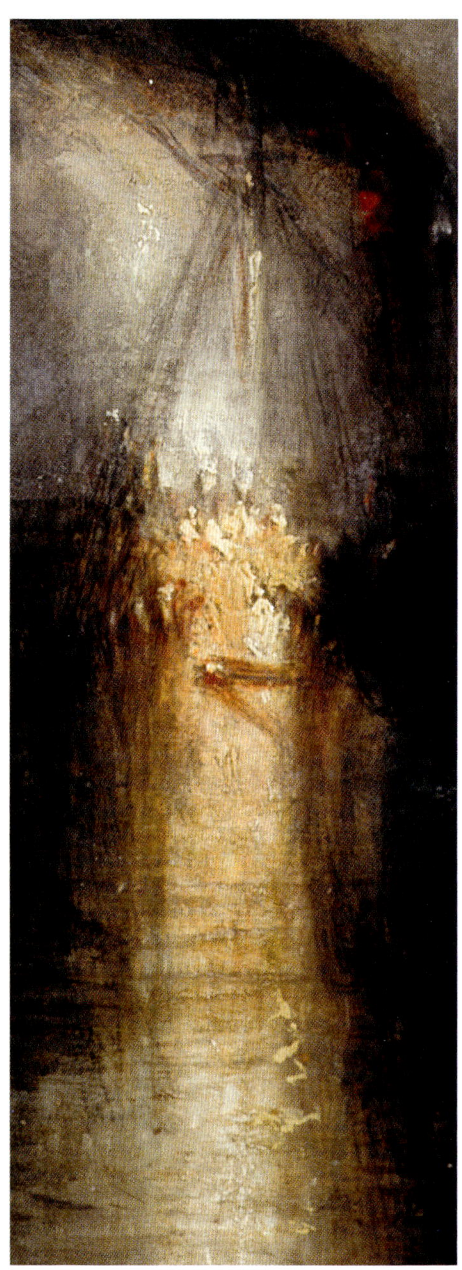

The coffin and lights

his shadow were added, as was Napoleon's shadow, and the rock limpet whose guilt-free freedom he contemplates (p. 88, above right).

Its pendant, or counterpart, is *Peace – Burial at Sea* (ill. p. 89), in which Turner envisaged the funeral at sea of his friend, the artist David Wilkie (1785–1841), who died while travelling. It, too, was finished at the Royal Academy in its frame, which included an octagonal gold mat that covered all the corners. At the upper left (opposite, bottom left), earlier curved brushstrokes sweeping across the sky to create white clouds had been overlain with a lot of wax-based white paint, applied thickly with a brush and then manipulated with a palette knife. The sky was the area to which Turner habitually applied less megilp and transparent glazes, so the covered corner is not distinctly different from the sky he could access and modify.

The lower corners make it clear what Turner could achieve during the varnishing days. In the one at the left (opposite, top left), thin, dark megilp glazes in the foreground have dramatically increased contrast and added local gloss, and make it clear that the shore is near, the water far more shallow than where the ship is anchored, hence greener in appearance and with more reflections. This was achieved through the use of virtually uncoloured glazes with slightly yellow megilp. The very black cormorant casting an equally dark shadow was introduced last, also in megilp.

The warm lights centred round the coffin being lowered into the sea are reflected in the still water, and make the coffin, as well as the sails and their reflections look dramatically black in contrast (opposite, right), despite the cooler, whiter light of the low moon, also reflected in the water. The moon, its reflection and the distant lighthouse are painted without medium modifier in stiff oil paint, and are therefore more white than the deck lit by flaming torches.

Interestingly, both *War* and *Peace* were nonetheless criticized by contemporaries for their respective lack of finish.[56]

FOUR

TURNER'S TOOLKIT: PROCESSES FOR CREATING A COMPOSITION

Assembling ideas and source material

That three hundred of Turner's sketchbooks survive in the Turner Bequest,[57] and a few in other collections, attests to their value to him. Some date to the late 1790s, the period when Turner first had commissions, and some are numbered or dated in his own hand. There were clearly some attempts to make them more organized and accessible when he wanted to mine them for information in later years (right, top).

The sketchbooks give the best clue to Turner's travels and interests over a working lifetime that exceeded fifty-five years, as well as charting his artistic development. He did not keep a diary or a formal accounts book, and his collected correspondence forms a relatively slim volume, with many letters devoted to obtaining a better deal from the engravers of his work.[58] This is typical of artists of Turner's era: when he was young, paper was expensive and was reserved for what mattered most, namely sketching and painting.

Turner clearly had what we would today call a 'photographic memory', and he devoted much of his life to close looking, using sketching to reinforce his observations, sometimes with just a few curving lines in graphite pencil to capture the form of a landscape or a few boats on the water from a given viewpoint (right, bottom). It is the more detailed drawings, and the sketches of distinctive architecture, that enable identification of his locations. Turner never annotated each sketch with a location, but on occasion he noted

a few words of description of particularly impressive storms or sunsets, colourful details in costume, or the building material of a town he was visiting for the first time.

Durham, North Shore sketchbook, 1817. Tate, London, title inscribed by Turner

Hulks, Probably on the Hamoaze, 1811. Tate, London

There are no written clues, not even cryptic ones, to the use he planned to make of any particular sketch – if he did plan at all. Sometimes one would be used years later. A few anecdotes related by friends suggest that the plan for future use of a sketch on occasion arose as early as the rapid capturing of a real scene: he once said to the son of his friend Walter Fawkes, as he sketched: '...in two years you will see this again, and call it *Hannibal Crossing the Alps*.'[59]

Over his lifetime, Turner tried out many types of paper and graphic media at least once, but the bulk of his sketches were made using graphite pencil, which would have been in a wooden casing like today's pencils, an improvement then newly available, and far more suited to rapid work outdoors than the rather powdery black, white or coloured chalks gripped in a *porte-crayon*, the drawing tool used by his predecessors. Frequently, he would use a soft pencil for the foreground and a harder one that gave a finer line for the background, thus economically providing a sense of distance and recession in the landscape with only two tools.

Numerous contemporary accounts suggest that Turner's verbal and writing skills were as poor as his skill at visual synthesis was excellent. He was nonetheless a good teacher, and even a committed one, when he got down to it. In 1808 he became Professor of Perspective at the Royal Academy, an honorary position with the annual obligation of addressing the students and Academicians of the day at a lecture, with interested members of the public, including his father William, also in attendance.

Turner prepared for his first lecture in 1811 with an extensive course of reading, before creating large-scale visual material to illustrate the rules of perspective as they applied to buildings his audience might have visited, such as Pulteney Bridge in Bath. His notes and delivery, according to those who attended, grew ever more chaotic as he mumbled and lost his place. Each year, he would add and move around material by cutting and pasting it, crossing out and inserting words. Turner's patient audience withstood all of this, because his visual material was so lucid.

One of his prepared sheets, at close to 1 m wide (3 ft), shows how to create a light underdrawing of ruled lines in graphite pencil, based on perspective lines that meet at a vanishing point (opposite, top); another shows the finished watercolour created from such a construction (opposite, bottom). Other related visual aids show how to build up the colonnade seen at the right of his diagram, from the first outline of a column and its capital (p. 96, left) to the perspective lines used to place it (p. 96, middle), and then how to use either shading in grey or a graduated wash of colour for representing sunlit and shadowed stonework to depict the roundness of the columns (p. 96, right).

To create duplicate visual material, Turner used a copying process that would generate non-reversed copies, which could be made cheaply and simply at home, involving lamp black and eggs applied to produce double-sided copying paper, and a straight-edge for scoring a line against with a sharp tool. This created copies on two sheets, separated by the copying paper, a process that might have involved his father's assistance.[60]

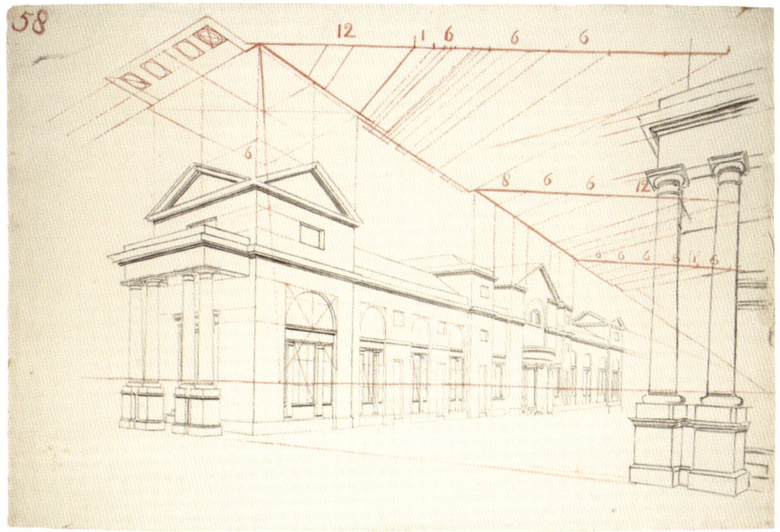

Lecture Diagram 58: Perspective Construction of Pulteney Bridge, Bath (after Thomas Malton Junior), c. 1810. Tate, London

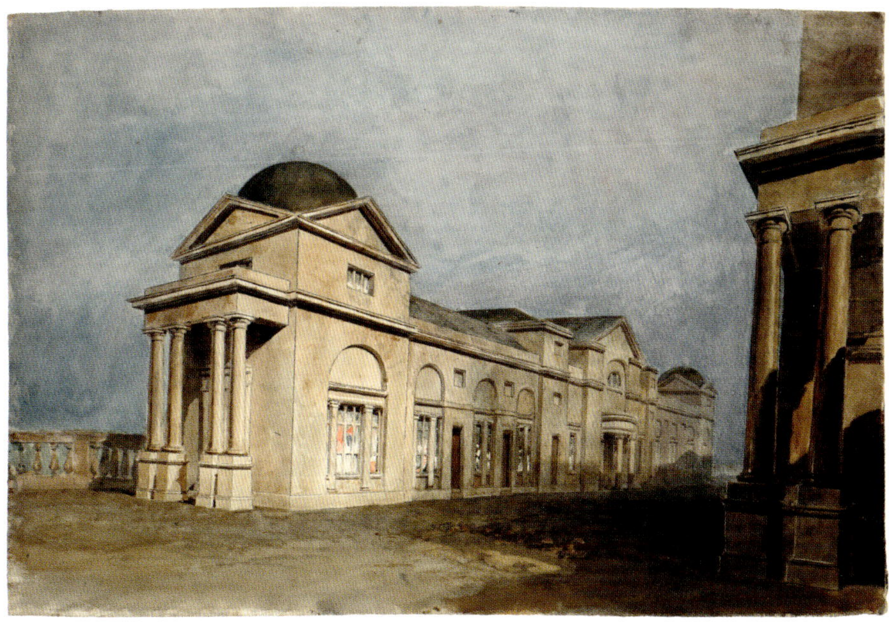

Lecture Diagram 59: Pulteney Bridge, Bath, in Perspective (after Thomas Malton Junior), c. 1810. Tate, London

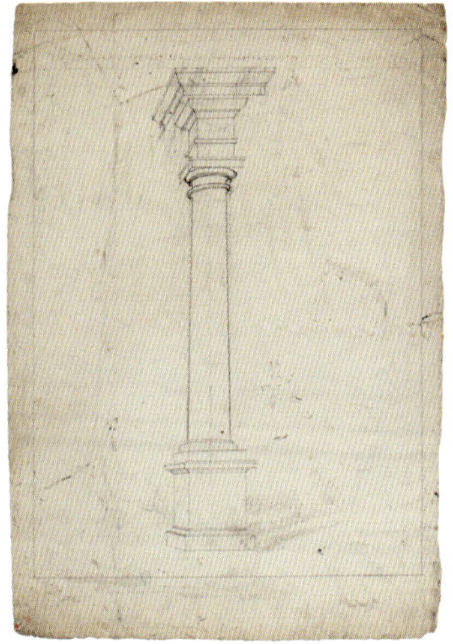

Perspective Study of a Tuscan Column,
c. 1810. Tate, London

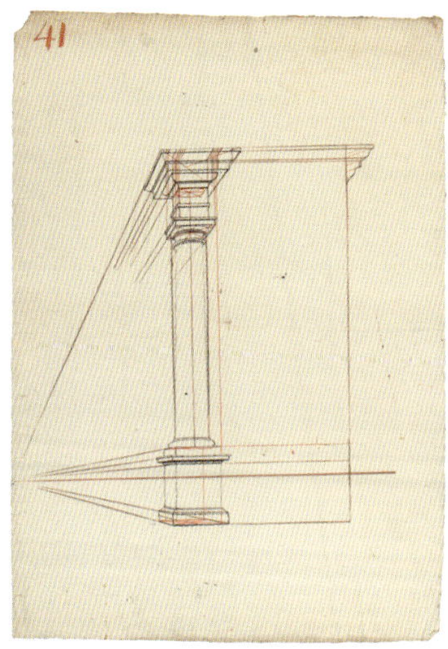

Lecture Diagram 41: Perspective
Construction of a Tuscan Column,
c. 1810. Tate, London

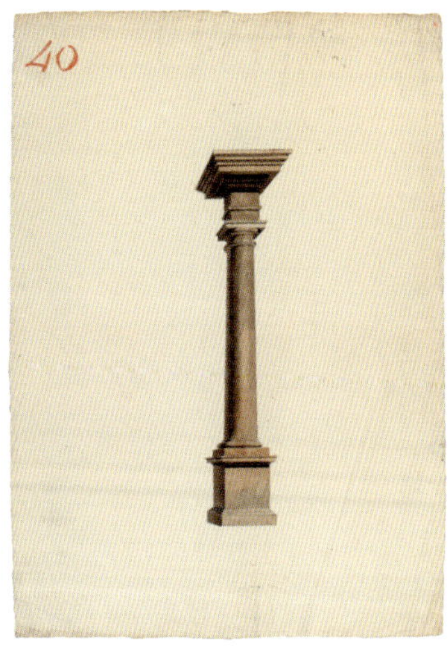

Lecture Diagram 40: Tuscan Column
in Perspective, c. 1810. Tate, London

In his own practice, however, Turner bent the rules of perspective, quite literally, to produce an original architectural composition that would convince a viewer who had never seen the city portrayed, as well as attract admiration from those travellers who recognized how he had warped space and moved buildings around to improve on reality (opposite, top). The same process of improvement and refinement of a natural landscape was universal in his era, and was a key aim of painters of the sublime, who sought to intensify and engage the emotion of the viewer. Occasionally he would draw the line of a mountain range in light pencil on paper, but the paint often overreached the drawn line, as the mountain gained in dramatic effect during the painting. Indeed, in later life Turner used ruled perspective lines in only a few, quite specific cases, such as for the complex façades of buildings or the numerous gun-ports of a well-known battleship. He did not usually draw the horizon line for a seascape, and the critical observer can see that his horizons often slope or include a step or two. His aim, instead, was to evoke atmosphere, immerse the viewer in the depicted scene and tell a story through the use of colour, rather than line.

The earliest stages of his compositions, therefore, evolved in terms of colour and tone, sometimes from the middle of the support outwards, but more often from the upper third downwards. We know this because the Turner Bequest includes all the beginnings on both paper (opposite, bottom) and canvas (overleaf) that were never developed into finished works. What we cannot know from an individual unfinished work is whether Turner felt

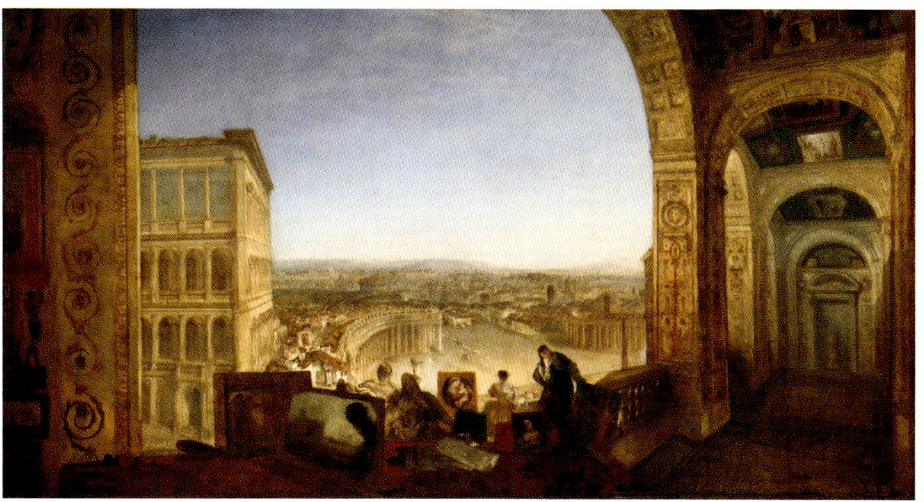

Rome, from the Vatican. Raffaelle, Accompanied by La Fornarina, Preparing his Pictures for the Decoration of the Loggia, exhibited 1820. Tate, London

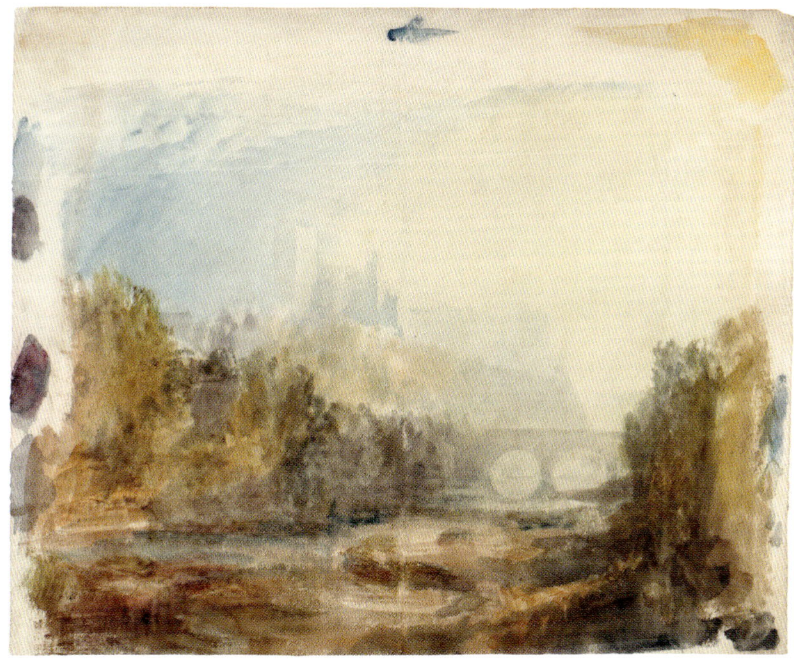

Richmond, Yorkshire, c. 1816–20. Tate, London

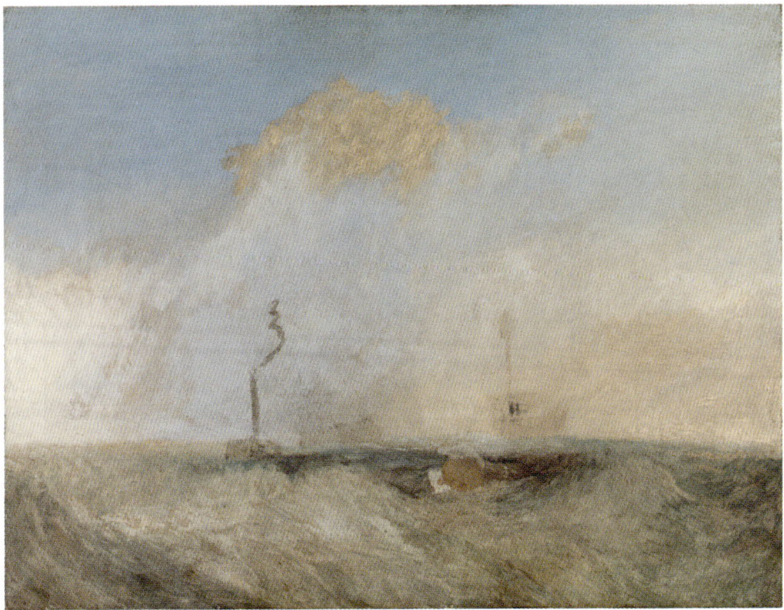

Steamer and Lightship; a study for 'The Fighting Temeraire', c. 1838–39. Tate, London,
seen after recent conservation treatment to alleviate damage caused by water and mould

it had failed and was beyond rescue, or was too good to spoil, given that a similar early stage could be essayed again and then developed on another support, or indeed whether circumstances simply compelled him to stop at that moment, and later distractions prevented the next stage of working. The sketchbooks that include colour beginnings, as they are known today, suggest that Turner often made five or ten on the same theme, and then developed one. He did not invite friends, still less clients, into his workspace, but those few who did manage it reported several occasions when he worked along a row of supports, either paper on canvas, moving from one to another with a brushload of colour.

It takes longer to work on a square metre or two of canvas than on a small sheet of paper, and it took more effort on Turner's part (or, more likely, his father's) to ensure a supply of canvases primed and ready for use, so there are fewer colour beginnings on canvas than on paper – one or two hundred (above), as opposed to thousands. Furthermore, canvas as a support is easier to reuse after wiping over with turpentine to remove recent paint, or scraping to reduce dried paint. A single canvas with a fully developed, exhibited image, in fact, conceals all of the earlier stages of development of the same image. Since Turner used similar colours at every stage, the most ingenious imaging techniques will never recover these separate steps. This development of a composition cannot even be explored very successfully by X-raying the painting, since all the elements in the image have somewhat fuzzy outlines, from their constant refinement during the painting process.

Practicality

It is already obvious that this working process is very efficient at capturing ideas, then working on them as time and circumstances dictated. A few lines in graphite pencil can be applied to paper in any circumstances: poor light, from a moving carriage, a fragment of historical architecture seen during a glance while passing. Liquid ink or a wet brushload of watercolour are far less amenable to working on the move. Turner generally travelled and sketched alone, or thoroughly ignored his companions once he began observing and sketching. He did not, at any time of his life, work with paid assistants who would hand him his tools. William Turner must have often been out on errands, showing visitors round his son's London studio, or cooking or cleaning, and cannot always have been to hand.

In Turner's youth, watercolour paints took considerable 'working-up' before a usable coloured wash could be coaxed from the block of 'hard' colour, so he tended to work in colour indoors, generally on only a small proportion of the pencil sketches. When we find colour used in a sketchbook that is still bound together, the page had to dry pretty well before another page could be turned over and used, which would also have been an unwelcome restriction to an impetuous artist. Using dry sketching materials like graphite pencil,

or very limited numbers of liquid ones such as irongall or Indian ink with a dip pen, and only one brush for washing in shadows, was practical, and reduced accidents in the field. Many sketchbooks were small, and the larger ones often had soft covers so that they could be rolled up and rammed into a pocket.

Oil paint was not supplied in tubes until the end of Turner's life. Instead, the colours came in small pigs' bladders (see p. 113), pieces of animal-derived, oil-proof and waterproof material cut into small squares, the corners pulled in over the blob of paint and bound with string, then trimmed off. The bladders were pierced with a pin, allowing paint to be squeezed onto the palette, before being 'closed' with a tack. They were messy to carry around, and prone to leaking all over the paintbox. Newly painted canvases posed an even bigger challenge if they had been worked on outdoors.

Instead, artists who painted outdoors in the early 19th century, like Constable, often used small boards that would fit into slots beneath the paintbox for transport home. Turner tended to work on a larger scale in oil than watercolour, his canvases or other supports usually being over half a metre square in area and generally closer to a full square metre (5 to 10 sq ft) or more. He did possess a rowing boat in which he could stow materials while sketching Thames scenes.

Traditional ways of creating a composition

The painter and diarist Joseph Farington (1747–1821), who as Keeper of the Royal Academy (in effect, facilities manager) was well known to Turner, wrote that:

[He] has no systematic process for making drawings … he avoids any particular mode so that he may not fall into manner. By washing and occasionally rubbing out, he at last expresses in some degree the idea in his mind.'[61]

Later, he added, 'Turner has no settled process, but drives the colours about until he has expressed the ideas in his mind.'[62] Farington noted this at a date when Turner had just begun to paint in oil, using conventional compositions only for the few years it took him to master that medium, as well as watercolour. The surviving body of work in the Turner Bequest makes clear how good a summary this was.

While pencil sketches can be related to his exhibited paintings, Turner certainly did not make a sketch for each element of a composition, and particularly did not do so for the groups of figures that populate many of his foregrounds, nor the foreground foliage other artists often painted with mimetic realism, after his first decade of painting. A small oil sketch would seldom be scaled up to a larger painting, or a same-scale oil study for refining the composition, as Constable would make for his large-scale works.

In a few cases, an unfinished Turner oil with the same topography as in a finished painting exists, but it seems more likely that the unfinished work had simply been put aside at an earlier stage, rather than made as a study for a planned composition. Turner also did not produce replicas of his work, as the previous generation of artists and many of his contemporaries did quite readily. Instead, he developed a system of painting that bypassed all of these stages, allowing him to continue in full creative flow, painting on the same canvas with which he had begun.

A watercolourist working with oils

The essence of traditional watercolour is transparency: thin washes of colour in water and gum, applied to an off-white or white paper, which provide every tint in the spectrum and every tone from pale to dark, with the paper itself serving as the lightest white in the composition (opposite). No one could appreciate this better than Turner. With very few exceptions (in works where he sought to create a gloomy atmosphere befitting his subject), he began his oils on a pale off-white ground, most often on canvas, but sometimes on a panel support.

Compared to other artists, Turner's grounds were whiter than most. The only artist who habitually used even brighter white grounds in Turner's early years was Joseph Wright of Derby (1734–1797), who also depicted intense, natural sources of colour, such as white-hot metal and glowing lava, much as Turner would depict the sun itself. With such subjects, neither artist could afford to compromise brilliance by applying colour over a dark or mid-toned ground, as had been done in the 17th century, or over a pale grey or warm off-white ground, as some artists did in the 18th century.

In oils, Turner usually began with coloured transparent washes comprising thinned-down, previously prepared oil paint, unless there was a need for a detailed drawing in pencil of some element that required correct perspective and detail. A battleship

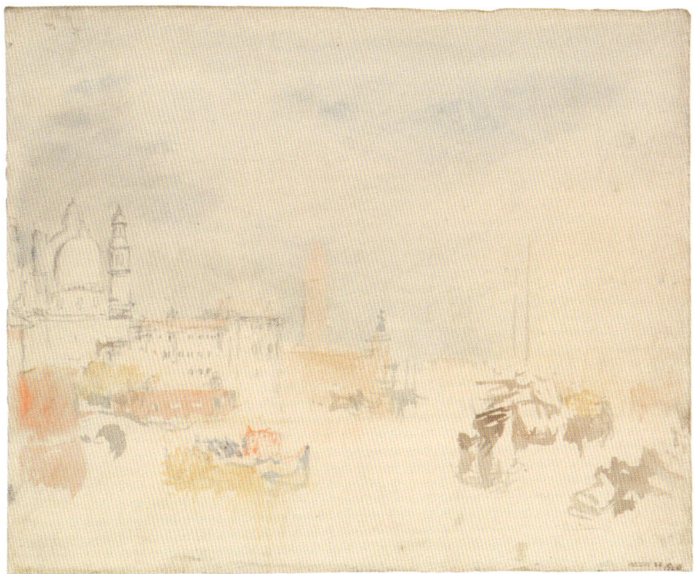

Boats Moored in the Giudecca Canal, near the Dogana, with the Back of the Salute, 1840. Tate, London

that had seen service against Napoleon at Trafalgar or a recognizable building in Venice dominating the composition required such detail, because viewers would spot and note mistakes, but a landscape never did.

Turner's first thin applications of paint were applied in the same tints that would appear in the final composition. The areas he knew would be lightest – often water, sometimes the sky and always the position of the sun – were left as bare white ground at this stage. Thus a canvas just begun, then put aside, might have paint on only half of its area, typically with colours that included a brown or brownish green for foliage, and some dull yellow or pale blue washes, like *Sketch for 'Harvest Dinner, Kingston Bank'* (overleaf). The water is not painted at all, but is implicit. Taken

one stage further, the transparent washes overlap, and begin to create darks. Such washes were harder to remove with turpentine than a watercolour wash is with water, and far more difficult to efface completely with clean turpentine, so areas were left 'in reserve', so that the paint applied later would be laid over white, maximizing the intensity of the lights.

The next stage would be to add localized brighter colour, often red, into these reserves of white. This balanced the composition: at a later stage Turner would, if necessary, make the colour fit into the scene depicted. In unfinished Italianate landscapes, for example, it is apparent that a patch of bright red or pale blue in the foreground could have been resolved into a single peasant in colourful costume, or two or three of them, their

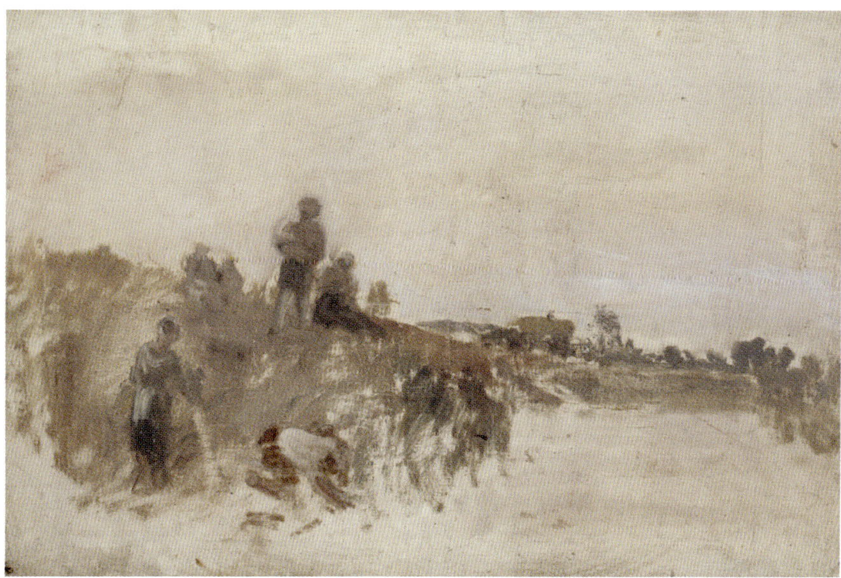

Sketch for 'Harvest Dinner, Kingston Bank', c. 1806–7. Tate, London

social interaction to be determined later. Where the paint is thin, the individual brushstrokes are just visible. Opaque paint, which included lead white and the colours used already, came next. A sea might consist of overlapping curved strokes of opaque paint, made with the full sweep of his arm, wielding a half-inch brush. Even a thin application like this looks opaque in oil, so contrasts between opaque light areas and glossy transparent shadows, some of them quite extensive, could be developed without introducing much texture.

Adding imagination

Turner had a lifelong interest in depicting weather, especially when it was dramatic, rather than calm. His predilection for drama places him firmly among the Romantic artists of the era, but a case has also been made that his well-observed and realistic depiction of storms and wild skies places him within a rising interest in meteorology and other sciences, all of which developed through the early 19th century, from observations and later interpretation of causes. Turner's earliest works in watercolour mostly include rather fine skies that are also completely believable, because they are so well observed. Even in his teens, while studying with Thomas Malton, Turner was soon the pupil chosen to apply skies.

His early years, in other words, were devoted to close observation to acquire the material, skills and muscle memory that would allow him to capture fleeting conditions of light and weather in an abbreviated form, which in turn would aid full recall long afterwards. Turner's effortless

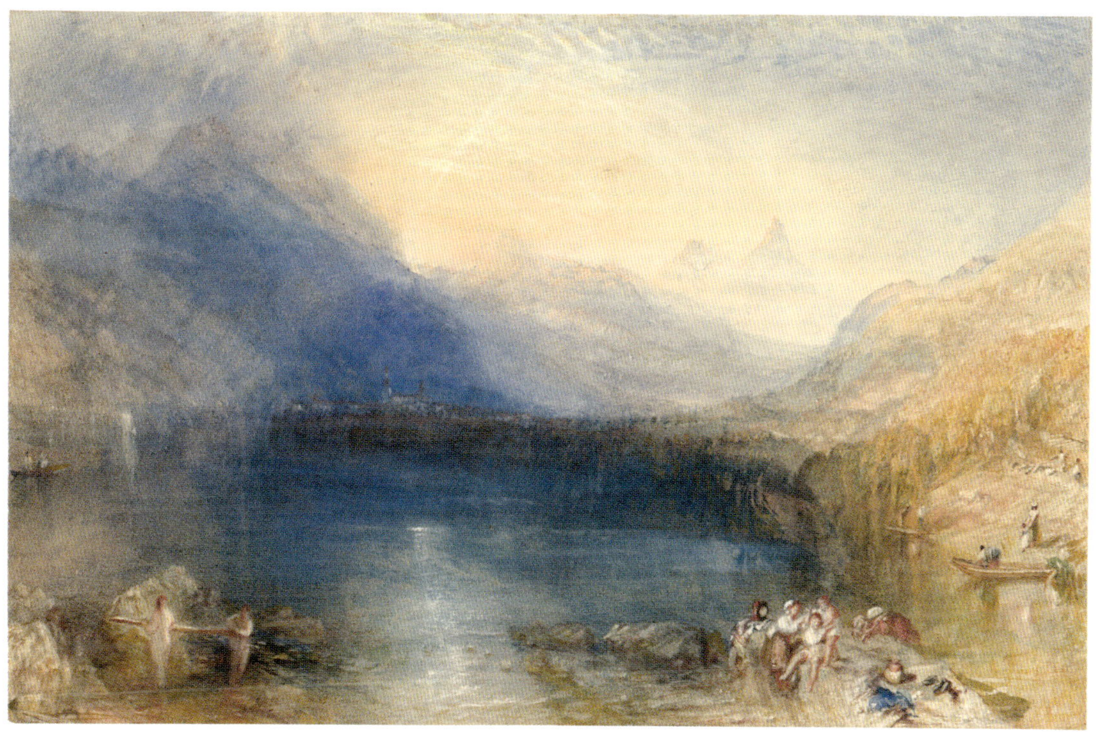

The Lake of Zug, 1843. The Metropolitan Museum of Art, New York

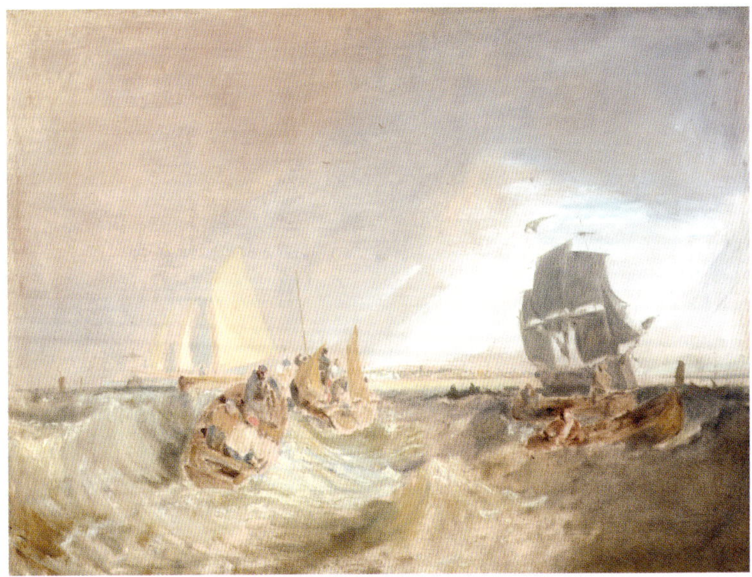

Shipping at the Mouth of the Thames, c. 1806–7. Tate, London

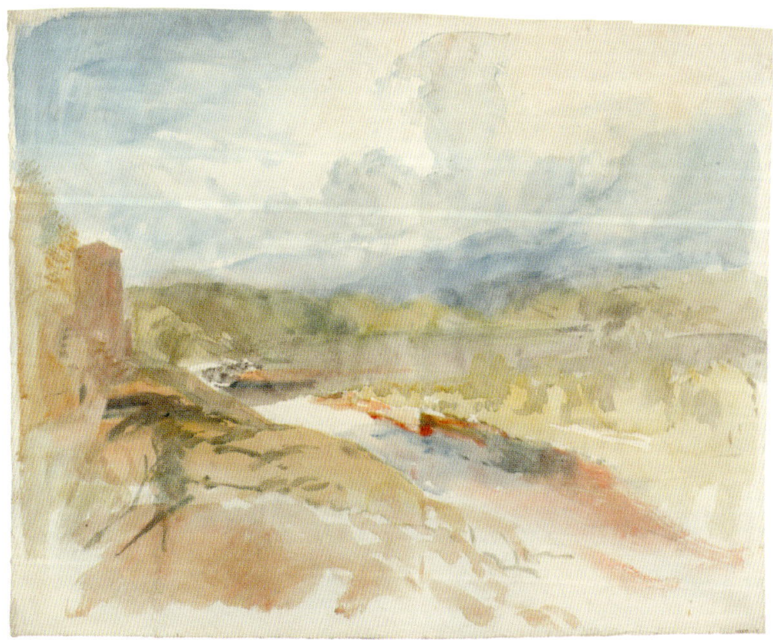

Kirkby Lonsdale, c. 1817. Tate, London

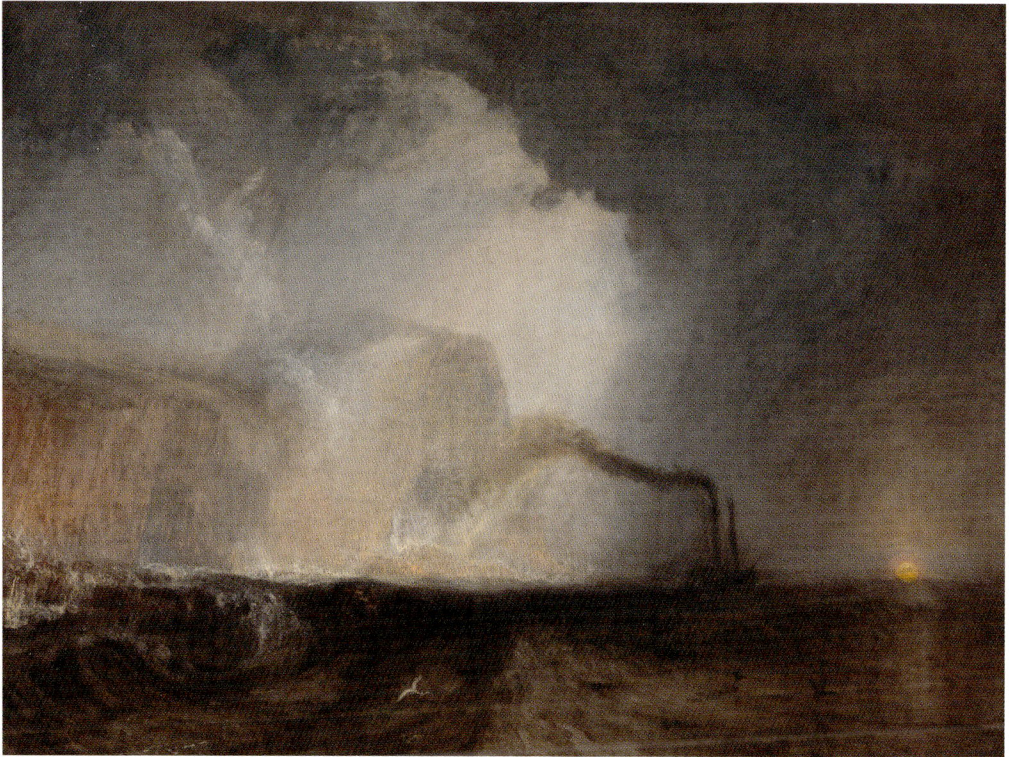

Staffa, Fingal's Cave, c. 1831–32. Yale Center for British Art, New Haven

and constantly practised execution enabled him to synthesize the scenery in front of him with remembered weather conditions, and to make the disparate visual resources blend seamlessly together through a sensitive deployment of colour.

Using warm and cool colours

Many of the late watercolours that owe their genesis to Turner's travels in Germany and Switzerland in the 1830s and early '40s have a common feature: they consist mainly of red, yellow and blue transparent washes applied to white paper, such as

The Lake of Zug (ill. p. 103), with only small details showing a wider gamut of colours. In fact, working with washes of a warm colour (most often a pure yellow, rather than a redder shade) and then a cool blue is a signature approach that Turner had developed much earlier and used across various media. In watercolours, this technique is wholly absent only in work done in his teens. In early oil paintings, such as *Dolbadarn Castle, North Wales* (ill. p. 14), he did not use this method, nor did he in the history paintings exhibited in the first years he was using this medium. Using warm

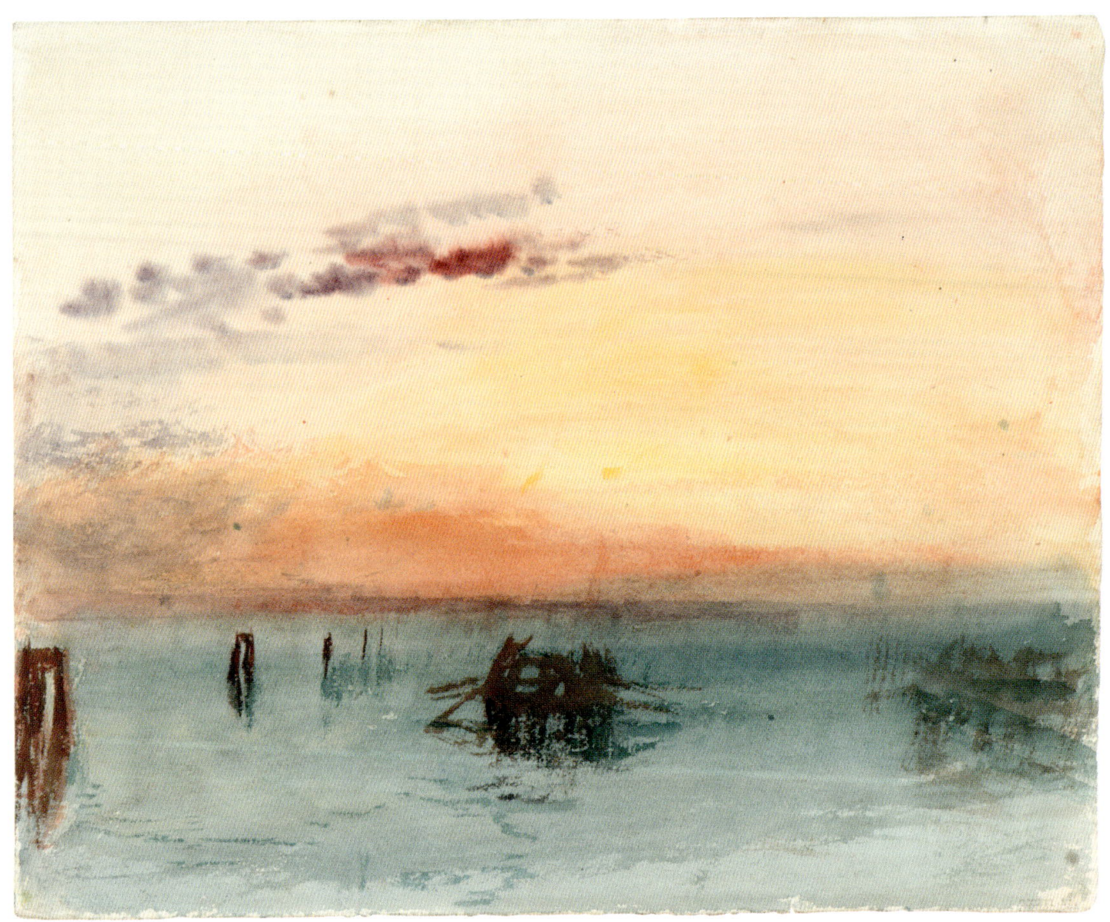

Venice: Looking across the Lagoon at Sunset, 1840. Tate, London

and cool colours, as opposed to sketching or working tonally, was not a traditional way of working: some artists of the later 18th century still built their individual working processes on a tonal beginning in a more or less warm brown, before adding colour, without deviating from the composition thus established.

The first indications that Turner used warm washes followed by cool ones to begin an oil painting are obvious before 1810 on canvases that had been abandoned early, such as *Shipping at the Mouth of the Thames* (ill. p. 104, top), which was taken one step further to include spots of bright red. A good example in watercolour is *Kirkby Lonsdale* (ill. p. 104, bottom), in which all of the primary colours were used. There are endless variations possible with such a method, one being to use a narrow tonal range for the vast bulk of a composition, which makes a magnificent contrast with a small amount of the complementary

colour. This can be seen in *Staffa, Fingal's Cave* (ill. p. 105), an oil painting that could, when seen in reproduction, be taken for a watercolour.

Venice: Looking across the Lagoon at Sunset (opposite) is a wonderfully simple yet stunning example of the technique that Turner used most: the contrast of warm and cool colours, elaborated endlessly and often in a complex way.[63] The initial applications to off-white paper of warm yellow for the sky and a greenish blue for the sea have been mingled to create a horizon disappearing into the twilight, while the band of yellow sky is warmed by the orange sunset on one side and cooled by purplish night clouds on the other. As well as having balanced but abstract colour, the clouds have been teased out to represent atmospheric conditions; the dark mooring posts in the foreground further ground a sophisticated colour study in a recognizable locality.

FIVE

PAINTBOXES, PALETTES AND COLOURS IN AN INDUSTRIAL AGE

Traditional watercolour materials[64]

Artists in the later 18th century, who regarded watercolours as 'coloured drawings', always used an array of transparent pigments, applied in a colloidal suspension of gum and water. The same medium is still used today in watercolour paints. Turner applied it to off-white paper of different textures, made non-absorbent to varying degrees by a size made from animal glue. The gum keeps these coloured pigments, usually very fine-grained, in suspension during the brushing process. As the wash dries, however, not only do the pigment particles lodge among the sized paper fibres, but also weak chemical bonds begin to develop between the size and the gum medium.

Freshly applied washes can be lifted off with a brushful of clean water, and a very new watercolour would be damaged by accidental splashes of water (such as raindrops). A watercolour that is fifty years old or so can be immersed gently into water during conservation treatment, without loss of colour, owing to the increasing effect of this hydrogen bonding.

All watercolour paints sold today have a medium of gum arabic. This was not the only gum available in the 18th and 19th centuries: tragacanth, sarcocolla and cherry gum, all with different properties, were also readily available. Gum arabic is the most soluble – and thus the easiest to lift off with fresh water – and the most suitable for an artist who likes to stir wet colours about on the paper. Gum tragacanth, on the other hand, is a better choice for the artist who wants to add more washes on top without picking up and redistributing earlier paint. It remains challenging to analyse the type used from the tiny sample of thicker gum occasionally found at the edge of a watercolour, but we do know that these alternative gums, as well as gum arabic, were present in Turner's paint. Both *Venice: Looking across the Lagoon at Sunset* (ill. p. 106) and *Funeral of Sir Thomas Lawrence* (ill. p. 117) have a medium of gum arabic, gum tragacanth and sugar.

Gum could be applied locally, to give texture and increase gloss, or to protect one key detail by stopping out (in Turner's case, often a circle of reserved white paper for the moon), while the surrounding area was worked up. A wash of glue size would do the same job, and appears to have done so for *Dolbadarn Castle: Colour Study* (ill. p. 24), another example of the use of gum tragacanth in the medium. Both gum and glue would be attenuated by the working up, and could be removed later without too much effort, leaving very little to be discovered today of the actual material used for this stopping out process.

The colourmen firms of Reeves, Rowney and Roberson all supplied watercolour blocks that included a mixture of gum arabic and gum tragacanth, which have been found by materials analysis in many of their colours. These were 'hard' watercolour blocks that took a lot of wetting and scratching before use, the only type available in Turner's youth when Reeves was a major supplier.

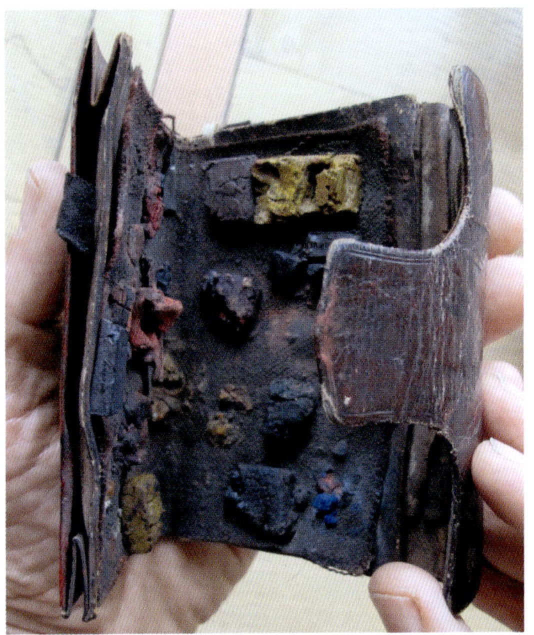

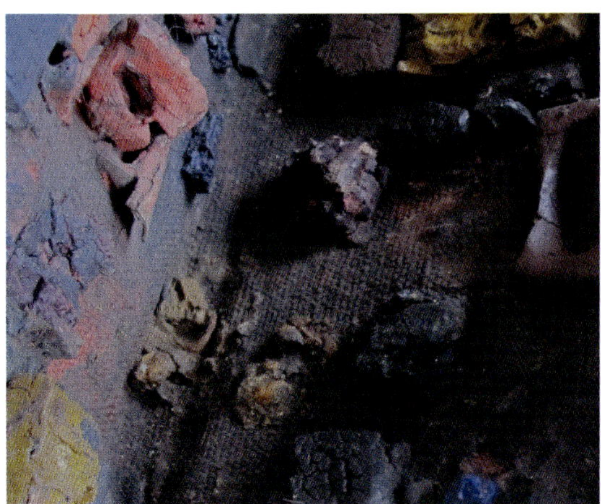

Travelling watercolour palette, ?1840s.
Private collection, UK

In a note in Turner's *Colour Bills* sketchbook from 1801, probably written by the seller, such blocks are called 'cakes', and it is clear that some colours cost ten times as much as others.[65] A professional artist chose from a range of colours and frequently had to replace the most commonly used in his paintbox with new cakes. If they chose, or if they could not afford to buy hard blocks, artists could buy dry pigments and grind them into gum with little effort, keeping the resulting paint wet and usable with the regular addition of water.

'Soft' watercolours that included honey or other sugars, or gum arabic alone, were made in increasing numbers for the amateur market: they behaved more like modern watercolour blocks, which can be simply wetted and used. The analytical evidence suggests that Turner often stuck to hard watercolour blocks, whose properties he knew well, and that he improvised travelling palettes from materials to hand, such as scraps of leather, pieces of canvas, and so on, replacing the blocks as they were used up. The blocks from this palette (above, left and right) were found to contain gum arabic alone, and may be soft. (Soft blocks show their colours over a century later, while hard blocks tend to blacken on the surface.)

The colours used by traditional watercolourists were limited in number, incapable of producing brilliant colours and mostly inexpensive. Brown bistre, blue indigo, sap green, several fast-fading yellow lake pigments (discussed later) and yellow gamboge were derived from domestic or imported plants, as were other fine-grained and transparent colours. All of the natural ochres, siennas and umbers were probably from local or regional sources that also supplied the users of larger quantities, such as house-painters. In his teens, Turner made rapid colour notes by the names of these pigments on some of his early sketches – using 'sap green' and 'ocker' (ochre) rather frequently – to remind himself how he would reproduce the scene in front of him in watercolour.[66] No pigment can be identified accurately by close looking alone – and some are difficult to detect analytically even today – so this is the only direct indication that Turner began his artistic career by using the traditional colours he would soon abandon for more intense, newly manufactured ones. This traditional range was often adequate for a British landscape in typically British weather, and, in Turner's case, for the occasional sketch.

The bright crimsons and reds so vital for soldiers' uniforms and flowers were plant-derived but far more expensive, and were usually used only in small amounts. The more costly bright colours, such as red vermilion, yellow orpiment, green and blue verditer and azurite, and Prussian blue, could also be bought as hard watercolour blocks by the close of the 18th century. Unused watercolour boxes from some of the major colourmen survive in museums today.[67]

A brief history of new colours[68]

Not only was Turner living in the best city in the world for obtaining artists' materials, but he was also living in a country where many new products were being developed and made, and overseas inventions quickly imported. Artists' colours had more commercial significance then than they do now, because watercolour was a vital tool for surveyors, military personnel, architects and explorers, as well as for artists. Newly discovered chemical elements were soon used in colourants for china production and colour printing, in addition to the fine arts.

One of the first new colours was Prussian blue, discovered in the first quarter of the 18th century and soon used in both oil painting and watercolour. It has a high tinting strength and greater intensity than indigo, which had previously been the only blue pigment deemed suitable in watercolours, where it was often combined with red earth pigments, such as red ochre or Indian red, to make a neutral or optical grey. Turner used Prussian blue by 1796 in watercolour, and may have used it earlier in works not yet analysed for this material, though he continued to use indigo, and sometimes both in different areas of one sheet of paper, for at least a decade. Indigo often fades badly, but Prussian blue – in its modern form, with very fine particles – is durable. Until the 1820s Turner was using the traditional variety, which is recognizable under magnification owing to its large flat particles, and is more variable in colour strength and stability.

The natural earth pigments, which include yellow and red ochre, raw and burnt sienna, Indian red, the more transparent Van Dyke brown, the umbers, and purplish-brown shades historically known as *caput mortuum*, were augmented with synthetic versions known as 'mars' colours. By the later 18th century, mars yellow and mars orange were available, followed by mars brown and mars red, which could rival red vermilion when it was painted over white. Their much finer particles

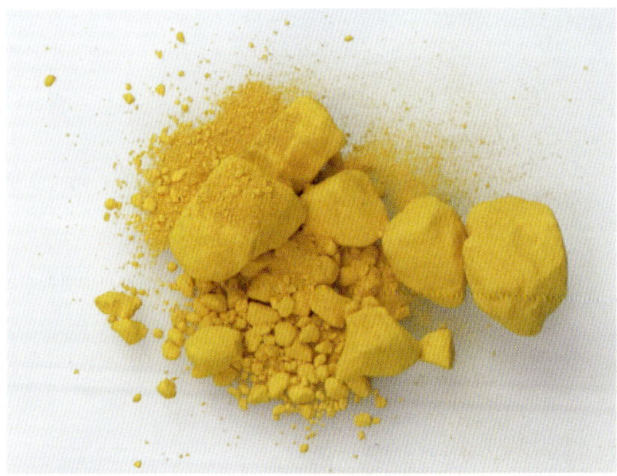

Modern chrome yellow pigment of the shade Turner frequently used.

(visible with a research microscope) meant that they provided greater intensity than the natural earth pigments. Mars orange, in particular, a shade not found among the natural earth pigments, can be seen in Turner's watercolours from 1795, as well as in his earliest works in oil. It remained a uniquely bright orange pigment until the 1820s, and one of Turner's most frequently used colours throughout his life.

Early in the new century, cobalt blue (cobalt aluminate) was developed in France, and produced there from 1807. War with France likely inhibited its importation and pushed up the cost, but Turner nonetheless managed to use it in a series of oil sketches of the Thames from *c.* 1807, which suggests great willingness to seek out and try a new material that would have been considerably more expensive than the home-produced blues. A slightly greenish blue, cobalt blue is good for sunlit skies. When Turner wanted a redder blue for an evening sky, he often employed the very traditional pigment smalt instead. This is not intensely coloured, and therefore should be used coarsely ground, which is what Turner did in both oil and watercolour: enormous glassy blue particles can be seen almost pushing their way from the paint layer. It is likely that he sought out supplies of brightly coloured smalt, unfazed by their unusual size, which must have made them feel very gritty when used in watercolour.

Important developments took place in yellow pigments, a colour favoured by Turner from his teens, well before the best new one would be produced. The poisonous orpiment (arsenic sulphide) was the most beautiful of the traditional yellows, and he certainly used it on occasion in the earlier decades. Patent yellow (lead oxychloride), known coincidentally as Turner's yellow for its maker, James Turner, who patented it in 1781, was a pale, clear shade of yellow that existing redder materials like yellow ochre or Naples yellow could not offer. It has been found in *Fishermen at Sea* and in *London from Greenwich Park*, exhibited in 1796 and 1809, respectively.

In 1808 Turner was still using the term 'patent yellow' in his sporadic colour notes.[69] Strontium yellow (strontium chromate), which has a similar pale, clear tone, appears in the *Battle of Trafalgar*, exhibited in 1806, and for a few more years after that. Significantly, all of these works were painted before the patenting in 1814 of what would become Turner's most regularly used yellow pigment: chrome yellow (lead chromate). The earlier yellows are only occasionally found thereafter. Orpiment also seems to have fallen out of use in this decade, in Turner's paintings and in his colour notes.

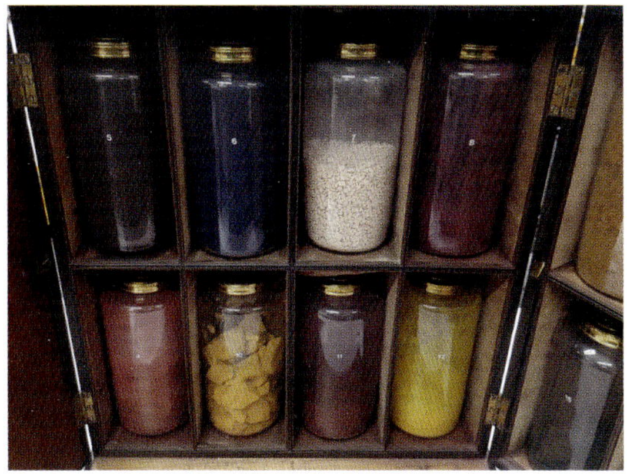

Large wooden cabinet with sixteen jars containing various pigments, ?1840s. Tate, London

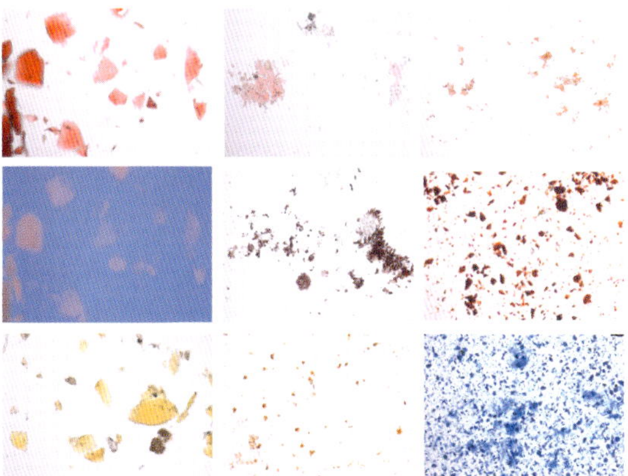

A selection of Turner's pigments, viewed in transmitted light. Three types of crimson madder (top row); the typical rose madder shade as it appears in ultraviolet light, followed by a brown and a scarlet madder (middle row); gamboge, a yellow lake of flavonoid type, and Prussian blue with the traditional type of particles (bottom row). All imaged at the same magnification.

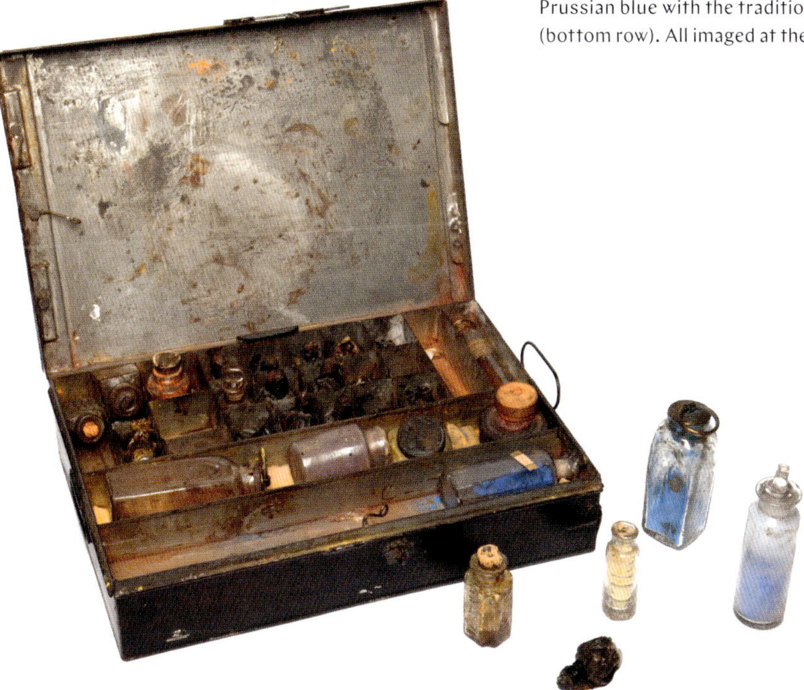

Turner's travelling paintbox, ?1840s. Tate, London

Chrome yellow was first available in a light yellow, with the same chemical composition but different shape of particles from the material available today. In the same decade, Turner first used a new mid-yellow shade (ill. p. 112); in the 1820s, it was made in a pale version that emulated patent yellow, which he used regularly ever after, usually also with the mid-tone, in oil and watercolour. It was available in scarlet by the last years of his life, with the later products including the shape of particles seen in today's pigments. Turner is to date the earliest known user in Britain by decades for every shade of chrome yellow, the mid-shade being one of his favourites. The single, newly invented tube of paint in his travelling paintbox contains chrome yellow (previous page, bottom).

Barium yellow (barium chromate), another pale, clear shade that is also intense, was made during this period. The exact date is unknown, as it was not patented until the 1840s, after it had been sold for some time. Turner seems to have used it first in *The Loretto Necklace* (1829) and ten years later in *The Fighting Temeraire* (ill. p. 149), but not regularly, which suggests that it was difficult to obtain.

Apart from mars red and chrome scarlet, the only other new opaque red pigment available in Turner's lifetime was iodine scarlet (mercuric iodide). Known today for its propensity to evaporate off the surface of paint, it may not have survived to be analysed in watercolours even if Turner had used it, as he did in oils for the sunset for *The Fighting Temeraire*, where an original varnish (which rarely survives on his paintings) has prevented its loss.[70]

Turner's friend, the colourman George Field, experimented and improved the manufacture of red lake pigments, the expensive transparent crimson and rose colours such as madder and cochineal, which had long been used in both watercolour and oil. A 'red lake' pigment is made from a dye, derived from the madder plant and the cochineal beetle, or – in the case of brasilwood – from a root, absorbed onto a 'substrate' of a fairly transparent white material like alumina, chalk or clay, or sometimes a metal other than aluminium. The substrate bonds with the dye, altering and intensifying its colour.

The bottles and jars of dried pigment that survive from Turner's studio (previous page, top left) include large numbers of red lakes in many tones.[71] Most are based on madder, many with unusual substrates that include copper or iron, giving bluer and browner tones than the rose madder available today. These have a wide range of particle sizes and shapes (previous page, top right), which can be recognized in some of Turner's paintings, and in a few of his watercolours. This wonderful and tempting range of shades had a drawback their maker sought to minimize by improving his production methods: some of them faded rapidly when exposed to light.

Greens for landscape had traditionally been made using optical mixtures: a blue and a yellow pigment for bright shades; a blue and a brown for dull ones; or black and yellow for olive tones. Prussian blue, yellow ochre and brown ochre are often featured in Turner's mixtures, which provided harmonious greens across the whole composition. There were developments in

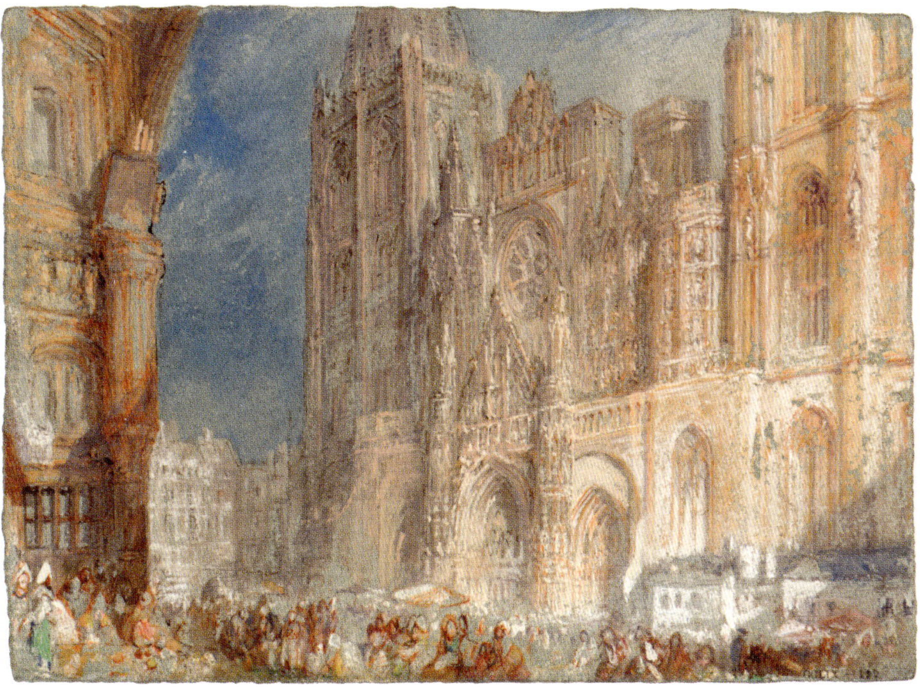

Rouen Cathedral, *c.* 1832. Tate, London

pure green pigments during Turner's lifetime, although many artists and critics felt them to be jarring when used alongside the more traditional mixtures. The earliest was Scheele's green (copper arsenite), invented in 1775, the year of Turner's birth, although he seems to have used it only rarely, and then with a greenish mixture in an unfinished work in oils from *c.* 1806–7 (in such mixtures, it would be easy to miss).

The more criticized emerald green (copper acetoarsenite), a bluer green, was made from 1814 but not in Britain, and has not been found (yet) in works earlier than *The Vision of Medea* and *East Cowes Castle*, both exhibited in 1828. Thereafter, Turner often used it in oil, and as small areas of pure

colour in watercolours from the 1830s, as he did in *Rouen Cathedral* (above). By this time, it was available in watercolour blocks, despite the criticism. The even bluer-toned viridian (hydrated chromium oxide), first made in 1838 in France, appeared in *The Opening of the Wallhalla, 1842* (ill. p. 61), exhibited in 1843. Like emerald green, Turner often used it pure, applied over white or a pale colour, for a small detail.

The options for black pigments did not grow at all over his lifetime, and browns – apart from mars brown, which came onto the market presumably as a more intense version of what had been available before as a natural earth pigment – did not increase either.

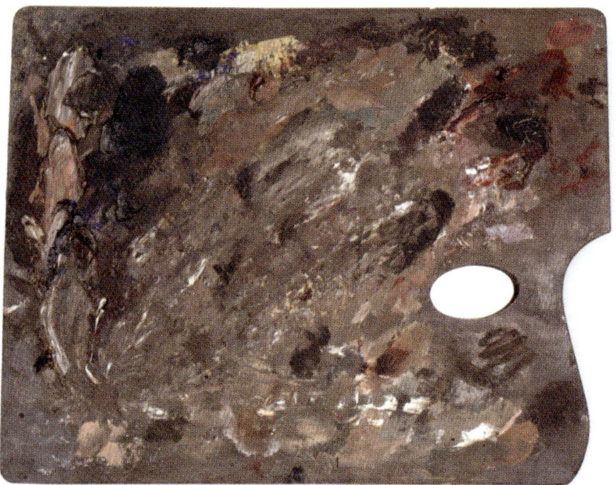

Turner's 'Chelsea' palette, used at the end of his life, ?1840s.
Tate, London

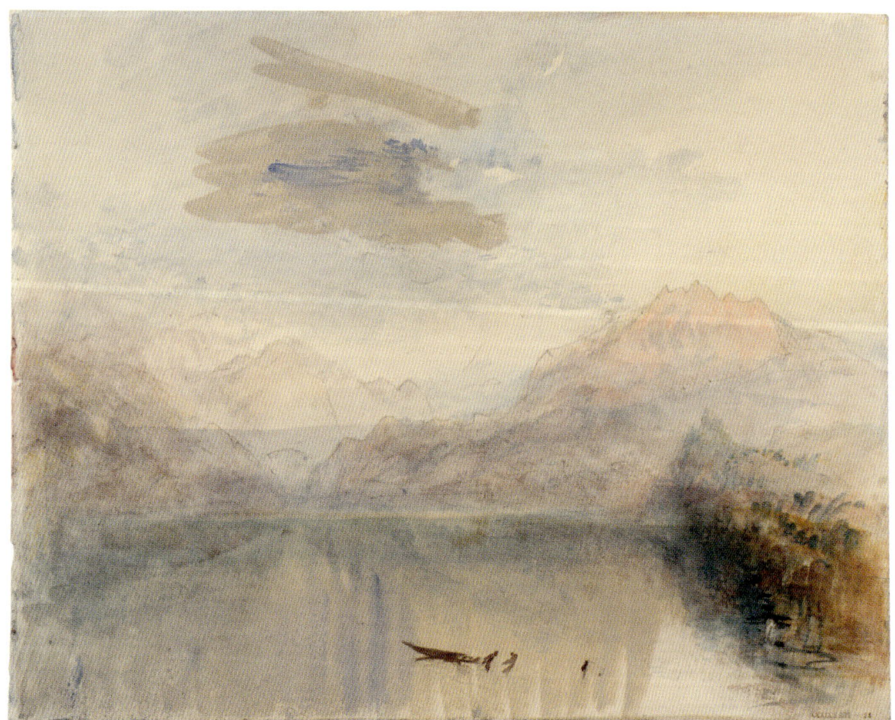

Mount Pilatus, from Lake Lucerne, 1841. Tate, London

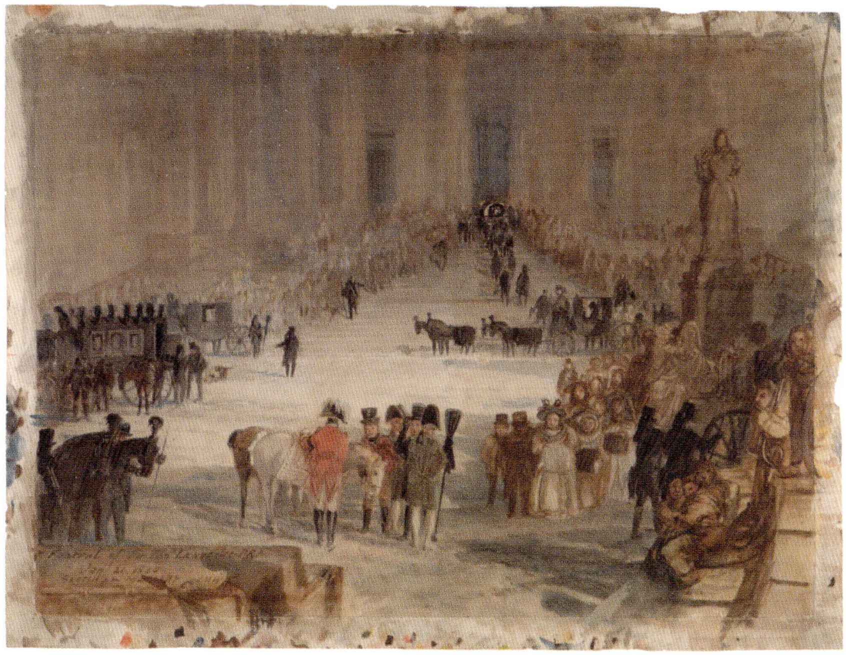

Funeral of Sir Thomas Lawrence: A Sketch from Memory, exhibited 1830. Tate, London

Lead white had been a universally used white pigment for some centuries, and even the invention in 1834 of a better zinc white, advertised as being sufficiently opaque for use in oil, did not discourage its use. Zinc white had been available in a rather transparent form for most of Turner's life, and he used it in watercolour in the *Tummel Bridge* sketchbook of 1801. It looks very transparent today (which is likely due to a known chemical alteration that can occur within years, or decades, of painting), and it is fortunate that Turner steered clear of it. There is no evidence as yet that he ever used it again on canvas or paper, though it seems to be present in traces on the palette said to be the last one he used (opposite, top).

Some of the works on paper with opaque white paint in gum applied as highlights include lead white – an innovative technique in watercolour of the earlier 19th century. Chalk (calcium carbonate) was the more predictable choice. In some watercolours, Turner used dolomite (magnesium carbonate), along with chalk, as he did in the sky in *Mount Pilatus, from Lake Lucerne* (opposite, bottom). Applied as thick gouache in gum medium, all three can look surprisingly similar, although in *Mount Pilatus* Turner atypically used oil as a medium as well as watercolour, the oil today appearing as a discoloured brown patch in the sky and, to a degree, in the foreground.

Turner clearly revelled in paler yellows, more natural-looking greenish blues that could be used for skies, and bright reds. By the first decade of the 19th century, some collectors and connoisseurs already thought that he used too much white (and, by implication, too little brown or yellow-brown, as seen in Old Master paintings that were covered in yellowed varnish).[72] Later in life, he was ridiculed by art critics for using too much yellow. Using pure green pigments, such as emerald green and, later, viridian, was unusual in oil painting in the 1830s, when he began to incorporate them to a striking degree, often contrasting them with red vermilion. Afterwards, he used pure green pigments less often, but more tellingly, and instead developed most compositions using yellow, blue and red.

For oils, Turner mixed the paint on a palette, generously and messily, without using any traditional system to arrange his colours, or, if impatient to begin, on the back of an unfinished painting, turned to the wall. For watercolours, he sometimes tried out colours on the edge of his paper (previous page), as well as mixing them on a white ceramic palette, more useful than a wooden one for showing how the colour would appear on off-white paper. Two such palettes survive (ill. p. 29 and right), both with red and blue paint and a rather similar appearance.[73]

Expanding choices across media

From his earliest years, Turner used precisely the same range of coloured pigments in both watercolours and oils. The new mars orange found in watercolours from the 1790s is the earliest example, as the same pigment also occurs in his early oils. Emerald green provides the most dramatic example, because he regularly used it locally, in details of pure colour, for watercolours on blue paper in the 1820s and '30s (see p. 115, bottom-left corner), and applied over areas of white highlight in many oil paintings, both for foreground details and within stormy seas.

Turner's travelling paintbox (ill. p. 113, bottom) illustrates his preparedness for work in any medium. Lockable, portable, yet large enough for use during an extended trip (it contains over seventy distinct colours), it includes small bladders of ready-to-use oil paint (which were indeed used, being pierced through the base so that the paint could be squeezed out) and bottles of dry pigments, including chrome yellow, cobalt blue and a little 'pill-box' of vermilion, all of which Turner used as the most prevalent colours in his later watercolours and oils. The box contains some brushes with handles short enough to fit inside – making them more suitable for watercolour, perhaps, since

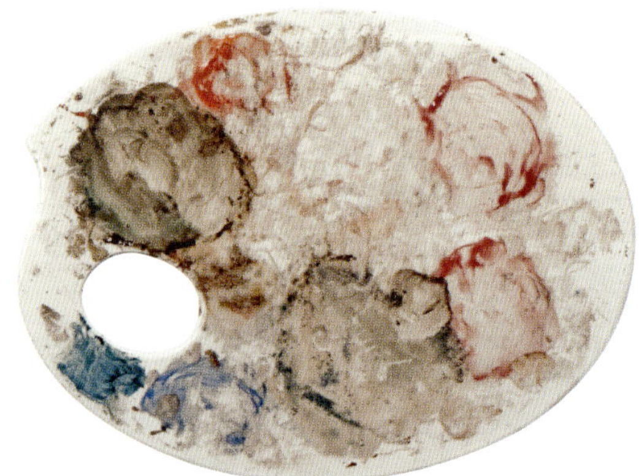

J.M.W. Turner's palette, c. 1790–1851. Ashmolean Museum, University of Oxford

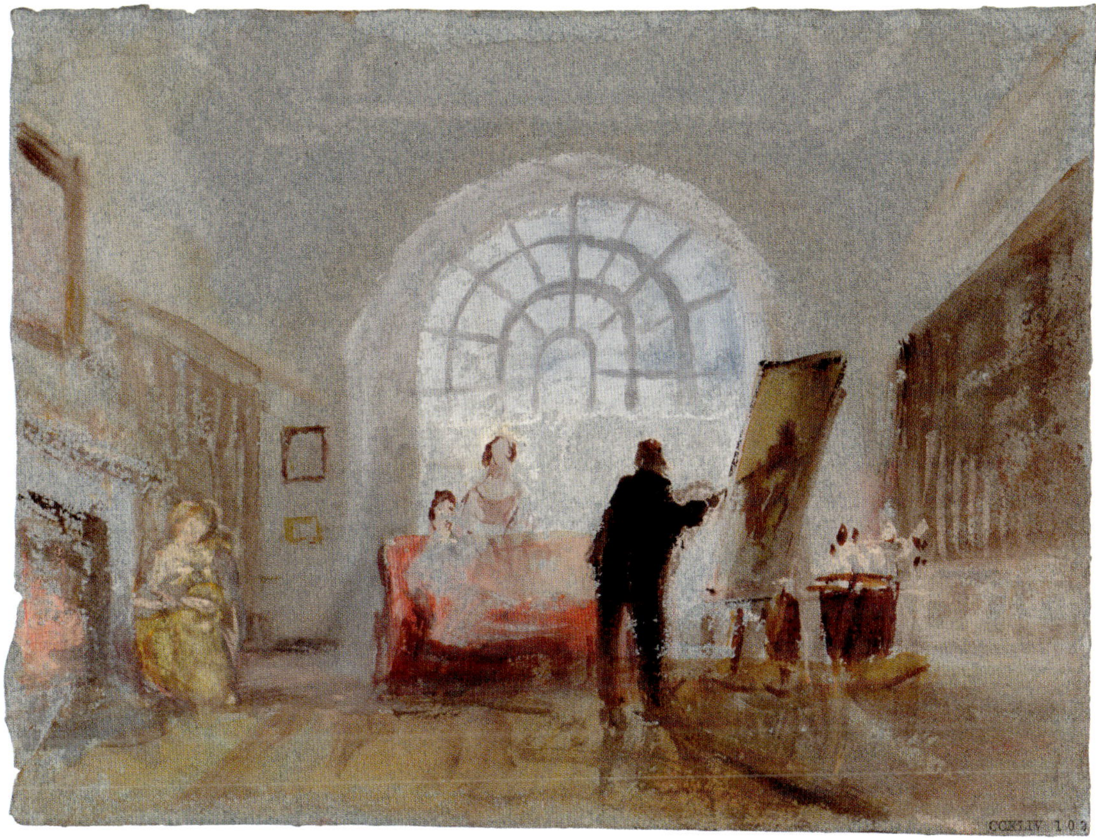

The Artist and his Admirers, 1827. Tate, London

his few surviving brushes for oil are too long to fit. Crucially, there are several (well-sealed) bottles of paint medium that might include gum for watercolour, or megilp. Turner clearly did work on an extensive scale when he was staying in the home of friends (above) and he needed a reasonable quantity of materials.

SIX

WORKING LIKE TURNER: A CONTEMPORARY ARTIST'S PERSPECTIVE

TONY SMIBERT

An experiment for painters

The exercise that follows is intended to give any artist, whether expert or aspiring, an insight into how Turner painted. Done under the technical guidance of Joyce Townsend, it simplifies a way of working used by Turner towards visual effects that are often seen in his unfinished oils, without being a copy of any specific painting. Towards the end of his life, many of his unfinished works approached what we would now call abstraction, although he must have seen many of them as 'complete'. Here, I have stopped at the 'indistinct' and 'unfinished' stage, but it could certainly be taken further, using Turner's oils as a model.

The materials needed include canvas boards, pre-primed with white acrylic gesso and with an additional ground of gesso, slightly warmed with yellow ochre to mimic Turner's lead white-based priming; hogshair brushes; tubes of oil paint in yellow ochre, cobalt blue, light red, burnt umber and Chinese white; and another tube of a 'thickener' for artists' paints. The exercise comprises five separate panels, with the fifth including all of the previous stages. At the end, a variation is given for completing the exercise in watercolour.

Panel 1

Start by wetting the board with white spirit. The amount of wetting will affect what comes next, so it should only be a low sheen of wetness. In the upper sky, make a horizontal wash of warm yellow ochre, using a wide arm movement, and carry the paint beyond the edges of the board. Repeat this across the lowest part of the panel. Next, strengthen the yellow ochre with the addition of light red, so that there are two horizontal bands of warmth across the upper and lower sections of the composition. I have also strengthened the area in the lower-left corner in preparation for the landform that is to follow. Finally, take a clean rag, load it with a cool colour (here, cobalt blue), and sweep this across the board to establish a cool band across the centre. Such a process would have allowed Turner to establish a warm evening or morning sky, reflected in a cool body of water receding into the far distance.

Panel 2

Press the rag into a darker colour (burnt umber, with a bit of yellow ochre and cobalt blue) to establish the broad but clearly defined mass of the tree, silhouetted against the sky. This can be achieved by gently pressing the bunched rag onto the surface, allowing the straggly bits to suggest foliage. The landscape painter Alexander Cozens (1717–1786), a great influence on Turner in his early years, used a system of 'blots' to suggest natural forms when composing landscapes. This can be extended down from the tree with a descending vertical 'smear' of the same tone and colour to establish the light form of the reflection in the water below. Next, press the rag, using the lightest of touches, to carry the shadow of the tree onto an imagined bank, which can be further suggested by applying

Panel 1

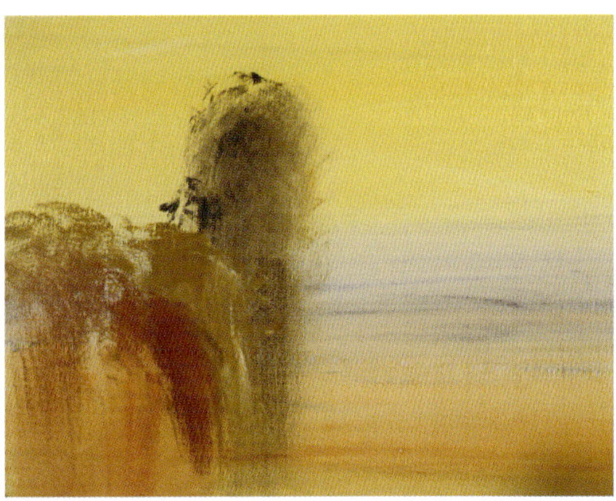

Panel 2

yellow ochre with the rag, and, in the foreground, a bolder application of light red, continued down into the water as another reflection.

Panel 3

This stage is a critical part of the process, and equivalent to a watercolour technique in which Turner was highly proficient: washing or sponging

out colour to introduce light. In oil, the suggestion of light is introduced with a thin application of opaque white; here, applied with a rag around and up to the edge of the tree and the ground, without obscuring the colours below. Note that the light is also reflected in the water, and that the paint has been applied in vertical strokes, suggesting a flood of light between the viewer and the horizon.

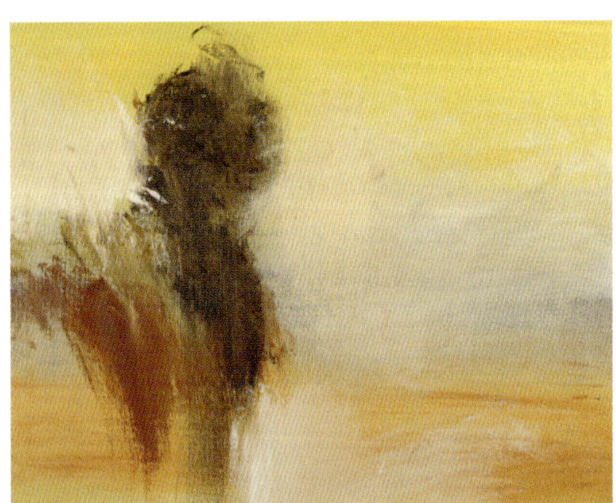

Panel 3

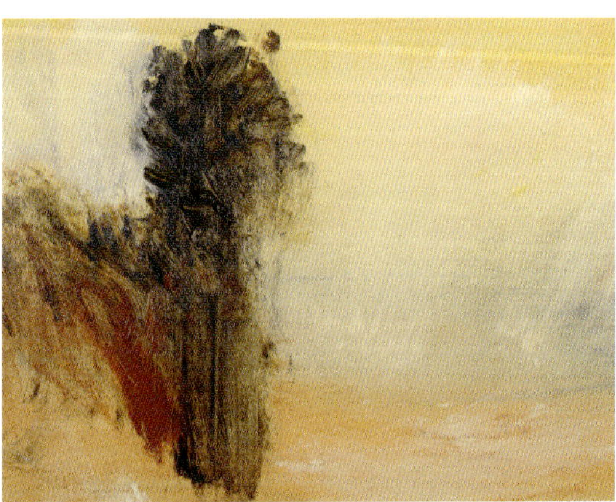

Panel 4

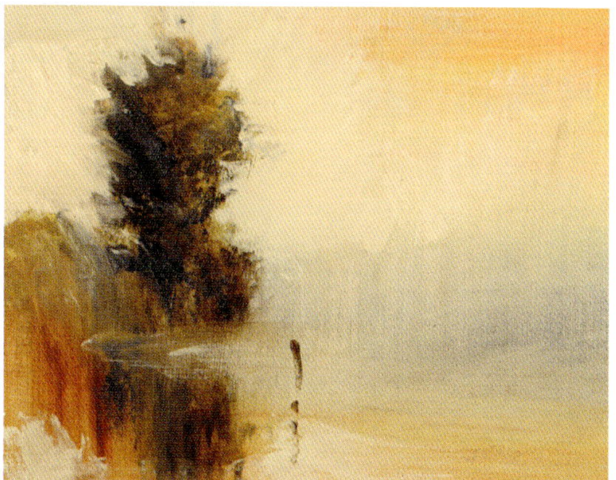

Panel 5

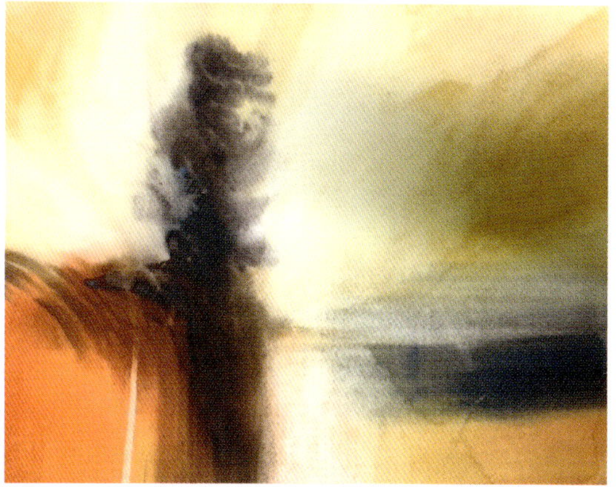

A variation in watercolour

Panel 4

Next, the darker mass of the tree is built up with heavier applications of paint, either with a rag or a brush. Most painters will probably find it easier to use the rag; Turner himself used rags to make a variety of marks, along with brushes, brush handles and fingertips. Add as much or as little of the landform necessary to suggest a Turner study.

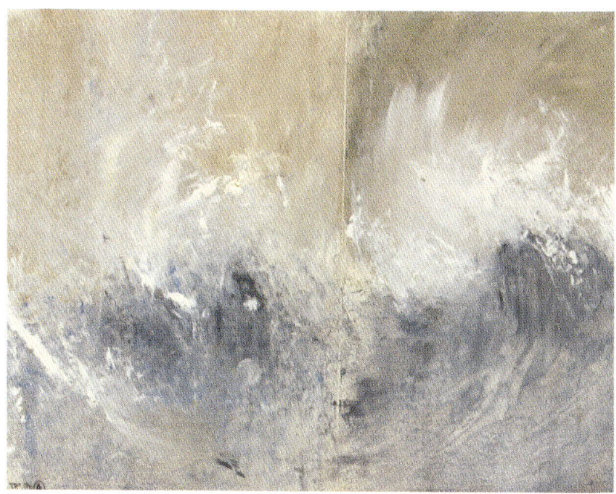

Recreation of the breaking wave

Panel 5

This panel completes the exercise with processes that Turner often applied in simple studies, but would also use in complex oils. A much heavier application of paint begins to create texture; with it, Turner might add foam to waves in a seascape, texture and form to clouds in a sky, a third dimension to architecture, and so on. This impasto provides an uneven surface from which light is reflected at many angles, bringing excitement to our perception of the play of light in his paintings. Here, the impasto is used sparingly to create light around the tree. It can be applied with a rag or brush, right up to the tree, helping to shape it with opaque white to which body has been added by mixing in thickener, rather than the megilp or wax-based medium that Turner often used. The direction of application can also suggest the direction of light: the best guide to doing it well is to stand in front of one of Turner's own paintings and look for the movement of his hand. Finally, notice that this heavier, brighter application

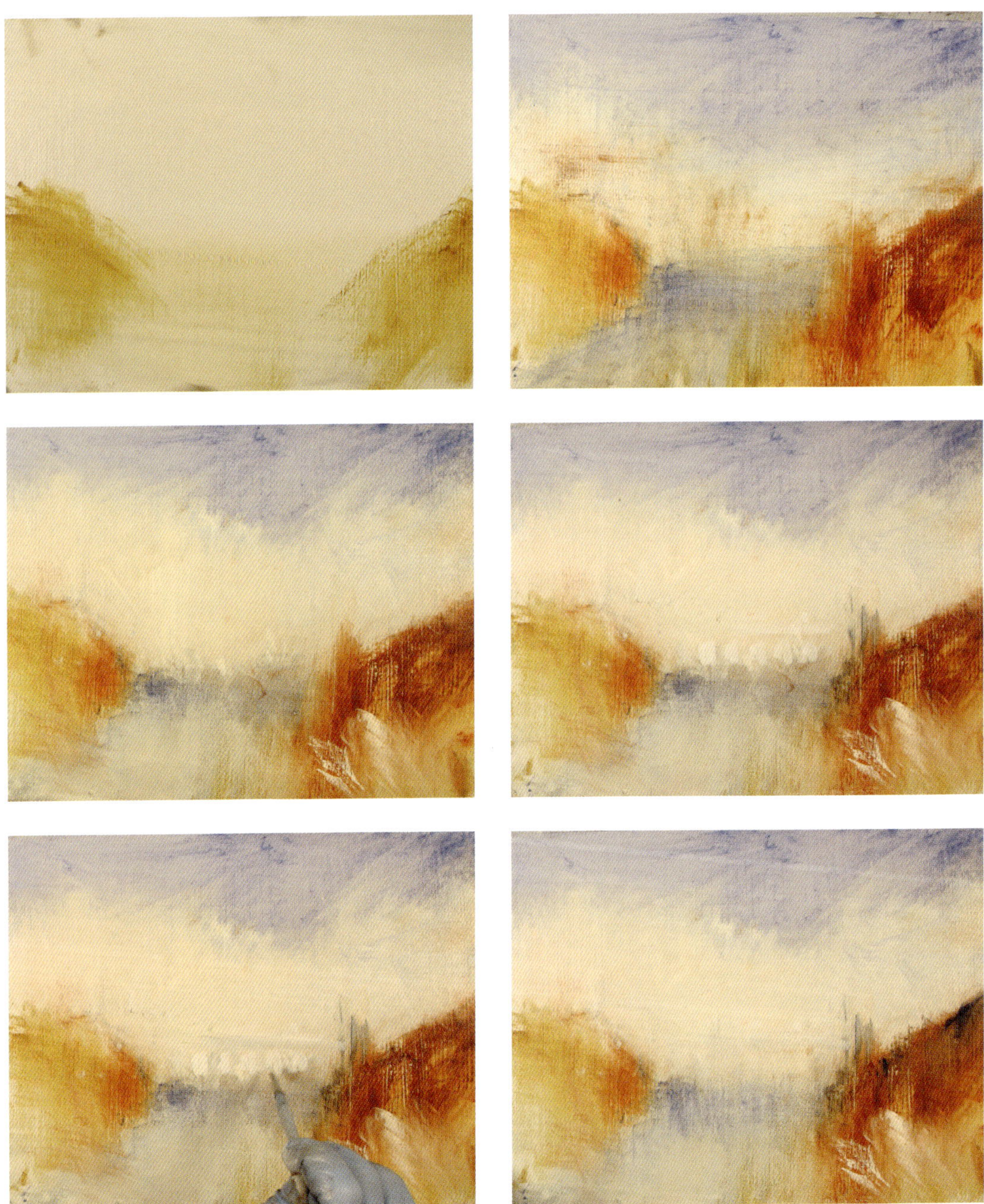

Landscape in six stages

of paint is echoed in the water below, and a suggestion of white light has been swept in horizontally from the water at the right into the shaded reflection of the bank at left. The next stage of Turner's core technical processes is also demonstrated in this panel, when he might add narrative elements with crisp details, such as a bird, a boat or a human form. Here, a very simple post is seen standing up from the water and reflected in it.

A variation in watercolour

The exercise can also be painted in watercolour on paper. The stages will all be the same (apart from being painted with broad brushes instead of a rag), but with a single critical difference: at stage 3, you should wash out the light-filled areas by removing colour with a tissue, a natural sponge or a brushful of water. In my own work, I favour washing out with a hand-held spray bottle, directing a forceful spray of clean water onto the area to be lightened, and sometimes tilting up the paper. As with most techniques, practice makes perfect, but the results can be wonderful. The materials used for this exercise include flat hake and sable watercolour brushes; watercolour paints in the same colours as used for the oil panels; and cold-pressed watercolour paper (300 grams per square metre) with a medium surface.

Further examples in oil

The work in oil shown on p. 123 (bottom) is a conscious attempt at recreating the breaking wave in Turner's *Waves Breaking against the Wind* (ill. p. 69), from *c.* 1840, using two of his methods. The left half was painted in one go, while the right half was left to dry at the stage when the form of the wave against the yellow sky was created. On another day – just as Turner would sometimes do – it was reworked, up to a comparable degree of finish.

This calm, sunny landscape (opposite) was inspired by *A River Seen from a Hill* from *c.* 1840–45 (ill. p. 81), which includes applications of white paint that both increase the sense of depth and bring down the intensity of the bright colours. This study is shown as six stages on the same board, starting with the first warm wash applied with a rag, through to the later brush applications of white paint, all completed in under fifteen minutes.

The simple seascape with storm clouds (overleaf, top) was created in four stages on one board by adding cadmium yellow to the same range of oil colours used before, as a substitute for Turner's more toxic mid-chrome yellow. The stages include the successive use of a rag, a brush and finally a finger to add form to the dabs of white paint. The small dark sailing vessel in the squall increases the sense of depth.

The next example (ill. p. 127), shown in twelve successive moments during its development over fifteen minutes or less, is a variant of the seascape with storm clouds, and developed to be more suggestive of a shipwreck. Both seascapes took about fifteen minutes to complete, and were begun with an intense yellow sky at the upper left and a dark threatening cloud at the right. As the second version developed, the yellow became less dominant in both sky and sea, as opaque white paint was applied and manipulated on top.

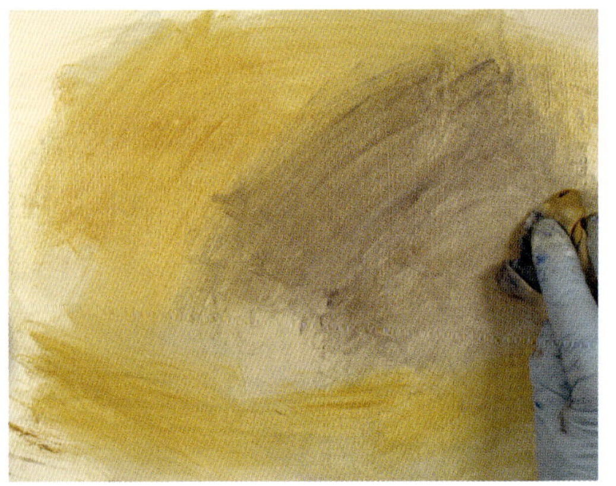

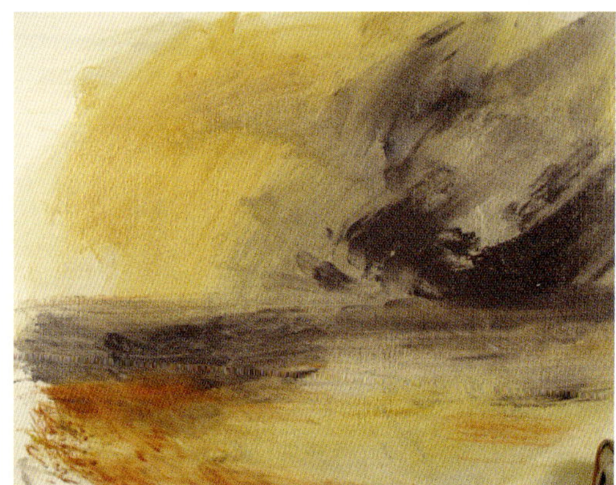

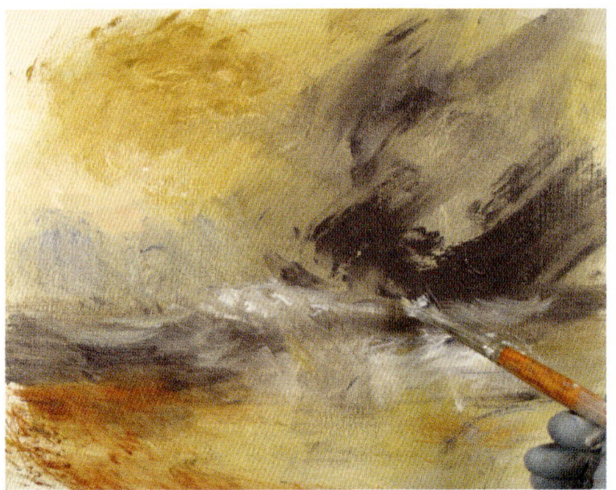

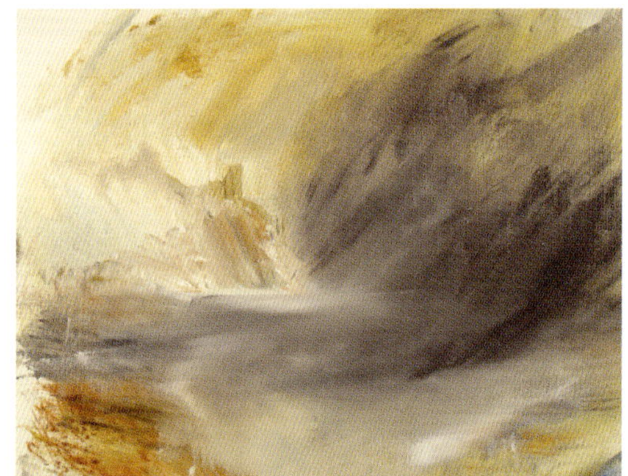

Seascape in four stages

The final panel (right) is another seascape, painted to suggest the water and spray of *The Slave Ship*, exhibited in 1840 and reproduced in a catalogue, which is shown overlying the panel on the right side.

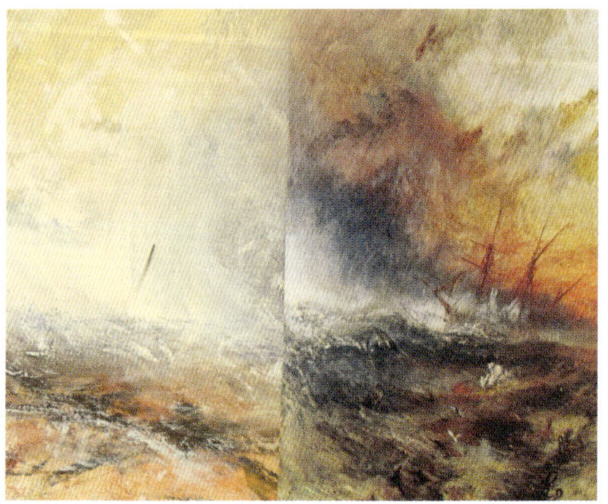

Water and spray

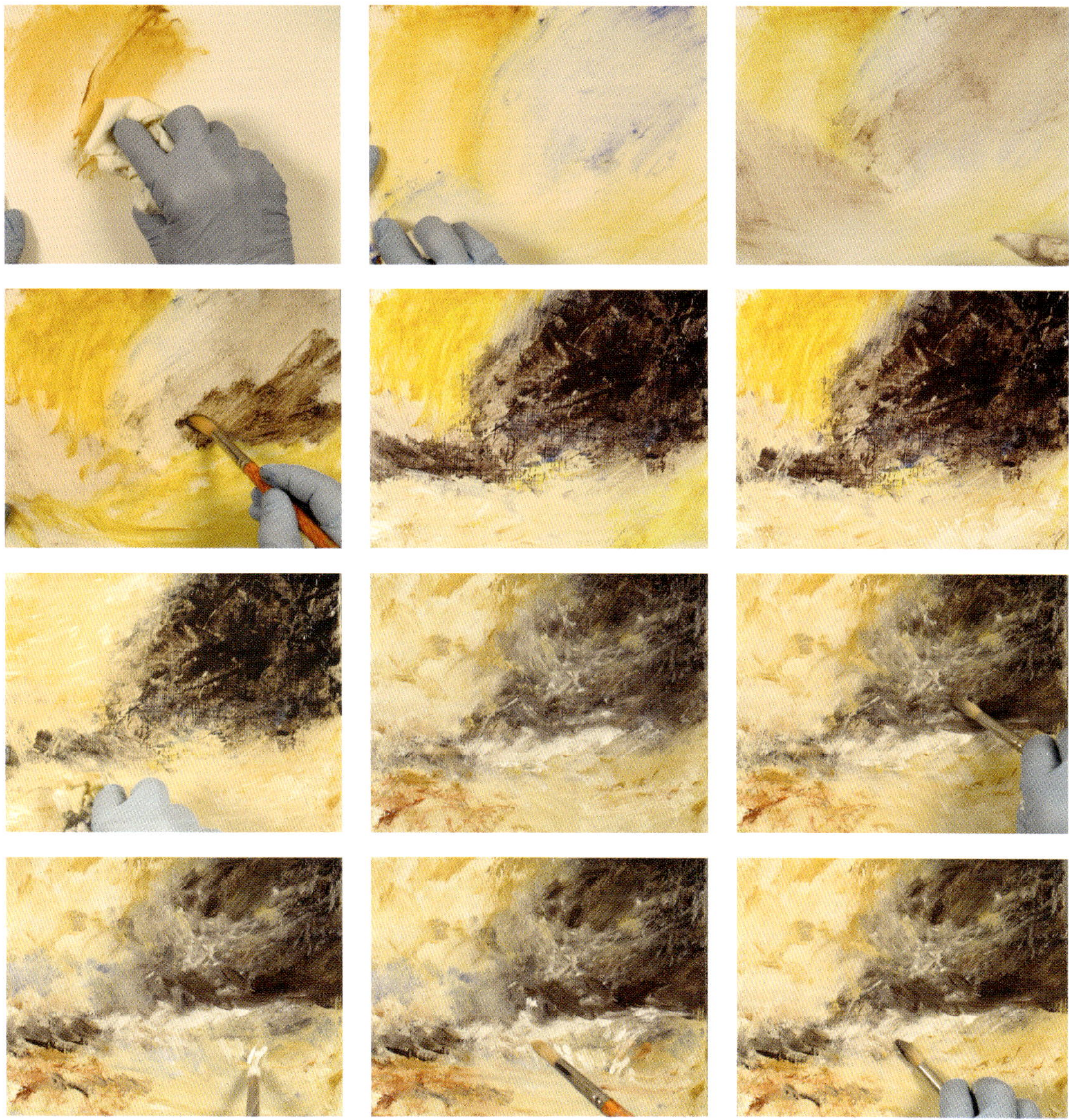

Seascape in twelve stages

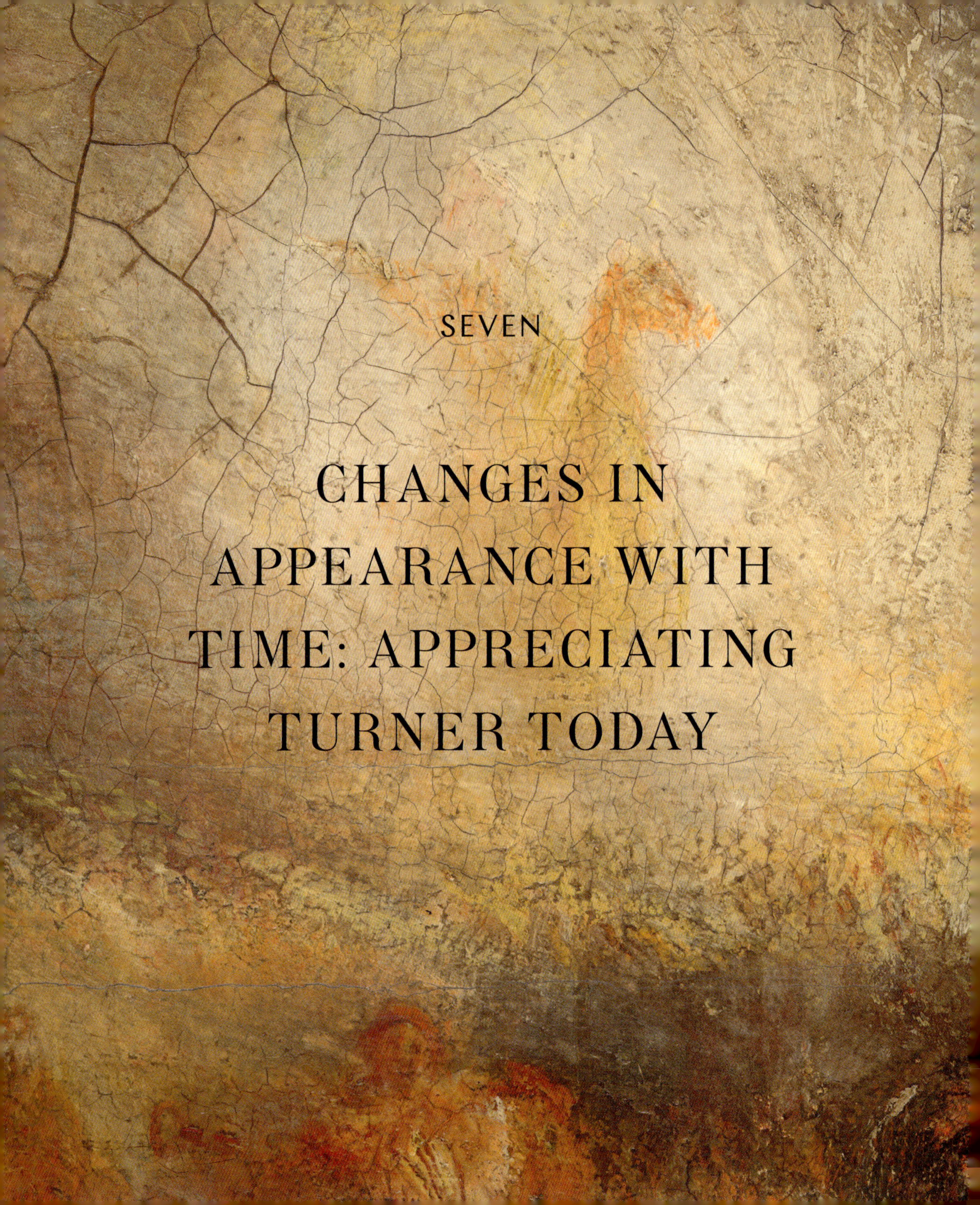

CHANGES IN APPEARANCE WITH TIME: APPRECIATING TURNER TODAY

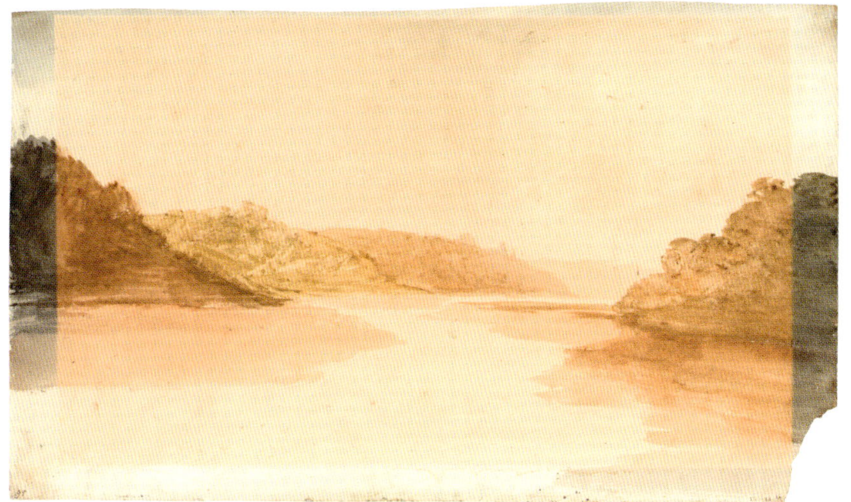

*Looking along a River between High Wooded Banks, with a Large Castle Just Visible in the Distance:
?Goodrich Castle on the River Wye*, 1798. Tate, London

Loss of colour is common in watercolours made in the mid- to later 18th century, because so many of the pigments commonly in use at the time faded rapidly if exposed to light. (When painted, these pictures were not intended for continuous display, but to be taken out for occasional appreciation.) Colour loss can also be seen in some of Turner's earliest works on paper, especially those displayed for long periods in the later 19th century, when public access was deliberately increased before its consequences for watercolours were realized.[74]

Looking along a River between High Wooded Banks (above), which was once covered by a window mount that obscured significant strips on both sides, is a striking example of a work by Turner where it is possible to see that mixed greens were used, very likely including blue indigo, as well as the yellow-brown ochre and a greener earth colour that alone survive. Another is *Heavy*

Clouds over a Landscape (overleaf), a sketch of the contrast between a purplish-grey cloudy sky and a brownish-green foreground landscape, made so rapidly that the artist did not make the horizon level (a later window mount was placed to level it). The colour alteration here is extreme, a combination of blue lost from the indigo and vermilion red mixture used for the grey sky, the same blue lost from the indigo and brown ochre mixtures used for the foreground landscape, and the off-white paper having yellowed severely where it was exposed to daylight for long periods.

It is still possible to see some of the intended effects in the sky. Greyer and darker clouds are to the left, which also had black mixed in; on the right, there was less red and more local variation, so that the clouds were more bluish purple, and paler towards the horizon. There seems to have been less shading in the landscape, judging by

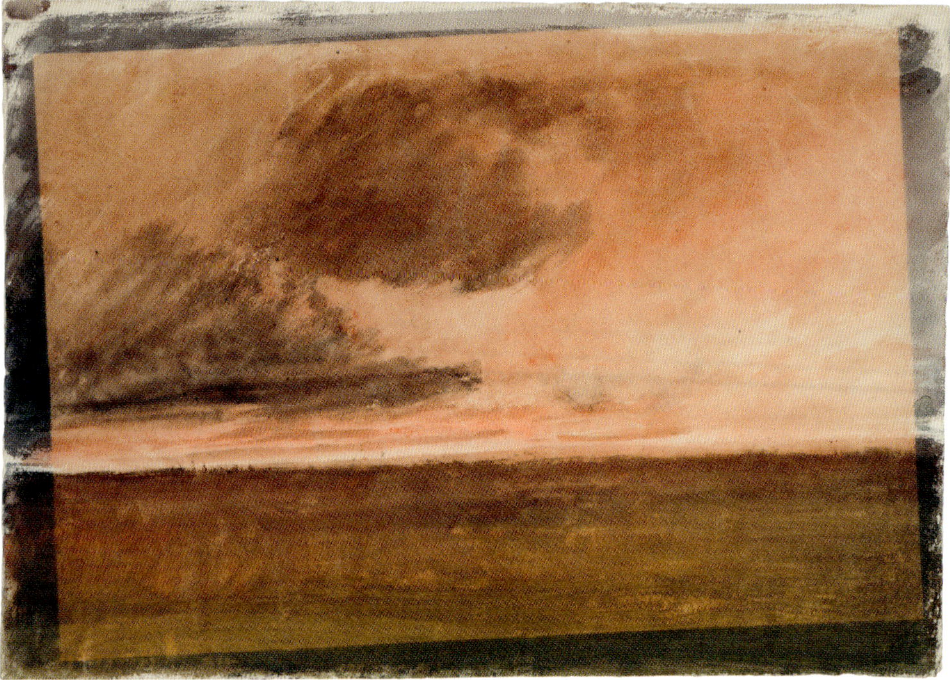

Heavy Clouds over a Landscape, c. 1820–40. Tate, London

what has survived round the edges. If there were any red lakes in the mixture, it is likely that they, too, have faded.

A more typical example of less severe colour loss that might be missed at first glance by the museum visitor is *The Pantheon, the Morning after the Fire* (opposite, top), where the volunteer firemen in the foreground now wear rather impractical pale red and pale blue outdoor jackets (opposite, bottom left and middle), and a crowd of wealthier but drably dressed onlookers can be seen near the burnt-out building. The sky is a rather anaemic blue for a morning scene, with dark and brownish clouds (opposite, bottom right).

Pallid red jackets, like that of the soldier further back, are a good indicator of colour loss. In fact, the clouds were painted with a madder lake produced with iron in the substrate, giving a browner tone than the usual crimson hue of madder made with a more conventional substrate containing alumina – but still a red, rather than a brown. Modifying the shade meant that the madder tended to fade more rapidly. A yellow lake was probably also used, suggesting that a lovely dawn light has been lost, and any pinkish glow on the icicles that formed overnight on the building is now completely faded. The light blue of both sky and jackets was likely to have been painted with indigo, long recognized

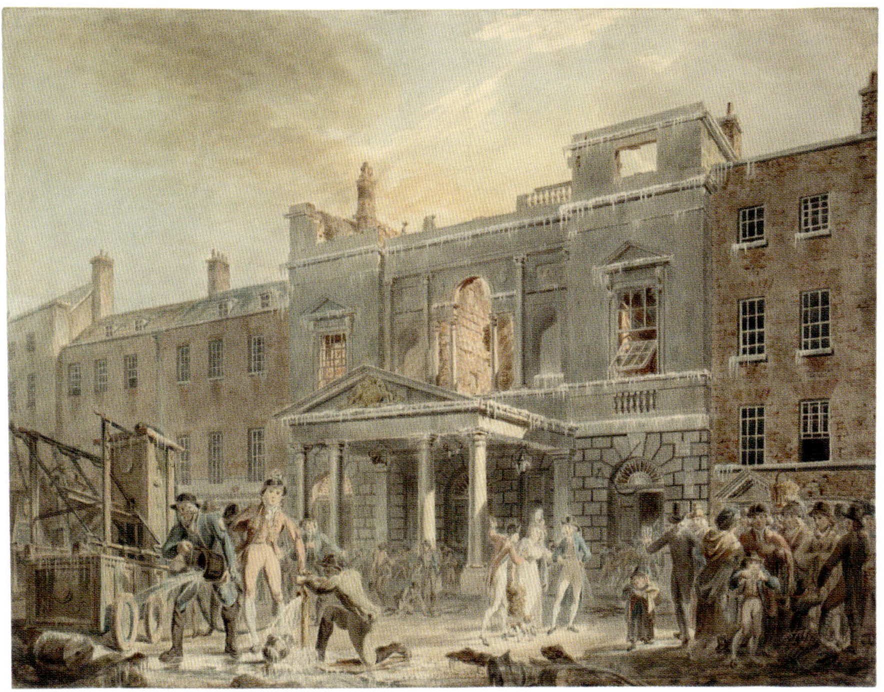

The Pantheon, the Morning after the Fire, 1792. Tate, London

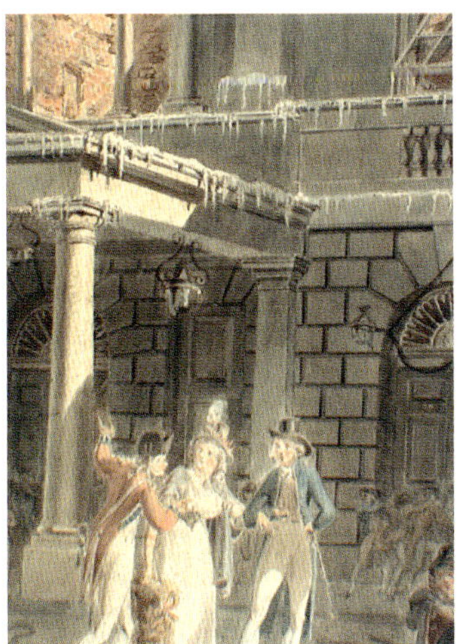

Detail of the figures

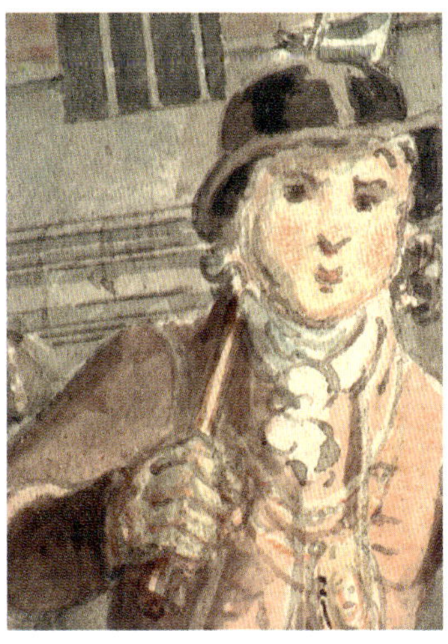

Detail of one figure

Detail of the sky at upper left

as a fugitive colour. Painted in more stable brown ochre and black pigments, the colour of the buildings will not have altered.

Red madder has also faded slightly from the optically mixed slate-grey sky in *Study for 'The Loss of an East Indiaman'* (ill. p. 41), which would have been more purplish in tone. The indigo, too, may have lost some colour. *Shields Lighthouse* (ill. p. 23) has a degree of colour change, not because the pigments have faded, but because the sheet had been displayed with the outer edges covered by a window mount, and the central area of the paper has yellowed irreversibly. The colour trials in Prussian blue at the outer edges were protected and retain their original blue, whereas the main image now appears greener than intended.

There is another class of lake pigments that is prone to fading: yellow lakes based on dyes extracted from plants, or pigments made with the same dyes, but without the laking process to intensify the colour and improve resistance to fading. The early sketchbooks do not name yellow lakes specifically, and few have been identified in Turner's watercolours; they are difficult to identify, even when fully present, and impossible to recognize, still less analyse, once faded.

Another yellow pigment of poor stability that Turner used in the earlier years is Indian yellow. It is easy to recognize in ultraviolet light, and was used in *View of Nuneham Courtenay from the Thames* (ill. p. 15) and *Trees by a Lake or River* (below), which do not look strikingly bright today and may have faded, and in other works from the 1780s and '90s. Because he moved so rapidly to using yellow earth colours, then to the chrome yellows in the 1810s, and more intense mixed greens and browns generally, these light-sensitive pigments may have been little used.

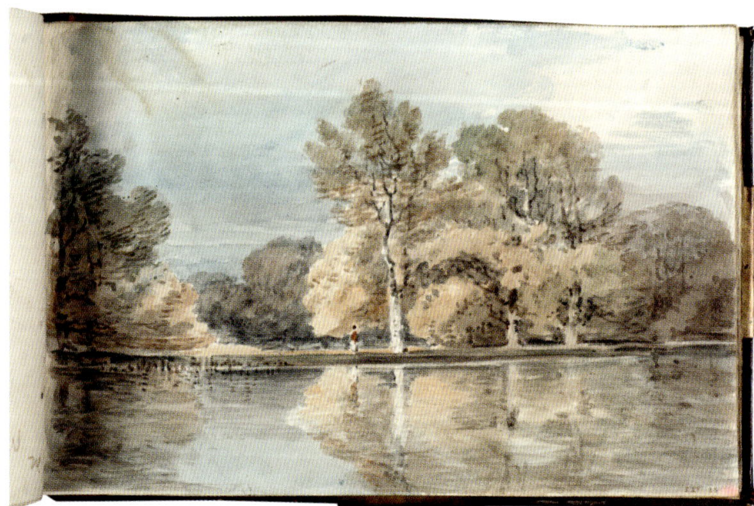

Trees by a Lake or River, c. 1795. Tate, London

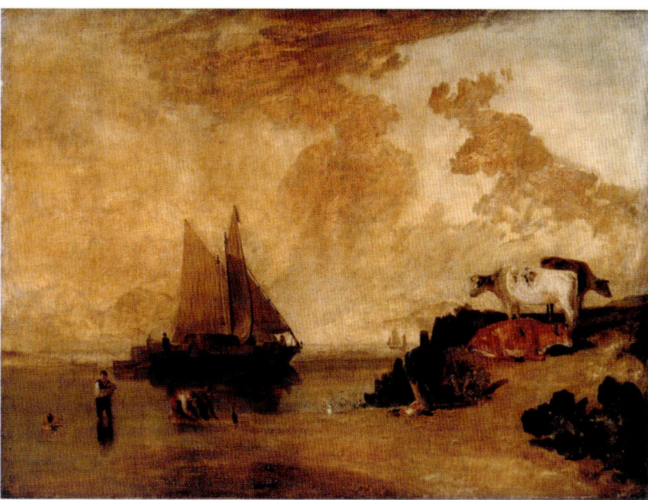

River Scene with Cattle, c. 1808. Tate, London

That some colours were light-sensitive was known to colourmen in Turner's lifetime. William Winsor, one of the founders of Winsor & Newton, is quoted in a company history:

'... noticing from time to time the very fugitive colours which Turner bought from us, [I] plucked up courage one day to remonstrate with him for so doing. Turner's answer ... "Your business Winsor is to make colours for Artists, mine is to use them".'[75]

A case can be made for Turner's seemingly cavalier attitude as a rational response to the lack of sound knowledge and abundance of conflicting anecdotal evidence that together comprised understanding of the longevity of different colours at that period. In reality, however, he was probably too caught up in the painting process to pause and consider later effects.

Oils: short-lived beauty due to fading?

Turner's oil paintings suffer from the loss of red lakes, as well. The pigments preserved from his studio (ill. pp. 9, 113) include a large number of red lakes in different shades, many of them madders with a wide range of substrates, which would confer many distinct shades. A few are based on cochineal, long known to fade readily. *River Scene with Cattle* (above) illustrates what happens when such pink and crimson shades are used in oil and exposed to too much light, though not necessarily too much for a typical work in oil. The clouds, which now look curiously brown, include a red lake with a copper-based substrate. It is even possible that the copper has reacted chemically with the paint, since this is an extreme example of darkening in paint that was once rosy and pale. Reviews of Turner's exhibited works that seem to describe colours we cannot see today may in fact indicate precisely what has been lost from some.

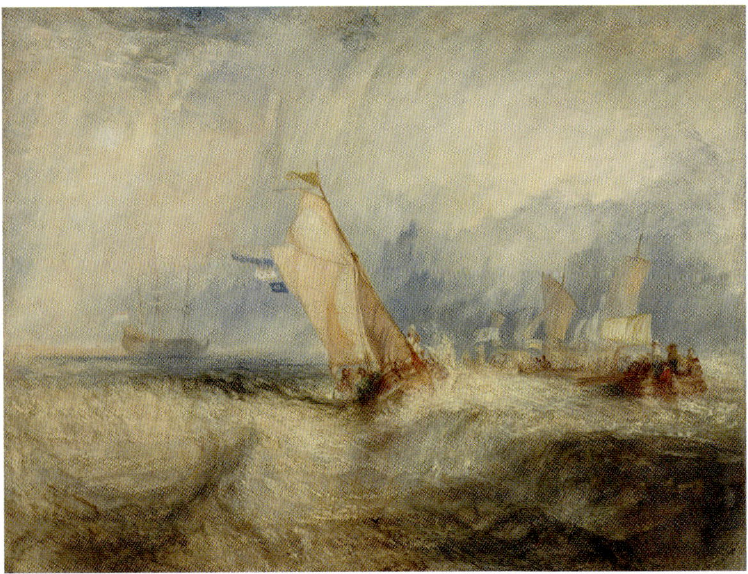

Van Tromp, going about to please his Masters, Ships a Sea, getting a Good Wetting,
1844. J. Paul Getty Museum, Los Angeles

Waves Breaking against the Wind (ill. p. 69) was a notable case, with the sunset, which extended over half of the sky, now lost because Turner used a salmon-pink lake pigment with a range of particle sizes. The same pigment occurs in *Steamer and Lightship; a study for 'The Fighting Temeraire'* (ill. p. 98), where its almost complete fading has also created a brown cloud and reflection in the water below. More obvious to the astute viewer is the complete loss of the upper red stripe in the red, white and blue Dutch flag atop the mast in *Van Tromp, going about to please his Masters, Ships a Sea, getting a Good Wetting* (above).

It is possible that the grey storm clouds that occur in many of Turner's seascapes have also lost some red lake, since it was his habit to mix slate greys and purples from blue or black, mixed with a red or crimson pigment. This alteration would leave little evidence, since the clouds were intended to vary greatly in tone, and most do not extend to the edges to make possible comparisons with unexposed areas. The near complete loss of red and pink tones from both *Waves Breaking against the Wind* and *Steamer and Lightship* are much more noticeable, simply because Turner habitually introduced the whole gamut of possible colours into any compositions that were developed to this degree. A preponderance of yellow and blue, dark and light, but no red should alert the viewer to the likelihood of colour loss.

Turner did not use indigo in oil paint, preferring several blue pigments more appropriately greenish in tone for depicting a sunlit sky. The blues he did choose – cobalt blue, smalt, natural ultramarine and Prussian blue – are fairly resistant to light-induced fading. The latter is the least stable of the group in this respect, but preserved and brighter blues at the edges, where they would have been covered by the frame, are not a feature of Turner's oils,[76] partly because he often reserved Prussian blue for local details in the body of the painting, making the comparison impossible.

Yellow lakes and yellow gamboge, often used in watercolour but less so by Turner, could be used in oil painting as a deep golden and transparent glazing colour, with the pigment simply added to oil or megilp. Even if the colours survived well, they would be difficult to spot on the surface, concealed by yellowed varnish. Far worse, such concealment might have led earlier generations of restorers, who worked without microscopes, to remove such glazes unwittingly, along with the varnish. They are not found on the surface of Turner's oils today, but it does not follow that this was a material he did not use in this way.

The majority of Turner's pigments, including the newly manufactured ones, are made from naturally occurring minerals. Most of these are resistant to fading, though in exceptional circumstances they may lose colour by other chemical reactions than light-induced fading.[77] His habit of not grinding pigments finely, or not purchasing already finely ground pigments, meant that the colours were as intense as the pigment could furnish. This lessens the risk of such reactions, which can proceed faster when the particles are fine. One exception is iodine scarlet: the fact that it was detected in *The Fighting Temeraire* (ill. p. 149) in the unusual circumstance of the original

varnish never having been removed to allow its evaporation raises the possibility that this intense colour has disappeared from other works.

Some of Turner's contemporaries feared the newly manufactured pigments would fade badly, and were especially concerned about the chrome yellows that he adopted so enthusiastically. There is no evidence of colour change in the extensive areas of chrome yellow he used in the skies, which often extend to the edges covered by the frame, where evidence of change would be obvious. The early forms of chrome yellow that he used differ in particle shape from those we see today; Turner's pigments had rounded particles, and examples from the later 19th century to the present day have very elongated ones. It is from the later 19th century that the darkening of such chrome yellow began to be noticed by artists, but Turner's chrome yellow does not behave in this way.

The much cheaper manufactured form of ultramarine also came under suspicion, and was adopted very slowly by most artists, even though it was far less expensive than the natural, mineral-based material. This is one of the only pigments that Turner did not use in oil despite its availability, the other being zinc white.

Oils: other colour changes[78]

The most dramatic colour change to be seen in oil paintings is the yellowing of the varnish over several decades, a short period of time compared to their overall lifetime. It is a permanent consequence of exposing the varnish to daylight, and will happen more slowly in museum conditions, with low lighting and all of the ultraviolet light filtered out. Varnishes also become yellow in the dark, and therefore can appear darker under the edges covered by a frame – as can be seen along the top of *George IV's Departure from the 'Royal George', 1822* (ill. p. 44), but this can be reversed gradually with light exposure.[79]

Varnishes have two functions: to protect the paint surface from accidental damage (meaning they should be hard, rather than soft), and to provide protection when accumulated dirt is removed. Just as importantly, they confer gloss and depth of colour, by wetting out the surface and counteracting the matte appearance of very pigment-rich and/or highly thinned paints. Contemporary connoisseurs and viewers expected to see a varnished surface with a degree of gloss, or a very newly painted surface that looked naturally glossy, rather than matte, because paint was still drying after its recent application.

Two types of varnish were common, though others existed: spirit varnishes, which were made from a soft triterpenoid resin, such as mastic or rosin, and dissolved in an alcohol, or oil varnishes, usually made and sold by artists' colourmen, who heated one or more of these resins with others, such as a harder diterpenoid resin, and with linseed oil or similar to produce a glossier, harder, more protective product. We know little directly about what Turner varnished with, because removal of a yellowed varnish from the oils has been the standard response to this colour change since the later 19th century. This means that the earliest of several varnish layers that may be present is usually not the one associated with Turner, but one applied later by a restorer.

The majority of paintings in the Turner Bequest – unfinished and never exhibited – were never varnished in Turner's lifetime. His exhibited paintings were varnished, some possibly, from the evidence of cross-sections, during the varnishing days when his paint was still wet. Some of the unfinished paintings were varnished after his death, but prior to the mid-20th century.[80] There is a single example that may well include the earliest varnish – *Moonlight, a Study at Millbank* (ill. p. 59) – as well as some later ones that conceal the original degree of gloss.

Turner's correspondence includes the occasional instruction to his father about ordering materials or sending off finished pictures to clients, and a single letter on varnishing, which implies that the varnish would dry overnight.[81] From this, it can be inferred that the varnish applied was of the 'spirit' type, because oil-based varieties would take longer to dry sufficiently for packing the painting for travel. It is likely that in this case William Turner did the varnishing himself.

Varnish removal is ordinarily possible by a conservator with skill and experience, and is typically done using solvents, which may be applied as a gel. The goal, difficult to achieve in practice, is often to remove later varnishes yet leave the earliest one as a protective layer, or sometimes to thin it to reduce visible yellowing. Sometimes this early layer has to be removed along with the later ones, because it has similar solubility. Removing varnishes from a finished oil painting by Turner requires conservator skills at a very high level, because the varnish so often lies over paint media that has been modified by Turner in different ways,

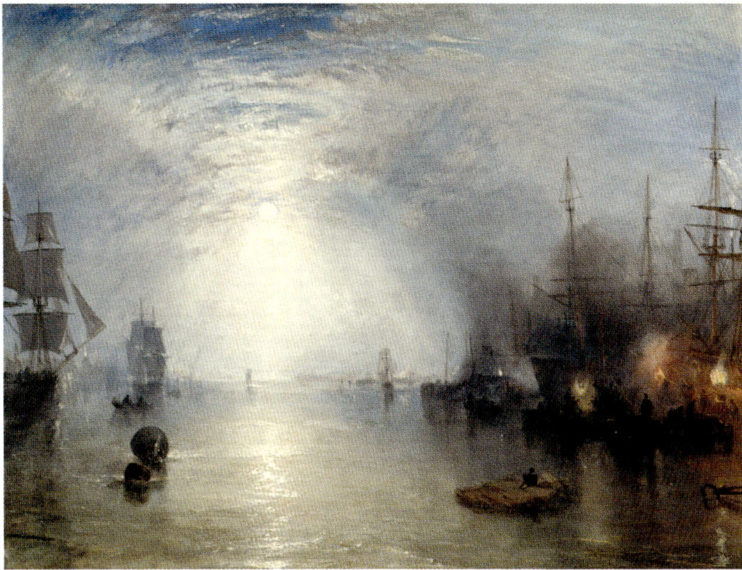

Keelmen Heaving in Coals by Moonlight, 1835. National Gallery of Art, Washington, DC

each different medium modifier localized and not obvious through the yellowed varnish, even with the aid of a microscope. Some of the paint may consist of precisely the same material as the varnish itself, and therefore have similar solubility.

The effect of removing a yellowed varnish is more than the recovery of cool tones that look too warm. Blue and cooler colours are changed most by a yellowed varnish. After its removal, colour contrast appears to be increased overall, with cool objects receding and hot reds standing out. This makes it possible to appreciate atmospheric perspective once more, with the slightly blue haze of the far distance seemingly increasing the recession. Varnish removal is surprisingly similar in perceptual terms to the added depth noticeable when the sun comes out on a previously overcast day. The paintings shown here have mostly had yellowed layers of varnish removed, the main exceptions being *Sunset* (ill. p. 67), with one or more very yellow varnishes that make it look too warm; *Moonlight, a Study at Millbank*, where the thick layers of several varnishes make the cool moonlight look much too yellow and the land too brown; and *The Fighting Temeraire*, which has the least yellowed varnish of them all, known to be the original with no further varnishes applied on top.[82] With such a bright yellow and red sunset, the slight yellowing is not obtrusive. In fact, this suggests that the original varnish must have been thin, and therefore not tremendously glossy.

All of the following types of colour change are incapable of being reversed, and require a leap of imagination to visualize the unaltered work.

The yellowing of megilp is one, because it includes the same mastic resin most often used for spirit varnishes, but the megilp is part of the paint itself, and the yellowing slowly intensifies over time. The least noticeable yellowing of megilp is in those soft, creamy clouds without hard edges in many of Turner's skies, which look a little more yellow than when first painted. In a sunset or in a depiction of afternoon light, this does not seem much of an alteration. Artists could plan for it, and knowledgeable critics might even anticipate it. One wrote of *Keelmen Heaving in Coals by Moonlight* (previous page): '... the tone seems too like daylight; but in a year or two hence it will be as bright and true a night scene as ever – or rather never was painted.'[83]

Thick glazes of megilp to intensify shadows, all medium and virtually no pigment, look more noticeable when they have darkened. It is reasonable to assume that the glossy shadows in the foregrounds of Italianate landscapes, and the glossy depths of Turner's seas, are warmer and darker than he knew them. Any obvious tonal imbalance between light sky and shadowed landscape is likely not what was intended. Wax-based medium modifiers yellow less severely, but asphalt-based ones (if Turner used any) can yellow more than his typical lead acetate-based megilps. The degree of change is difficult to estimate. The worst feature of megilps is their tendency to form wide shallow drying cracks that tear through the paint film and reveal the distinct colour of a layer below. Such cracks run over the point in a localized application, where the applied megilp went on most thickly, and can be very dramatic.

In 1847, when his health was not good and the deadline for the Royal Academy exhibitions loomed large, Turner repainted half the surface of a canvas he had first painted some forty years earlier, using huge quantities of megilp. The result is odd, to say the least. *The Hero of a Hundred Fights* (opposite, top) shows the annealing of a bronze equestrian figure, as it glows within a furnace (opposite, bottom), while the dark industrial interior can be seen as first portrayed in portions at the right.

The micrographs of the foreground and glowing furnace (p. 140, top) show the areas painted with megilp and lead white, chrome yellow and vermilion. They correspond pretty well with the white areas of the X-radiograph (p. 140, bottom), revealing lead white. When megilp was used extensively over the surface, it led to cracks of different widths and to varied depths, finer and wider-spaced, where the megilp was thinnest. This can be also seen in the details from *War. The Exile and the Rock Limpet* (ills. pp. 87, 88).

Ruskin wrote: 'No picture of Turner's is seen in perfection a month after it is painted. The "Wallhalla" cracked before it had been eight days in the Academy rooms.'[84] Today, its surface is extensively cracked in most of the sky, in the misty middle distance, in the impasted paint of the hillside, in some of the shadowed water and in many dark glossy areas of the figures in the foreground. Ruskin was very likely referring to cracking in the foreground, which indeed includes Turner's usual megilp – not just where it is obvious in the dark glossy areas as the last brushstroke, but also sometimes farther down within the painting. Such

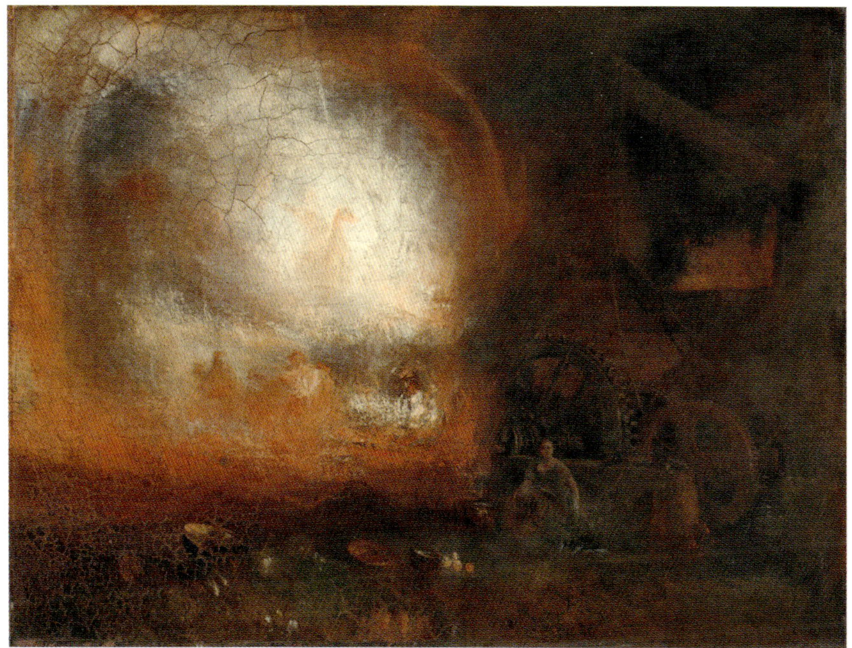

The Hero of a Hundred Fights, c. 1800–10, reworked and exhibited, 1847. Tate, London

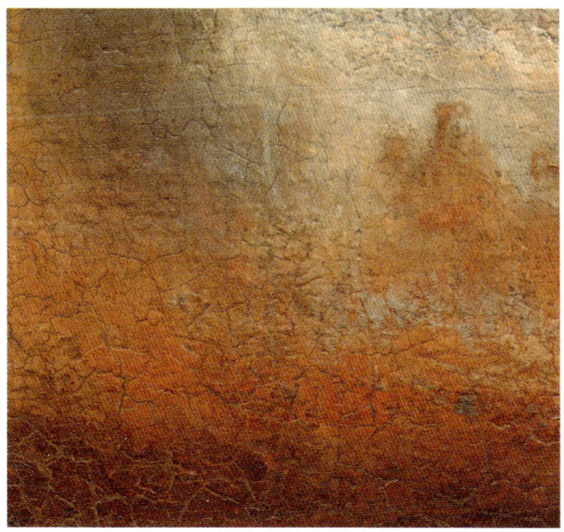

Detail of the left foreground

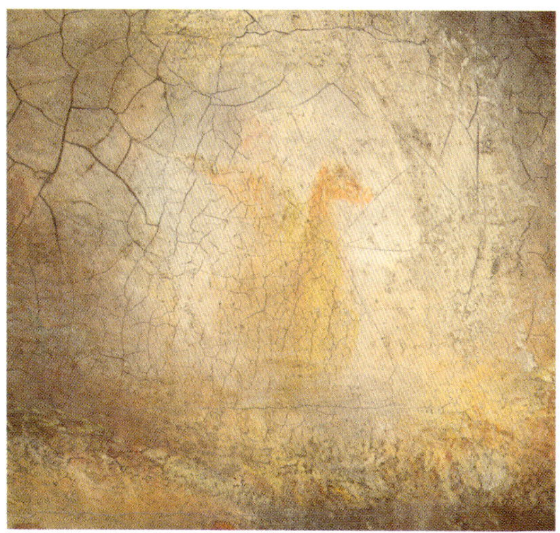

Detail of the white-hot metal of the sculpture in the furnace

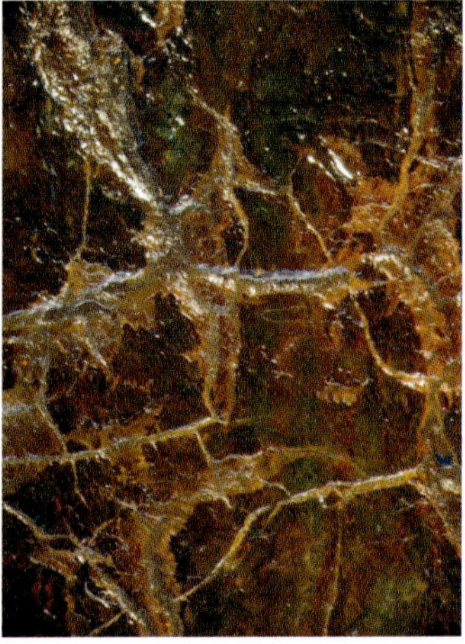

Micrograph of the green foreground

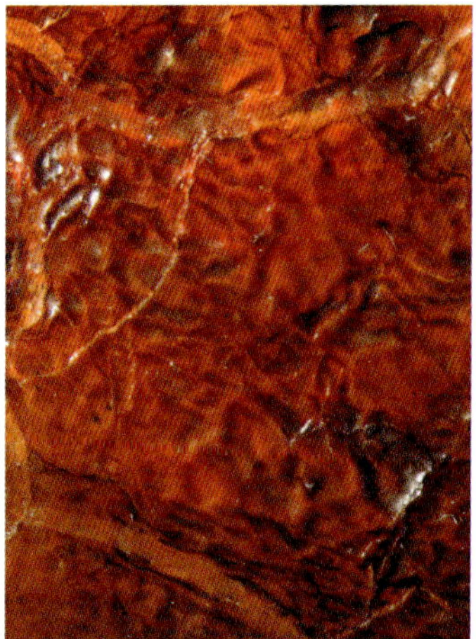

Micrograph of the glowing furnace

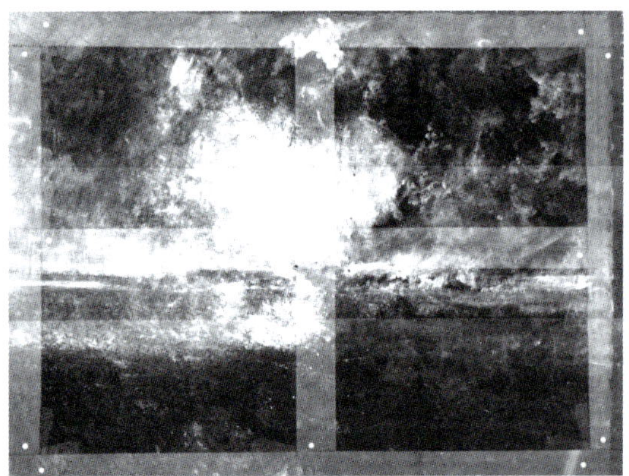

X-radiograph of *The Hero of a Hundred Fights* (ill. p. 139)

cracking was the price to be paid for using megilp liberally, instead of cautiously, applying it thinly and sparingly to paint that had dried thoroughly.

Optical changes arising from the use of large amounts of lead-based driers are harder to describe, and to reverse in the mind's eye (although it is the same chemistry that causes megilp to yellow). Turner's paintings in general are not too badly altered by the chemical reaction between lead-based pigments and driers, and, to a lesser extent, lead white pigment with oil medium to form lead soaps.[85] It proceeds at a much faster rate in the presence of lead-based driers, and makes the medium-rich and darker shades akin to much older paint in terms of increased transparency and a darkened appearance.

This aged paint also has a different response to the solvents used to remove varnishes, compared to pale and opaquely painted areas such as skies. Because Turner used a lot of lead white, often applied thickly, a slight attenuation of brightness and impact in the skies is rarely noticeable, except for thin applications over dark paint, or dashes of flying spray on top of a dark sea. In that case, the spray would look anaemic and undramatic. The fact that his grounds were white and very light mitigates the effect across the whole painting.

Dort, or Dordrecht, the Dort packet-boat from Rotterdam becalmed (below), inspired by the art of the Dutch Golden Age, would look less radiant and its calm morning light less convincing if the same composition had been painted over a mid-toned ground in the typical 17th-century manner. Many landscapes from this period look thin and insubstantial, with figures and foreground foliage shadowed, or even ghostly, because the increasingly transparent paint for such details has a dark underlayer. Turner's habit of leaving a reserve of white priming for the later painting of light-coloured features, including groups of figures such as the sailors in the largest boat in *Shipping at the Mouth of the Thames* (ill. p. 104), fortunately sidesteps the effect. It is nonetheless the reason why a few smaller figures added later to the foreground of a partly developed composition may seem insubstantial when compared to those he planned to apply in a reserve.

The effect is often more pronounced in early works, before 1810 or so, a period when Turner may have been experimenting with medium modifiers to create bodied paint, before finding the

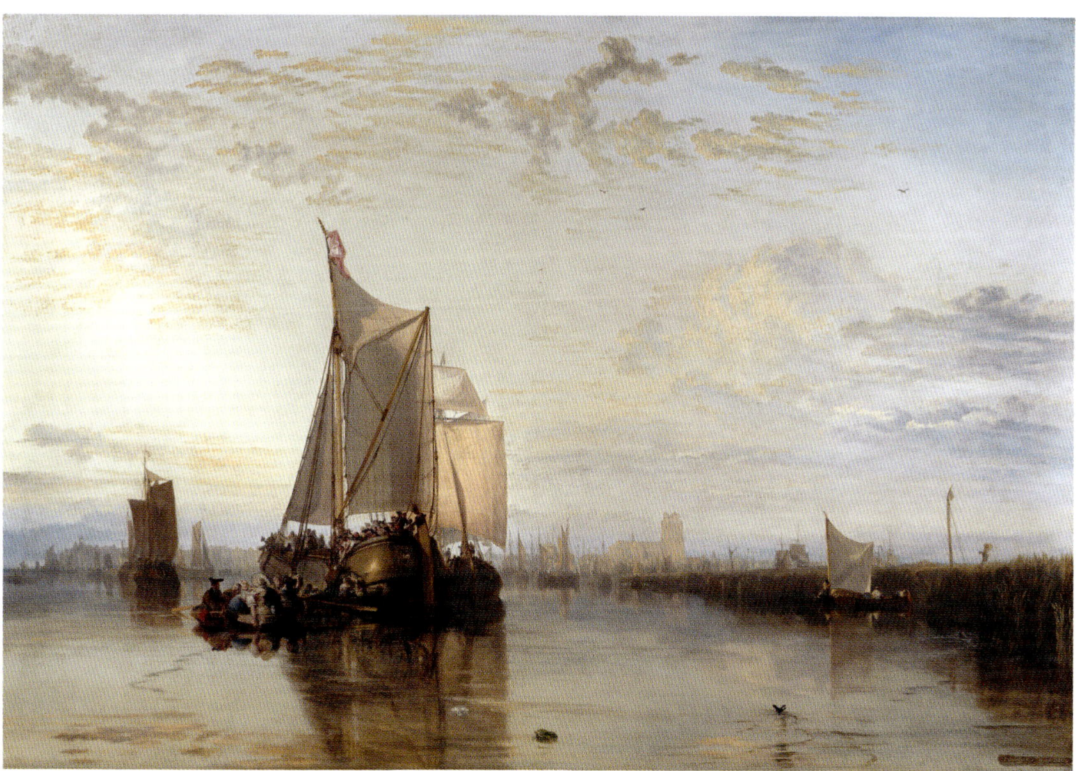

Dort, or Dordrecht, the Dort packet-boat from Rotterdam becalmed, 1818. Yale Center for British Art, New Haven

lead acetate-based megilp that so well answered his needs. His paints at this time seem to include extra ingredients and modifiers not seen in later decades; there is also evidence for large amounts of lead-based driers.

In central London, the air was heavy with soot and urban pollutants, with far more sulphur-based gases than we experience today, which made the exposed and unvarnished lead white in the primings of oil paintings and the highlights of watercolours alter chemically and darken, sometimes to a deep brown.[86] Some of the 'grime' on *A River Seen from a Hill* (ill. p. 81), which was reported to have obscured the bright blue sky and quite intense yellow of the foreground completely, must have been due to this phenomenon, as well as to an accumulation of soot and smuts from coal-burning. Non-varnished paint was susceptible, especially the coarse stack process type of lead white that Turner used exclusively in earlier decades and still occasionally towards the end of his life. Some types of oil made the reaction more likely.[87] Documented surface cleaning of unfinished paintings suggest that this discolouration was very common, but so successful was the cleaning that it is very rare to come across it now.

A dramatic surviving example is *Venice, the Piazzetta with the Ceremony of the Doge Marrying the Sea* (opposite, above), the untrimmed tacking margins of which are covered in Turner's typical lean and absorbent priming, made from lead white (opposite, below; and see p. 46, right). These areas are now a dark brown. In the medium-rich impasto for the clouds, there is an obvious colour change (p. 144, above left), while the leaner paint at upper right now looks like two discordant brown patches (p. 144, above right). It is fortunately rare to find such a visually disturbing change, but an intermediate stage, a light grey or brown (p. 144, below), is not uncommon in unfinished works from the 1830s and '40s, never protected by varnish.

The effect of Turner's habits on preservation

Turner himself was hardy and healthy until almost the end of his life, and could work long hours in conditions that many visitors to his studio described as damp, cold and neglected. Some implied that rain came in through the cracked windows, and canvases in the Turner Bequest show evidence of water damage that could date from this period. His cats came in and out through opened windows. In winter, especially, damp cold conditions make canvases slacken, and flap when disturbed by footfall or vibrations from moving frames. This induces ageing cracks in the paint.

After his father died in 1829, Turner would have moved paintings and frames around by himself, and accidents must have happened as increasing numbers of unsold paintings piled up in the studio and in other rooms. One such incident befell *Regulus* in the 1830s (see pp. 83–87), while some canvases show circular crack formations that are the evidence of a sharp impact, most likely from a corner colliding with a canvas farther back in the stack. The canvases with egg-white primings all too readily supported mould growth in damp conditions; this causes dark spots on the paint, which have nibbled into the surface where they were neglected for a hundred years, as befell the least finished paintings.

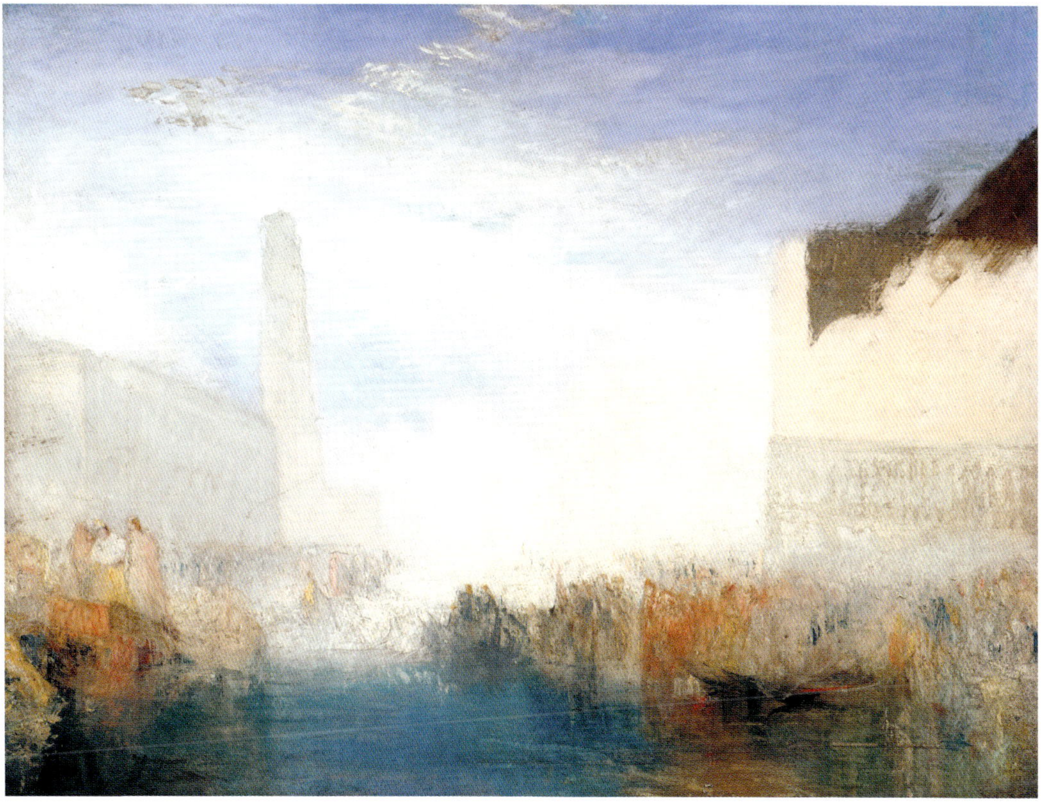

Venice, the Piazzetta with the Ceremony of the Doge Marrying the Sea, c. 1835. Tate, London

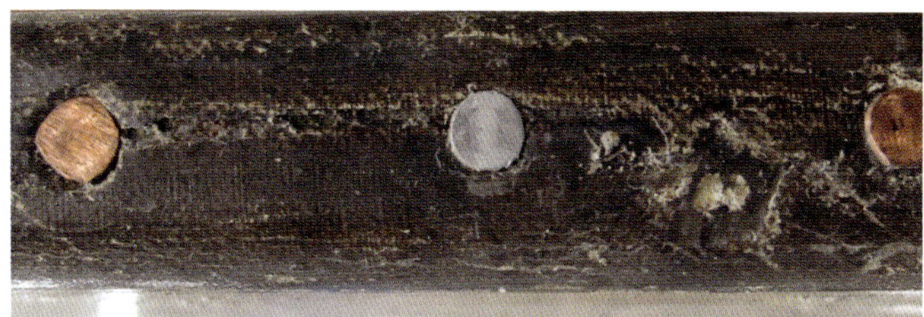

A rare survival of untrimmed tacking margins, showing darkening to deep brown of the lead white-based priming

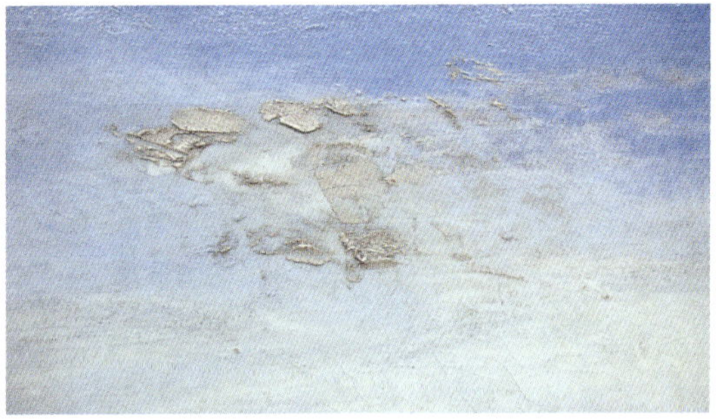

Lead white-based impasto in a cloud, discoloured noticeably

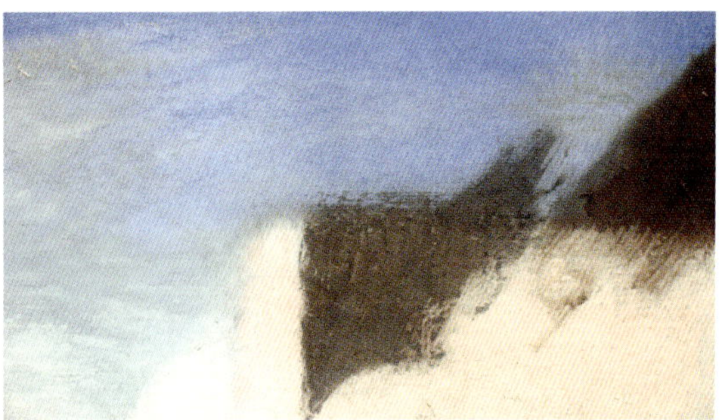

Lean lead white paint at the upper right, now a dark brown

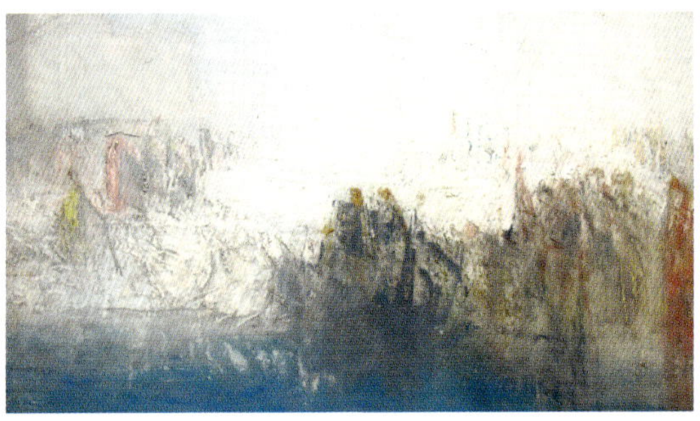

Discordant mid-grey paint in the foreground water

Given the location of Turner's studio in central London, there must have been a lot of dirt and soot in the air from coal fires and urban pollutants. Sometimes there is a layer of dirt on the priming, visible in cross-section, indicating that a primed support was lying around in the studio for some time. Such a layer is present on the priming beneath *The Opening of the Wallhalla, 1842* (ill. p. 61), which has an unusual support – not canvas, but a rather splendid piece of hardwood, pre-primed by the colourman and matching the hardwood support of *The Story of Apollo and Daphne*, exhibited in 1837. If Turner purchased the pre-primed panels

together, then the priming for the *Wallhalla* might have had five or six years of London grime on it, difficult to remove, even if he had uncharacteristically cleaned the surface carefully.

Turner's worst habit in regard to the preservation of his work was his own impetuous and spontaneous approach to painting. Sound practice dictates that new paint should be applied either to paint that is wet enough to combine with it, or to properly dried paint, but not to paint that is part-dry and forming a thin skin on top. The medium-lean priming should also be systematically painted over with successively more medium-rich paint, applied in thin layers, while medium modifiers should just be used – sparingly – in the topmost layers.

These rules would work with a carefully constructed composition, built up gradually with time allowed for each session of painting to dry. Samples of Turner's paint made into cross-sections show instead a wild alternation of thick and thin paint applications, with solid blobs of lead white in stiff oil landing on thin megilp layers and thick, soft, wax-based layers alike, with thin coloured glazes between, applications of megilp that dried in fine wrinkles, and every possible sequence imaginable. It is obvious from examining his paint with a microscope that no two spots would have the same layer structure. Turner knew what he wanted to paint and, by his later years, knew that he could achieve particular effects by more than one set of processes, so he let instinct take over, and broke all the rules of sound painting.

The result was beautiful, of course. The consequence today of such haphazard, unsystematic paint application is flaking spots of paint from earlier paint layers, some of the paint cleaving in its entirety off the priming, and lots of very localized cracking. Such problems were reported in the 19th century, and by visitors to Turner's studio. Until the Turner Bequest moved to a controlled environment in 1987, it was documented that cracks grew and paint flaked off canvases with depressing regularity. Many of the finished paintings have been repeatedly treated for paint detachment for more than a century, both by reattaching flakes of paint and by retouching areas of loss. The way Turner painted would inevitably have led to such treatments becoming necessary, but the conditions in his studio can only have made things worse.

The effects of past conservation

A treatment that is avoided today but was common in the 19th century and, indeed, until the 1970s in public collections, has been applied to the great majority of Turner's oils, as it was to most other paintings of that age or older: lining. It was done because canvas that is a century old, exposed to intense urban pollution, loses strength and becomes very fragile where it is turned over the

sides of the stretcher. Lining traditionally involved adhering thin paper to the paint with animal glue to prevent any losses of paint flakes, removal from the stretcher, turning the painting face down on a table, brushing on adhesive (usually glue paste in the UK), laying a new canvas over the top, and melting the adhesive into action using heated irons of the type used for ironing clothes.

Only when the painting was turned over did the damage to wax-based paint become apparent, far too late to save the impasto from softening, or even flattening. In the 20th century the process evolved, with the use of tables that gave controlled heating to the lining canvas underneath, with the painting on top, so that its response to heat was visible during the process. By the 1960s and '70s, a wax mixture was used instead of glue paste, impregnating the paint, as well as attaching the new canvas. This was the treatment applied to many unfinished paintings in the Turner Bequest. Today, the required strengthening of the turnover edges can be effected by the local application of supporting strips of canvas to the unpainted edges only. This process of striplining is common in public galleries, thus avoiding full lining.

Traditional lining, though carried out by skilled liners who undertook only this treatment, gave uneven heating of the paint, so that some wax-containing areas might be melted smooth, but others would not. It is very telling that the spermaceti wax found in some unlined Turner oils on panel supports, which render lining unnecessary, has not been found by analysis in any lined works. Spermaceti wax has such a low melting point, as noted earlier, that it must have melted and dispersed too far into the paint to be detected now. Even Turner's unrefined beeswax, which melts more readily that typical beeswax, presented unforeseen problems to traditional liners. The worst examples have local impasto pushed right down into the plane of the paint, surrounded by a 'moat' of even flatter surface.

The first restorers of Turner's paintings worked without microscopes or knowledge of his wax-based paint, and at a pace that seems unbelievable today. It gave no time for any more than the application of a standard treatment, without time to look much at the individual painting. When *Regulus* was attacked with a knife in 1863, the canvas was sent out to a company that specialized in lining, and returned in ten days. The varnish removal and its replacement followed by retouching took under a month.

Because of the earlier accident to the painting in Turner's studio, this was the second time the painting had been lined.[88] The very thick paint he used to disguise that first repair has been prone to flaking off ever since, and between the numerous surface cracks it does not lie flat, but is cupped. There are numerous recorded treatments to secure and resecure it. A detail of the water (opposite) illustrates its appearance now. Sadly, this is but an extreme example of where early lining and multiple campaigns of treatment made necessary by Turner's painting processes may lead.

Turner oils at their best

Because of the subtle visual changes brought about by the natural ageing of paint like Turner's, rich in megilps and lead-based driers, the very best-preserved of Turner's oils are often those that he put aside before the megilp stage. *Waves Breaking against the Wind* (ill. p. 69) provides a wonderful example of his skill at depicting spray, breaking waves and a shoreline still wet from a receding wave.[89] The breaking wave at the centre (see p. 70, top) is a dynamic and detailed study of water, made with very few colours (if we ignore the lost pinks in the sky, its background is a simple and uniform yellow for the moving wave to stand out against) and mainly in shades of grey.

The wave has all the immediacy of a highly accomplished *plein air* sketch, but is actually a work of the imagination, distilled from decades of experience of intense looking at the sea in all its moods. The surface is free from cracks, certainly never damaged by early varnish removal since it had never even been freed from a century's grime until more benign methods of cleaning paint had been developed. It is tempting to wonder if Turner himself liked it too much to proceed further. There are several similar studies of almost equal beauty in the Turner Bequest, most appearing in near-perfect condition – except that reds and pinks are largely absent from all of them.

Among Turner's landscapes and cityscapes, *The Arch of Constantine, Rome* (ill. p. 148) is today very little altered, because he had not developed it to the point of adding texture and gloss through the addition of medium modifiers. There is no evidence for colour loss, and little disruption of the surface other than fine ageing cracks. *Norham Castle, Sunrise* (ill. p. 13) is also in excellent condition, an example of a finished work (in Turner's estimation, if not that of his contemporaries) which

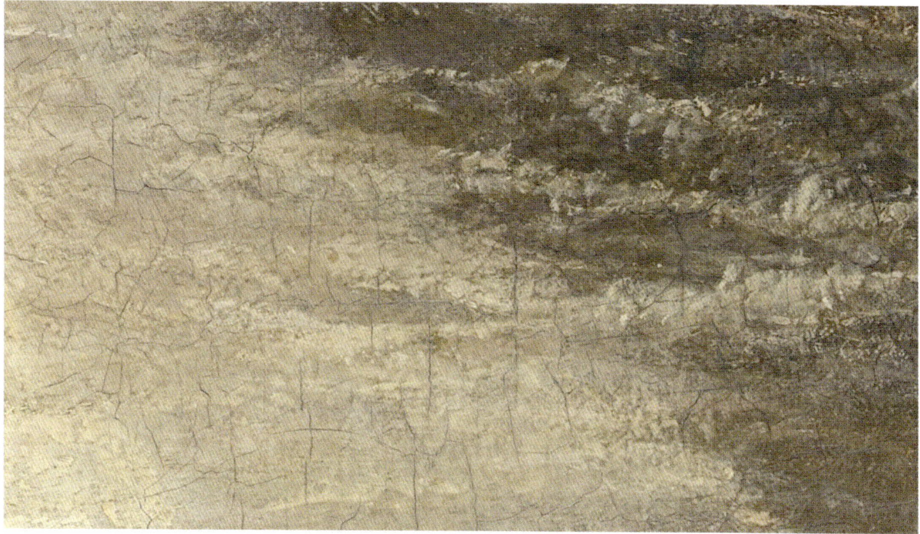

Detail showing the water in *Regulus*, with cupped paint and retouches (full work ill. p. 83)

relies more on subtle contrasts of colour than of texture or gloss, thus avoiding the disadvantages of using megilp and other medium modifiers to excess.

The best preserved of the finished works are often those Turner sold soon after their completion: they escaped from the cold and damp of his studio and gallery in his later years, and likely found a better environment in the home of their purchaser. This has certainly been the case with *The Fighting Temeraire* (ill. p. 149), a painting also fortunate in that it escaped all restoration treatments in the later 19th and early 20th centuries, was always protected from soot and pollution by glass, remained unlined until 1963, when it was replaced on its original stretcher, and still retains its original varnish.[90] Detailed materials analysis of the pigments and paint media Turner used for it has revealed not only the pigments he typically used at the time, but also some less than durable materials that would not have survived on any less fortunate canvas, including the brilliant red pigment iodine scarlet (used just above the sun, less strongly coloured now), barium chromate (used in addition to chrome yellow in various shades) and gum benzoin (used here as a glazing material, which would yellow less than megilp).[91] The intense sunset, the glossy depths of the water, and the extreme contrast between the light ship and the dark tug all show Turner, that supreme colourist, at his imaginative best.

Ruskin squarely blamed the artist himself for the rapid changes in the oil paintings, and his writings suggest we can never see Turner's paintings at their best, some two hundred years after they were created:

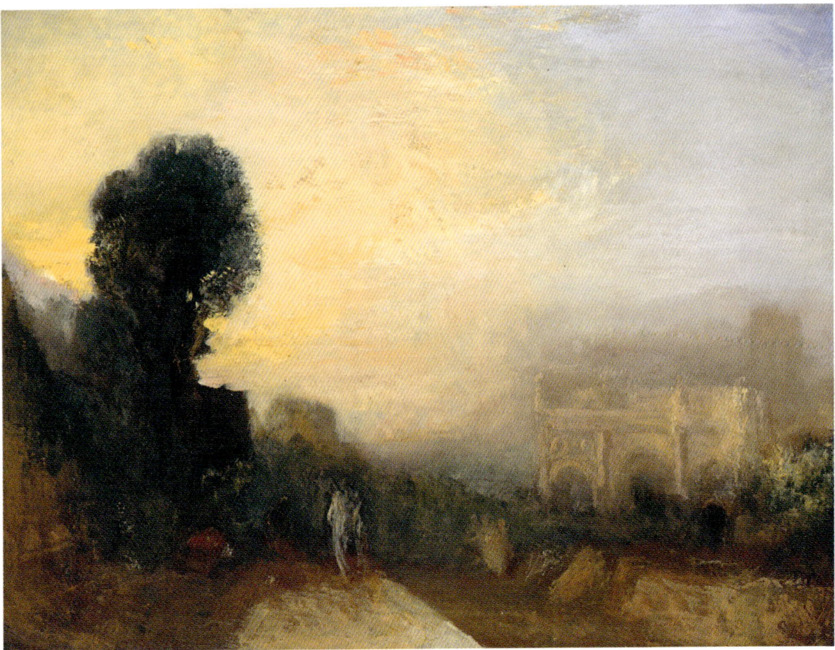

The Arch of Constantine, Rome, c. 1835. Tate, London

... The vermilions frequently lose lustre long before the [Royal Academy] exhibition is over; and when all the colours begin to get hard a year or two after the picture is painted, a painful deadness and opacity come over them, the whites especially becoming lifeless, and many of the warmer passages settling into a hard valueless brown ... in some measure these results are unavoidable, the colours being so peculiarly blended and mingled in Turner's present manner, as almost to necessitate their irregular drying ... the old *Temeraire* is nearly safe in colour, and quite firm ... The fact of him using means so imperfect, together with that of his utter neglect of his own pictures in his gallery, area phenomenon of human mind which appears to me utterly inexplicable, and both are without excuse.[92]

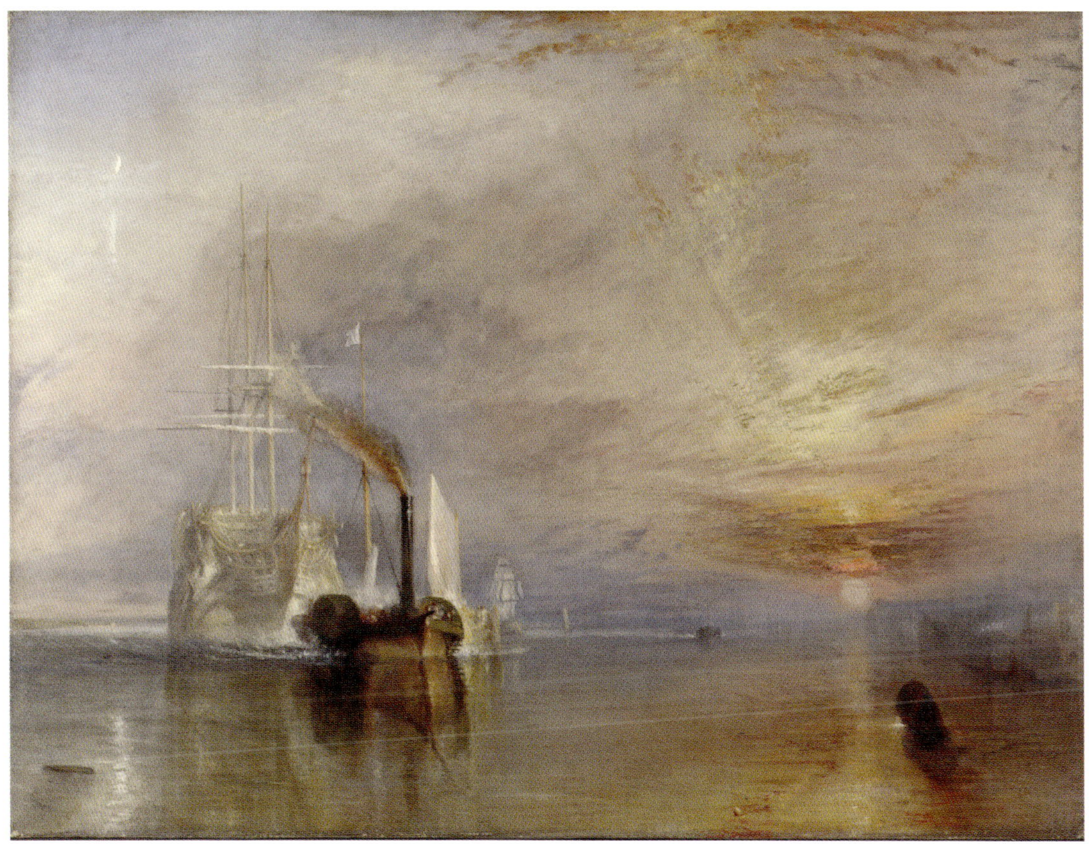

The Fighting Temeraire tugged to her last berth to be broken up, 1838, 1839. National Gallery, London

NOTES

1. For watercolours, see Moorby, Nicola, and Ian Warrell, *How to Paint Like Turner* (London: Tate, 2010), and Smibert, Tony, and Joyce H. Townsend, *Tate Watercolour Manual: Lessons from the Great Masters* (London: Tate, 2014). For oil paintings, see Townsend, Joyce H., ed., *Turner's Painting Techniques in Context* (London: UK Institute for Conservation of Historic and Artistic Works, 1995); and Townsend, Joyce H., *Turner's Painting Techniques* (London: Tate, 1993; 4th ed., 2005).

2. Appropriate analytical methods for paint are described in Stoner, Joyce Hill, and Rebecca Rushfield, eds, *The Conservation of Easel Paintings* (Oxford: Routledge, 2012), in particular chapters 17 and 18 for examination methods, including paint cross-section and dispersions, and chapter 22 for descriptions of the techniques of SEM-EDX, FTIR microscopy, GC-MS, Py-GC-MS and HPLC, used to analyse paint for this study.

3. An unpublished catalogue of the frames used with each Tate painting at different times has been created by Dr Ivan Houghton, and can be consulted in the Tate Conservation Department. See Houghton, Ivan T., and Gerry Alabone, 'Understanding the framing of the Turner Bequest', *The British Art Journal* 12:1 (2011): 42–51; for framing generally, see Alabone, Gerry, 'The picture frame: Knowing its place,' in Hermens, Erma, and Tina Fiske, eds, *Art, Conservation and Authenticities: Material, Concept, Context* (London: Archetype, 2008), 60–69.

4. For an expanding illustrated online catalogue of all Turner's works on paper, see 'Search the catalogue', in Blayney Brown, David, ed., *J.M.W. Turner: Sketchbooks, Drawings and Watercolours*, Tate Research Publication, December 2012, tate.org.uk/art/research-publications/jmw-turner/search-the-catalogue-r1176978. All public collections, including Tate, illustrate their Turner oil paintings on their websites.

5. The printed catalogue raisonné by Butlin, Martin and Evelyn Joll (*The Paintings of J.M.W. Turner*, 2 vols, New Haven and London: Yale University Press, 1984), ordered by 'BJ' numbers, has no online equivalent. The dates used here for paintings and watercolours in the Turner Bequest are those given as of March 2019 on tate.org.uk, rather than those in Butlin and Joll, as the Tate website incorporates the latest research into subject and date.

6. Forrester, Gillian, *Turner's 'Drawing Book': The Liber Studiorum*, exh. cat., London, Tate, 1996.

7. Riding, Christine, and Richard Johns, *Turner and the Sea*, exh. cat., London, Royal Museums Greenwich, 2013.

8. Wark, Robert R., ed., *Discourses on Art: Sir Joshua Reynolds* (New Haven and London: Yale University Press, 1959; rev. ed., 1997).

9. Turner's early years – up to 1815 – have been admirably described and works from that time illustrated in Shanes, Eric, *Young Mr Turner: The First Forty Years 1775–1815* (New Haven and London: Yale University Press, 2016); see also Warrell, Ian, 'J.M.W. Turner and the pursuit of fame', in Ian Warrell, ed., *J.M.W. Turner*, exh. cat., London, Tate, 2007, 12–21. For Turner's later life, see Smiles, Sam, *The Turner Book* (London, Tate, 2006), and Wilton, Andrew, *Turner in his Time* (London: Thames & Hudson, 2006).

10. In particular, *Snow Storm – Steam-boat off a Harbour's Mouth*, exhibited 1842 (ill. p. 77). Hamilton, James, *Turner and the Scientists*, exh. cat., London, Tate, 1998, 126–28 and chapter 7, 115–28.

11. Solkin, David H., ed., *Turner and the Masters*, exh. cat., London, Tate, 2009.

12. Warrell, Ian, *Turner's Sketchbooks* (London: Tate, 2014).

13. Shanes.

14. See Smibert, Tony, *Turner's Apprentice: The Essential Manual for Watercolour Success* (London: Thames & Hudson, 2019), on following in Turner's footsteps along his known travel routes to understand his working processes.

15. Cook, E.T., and Alexander Wedderburn, eds, *The Works of John Ruskin*, vol. 3 (London: George Allen, 1903–12), 128.

16. This fact has inspired many more recent exhibition organizers to use red walls. A historically inspired red, used at a similar date to that in Turner's gallery, can be seen in the main galleries of Dulwich Picture Gallery, London.

17. Wark.

18. See Bower, Peter, *Turner's Papers: A Study of the Manufacture, Selection and Use of his Drawing Papers 1787–1820*, exh. cat., London, Tate, 1990, and Bower, *Turner's Later Papers: A Study of the Manufacture, Selection and Use of his Drawing Papers 1820–1851*, exh. cat., London, Tate, 1999. The preceding and later summaries on his papers are drawn from these catalogues, which also provide a history of paper-making in Turner's era and valuable information on how different papers performed when used by an artist.

19. Studies by Bower and others have found strong evidence that the year incorporated into watermarks during Turner's earlier lifetime was not updated at each year end, but later. Whatman papers with watermarks for 1794 and 1801, used by Turner, do not imply use in that year, as is sometimes suggested, since paper endures for many years, whether used or not.

20. Bower, *Turner's Papers*, 71.

21. Egerton, Judy, *Turner: The Fighting Temeraire*, exh. cat., London, National Gallery, 1997, 70 and note 107.

22. Thornbury, Walter, *The Life of J.M.W. Turner, R.A.*, 2 vols (1862; London: Chatto & Windus, 1877; repr. 1970), 362.

23. Cook and Wedderburn, vol. 3, 293.

24. Thornbury, 363.

25. Here, I am following the convention that broad classes of paint (oil, watercolour) are media, while sub-classes (such as megilps) are mediums. Turner's contemporaries used these terms, and spoke of 'adding a vehicle' to paint, in the sense of adding something to the oil in which it has been ground.

26. Townsend, Joyce H., 'The materials of J.M.W. Turner: Primings and supports', *Studies in Conservation* 39 (1994): 145–53.

27. Ibid., 147.

28. Jones, Rica, et al., 'Observations on drying crackle and microcissing in early and mid-18th-century British paintings', in Arie Wallert, ed., *Painting Techniques: History, Materials and Studio Practice* (Amsterdam: Rijksmuseum, 2016), 174–81.

29. It is more likely that these observers saw spots or aggregates of lead soaps, which formed early because the paint contained driers (see chapter 7).

30. Cove, Sarah, 'Fit for purpose: 30 years of the Constable research project', in Joyce H. Townsend and Abbie Vandivere, eds, *Studying the European Visual Arts 1800–1850: Paintings, Sculpture, Interiors and Art on Paper* (London: Archetype, 2017), 94–108.

31. Turner's other habits of layering paint with different modifiers have caused paint to later flake off, and generations of restorers to re-adhere it with similar materials, including egg tempera paint. Analysis of the paint could not distinguish theirs from his.

32. Carlyle, Leslie, *The Artist's Assistant* (London: Archetype, 2001), 391–402.

33. Townsend, Joyce H., et al., 'Nineteenth-century paint media: The formulation and properties of megilps', in Ashok Roy and Perry Smith, eds, *Painting Techniques: History, Materials and Studio Practice* (London: International Institute for Conservation, 1998), 205–10. The article compares proportions of 3:1, 2:1, 1:1, 1:2 and 1:3 of lead-prepared drying oil to varnish, to simulate Turner's mixing practice. The more extreme proportions dried soft and tacky, and darkened further as they aged. Later in the 19th century, megilps included copal and mastic, and generally had the best proportions for minimizing yellowing, wrinkling, and so on, as the product was improved.

34. Ibid. Trials with carefully prepared recipes averaged from 19th-century sources, using historically appropriate materials, showed how easy megilp was to mix, how quickly it gelled and how exciting a material it was to paint with. Artists' suppliers today make a number of products that offer similar benefits, without the disadvantage of using toxic lead compounds.

35. Ibid, and Boon, Jaap J., et al., 'The Opening of the Wallhalla, 1842: The molecular signature of Turner's paint as revealed by temperature-resolved in-source pyrolysis mass spectrometry', in Townsend, ed., *Turner's Painting Techniques in Context*, 35–45.

36. 'Encaustic' painting methods, which involved working with hot painting materials and even a hot surface to paint upon, were also discussed in Reynolds's later lifetime and were postulated for use by George Stubbs (1724–1806). They all sound too impractical to consider for canvas paintings and for artists who work creatively and rapidly.

37. This is not a problem for present-day conservators, who use heat-controlled tools. Restorers in the 19th century could not control their heating irons to keep them below this temperature.

38. Smibert and Townsend, 19–22, for the making of quill brushes; for illustrations of housepainters' brushes, see Baty, Patrick, *The Anatomy of Colour* (London: Thames & Hudson, 2017), 78–81.

39. In effect it is necessary to make up the recipes, and then choose materials analysis applicable to cake, not to the basic ingredients that went into the cake. The original ingredients are completely altered during the cooking.

40. *The Opening of the Wallhalla, 1842* is a good example because it is on a hardwood panel, rather than canvas, and has not suffered from numerous paint losses or conservation treatments, as the late canvases have. It has been extensively analysed; see Boon, et al., 35–45.

41. Cook and Wedderburn, vol. 3, 293.

42. https://www.tate.org.uk/art/artworks/turner-sunset-n01876, accessed 5 August 2018, referring to Thornbury, 104, and suggesting this date.

43. Hellen, Rebecca, '"Three days or more …": Turner's varnishing day practice and the physical evidence', *British Art Journal* 15:2 (2014): 47–53.

44. Butlin and Joll, BJ401 catalogue entry.

45. At the time of writing, the Courtauld Institute of Art occupies this space, which is divided into a series of smaller display rooms. A planned programme of restoration beginning in 2018 will restore it to its original dimensions and appearance.

46. Solkin, David H., *Art on the Line: The Royal Academy Exhibitions at Somerset House 1780–1836* (New Haven and London: Yale University Press, 2001). The cover of this catalogue illustrates the crowded hang and the visiting crowds who came to the exhibition in Turner's lifetime. A useful resource on the experience of each year's exhibition from the foundation of the institution is being created at http://www.paul-mellon-centre.ac.uk/projects/ra250.

47. Hellen, 47–53.

48. Cook and Wedderburn, vol. 7, 247–48.

49. R.C. Leslie to Ruskin, letters 1 and 6 of 1884, in Cook and Wedderburn, vol. 35, 572.

50. By this time the unvarnished surface was so grimy the image was impossible to see, as recounted in Butlin and Joll, BJ532 catalogue entry.

51. Hellen, 51.

52. Hellen, 47–53.

53. Townsend, Joyce H., Rebecca Hellen and Ian Warrell, 'Turner's *Regulus*: A tale of violence, abuse and accident, illuminated by technical study', in Townsend and Vandivere, eds, 109–24.

54. The identical size means that the frames and mats can be swapped from one picture to another. Research has determined which went with which, and which of the extant frames correspond to those Turner used originally; see Houghton and Alabone, 42–51.

55. The frames of these square paintings have been discussed in Moore, Adrian, 'The framing of the Turner squares as a set', *The Picture Restorer* 46 (Spring 2015): 10–11.

56. See https://www.tate.org.uk/art/artworks/turner-peace-burial-at-sea-n00528, quoting a Tate gallery label for 2010.

57. Blayney Brown, ed., 'Search the catalogue'.

58. Gage, John, *Collected Correspondence of J.M.W. Turner* (Oxford: Oxford University Press, 1980).

59. Butlin and Joll, BJ126 catalogue entry.

60. See https://www.tate.org.uk/art/artworks/turner-lecture-diagram-58-perspective-construction-of-pulteney-bridge-bath-after-thomas-d17083.

61. Garlick, Kenneth, and Angus Macintyre, *The Diary of Joseph Farington 1793–1821*, vol. 1 (New Haven and London: Yale University Press, 1979), 270.

62. Ibid., 273.

63. Smibert and Townsend, 90–99; Moorby and Warrell, 60–61, 116–19 and 122–23.

64. Much of this section is based on Ormsby, Bronwyn A., et al, 'British watercolour cakes from the 18th to the early 20th century', *Studies in Conservation* 50 (2005): 45–66.

65. See https://www.tate.org.uk/art/artworks/turner-inscription-by-another-hand-and-turner-notes-of-artists-materials-and-prices-d03777. Three cakes of colour are listed as costing 2 shillings, and a single cake 8 shillings.

66. With Turner's capitalizations and spellings: 'the sky a lovely tint of Blue Lake and Indian red' (*Welsh and Marches* tours, XIII-H, 1792–93); 'Umber and S[ap] Green the broken part umber and Bister, the distance part a Blue Green Sap and B[istre]' (*Study of Foliage and a Turret at Battle Abbey, after Michael Angelo Rooker*, XVII-Q, 1793 and earlier); 'Pure Bt [bright?] Yellow Ocker Colour with Green [of 'Greys'], very little Lake' (*The Church of St Sepulchre, Northampton: The Tower and Spire, with the Circular Nave, South Porch and South Aisle*, XIX-7, 1794); 'Sky Warm Ocker Grey' (*Smaller South Wales sketchbook*, 1795, XXV-17; 'Bright Orange staines Bright S.G. [sap green] and Ocker R. [red] Irony grey on the D.B. [dark brown?] Umber' (*Kidwelly: The Castle Seen from the Opposite Bank of the River Gwendraeth*, XXVI-16, 1795). See Blayney Brown, David, ed., 'Search the catalogue'.

67. The Reeves Collection at the Museum of London includes many watercolour paintboxes from the late 18th to the late 19th centuries, along with the company's archives. Reeves was one of the earliest and most innovative artists' colourmen, and traded for over a century under different partnerships.

68. This section is based on Townsend, Joyce H., 'The materials of J.M.W. Turner: Pigments', *Studies in Conservation* 38 (1993): 231–54, and on numerous subsequent unpublished analyses of artworks.

69. See *Tabley No. 2* sketchbook (Tate, London), c. 1808, 'Large Eel Hooks. Patent Yellow'. See Blayney Brown, ed., 'Search the catalogue'.

70. Egerton, 121–23.

71. Townsend, 'The materials of J.M.W. Turner: Pigments', 231–54.

72. Warrell, 'J.M.W. Turner and the pursuit of Fame', 12–21; Owen, Felicity, David Blayney Brown and John Leighton, *Noble and Patriotic: The Beaumont Gift, 1828*, exh. cat., London, National Gallery, 1988, 25.

73. The other is in the Royal Academy, London.

74. The colour loss that resulted was one driver for the first critical research in this topic, published as Russell, William James, and William de Wiveleslie Abney, *Report to the Science and Art Department of the Committee of Council on Education on the Action of Light on Water Colours* (London, HMSO, 1888).

75. Killik, William E., *A Short History of Winsor & Newton* (London: Winsor & Newton, 1925), n.p.

76. A fairly common feature in the Prussian-blue skies of some 18th-century works, and not unknown in the later 19th century.

77. Such circumstances, to which much older paintings are more prone than those of Turner's era, include: deterioration of the oil medium leading to loss of blue from smalt; cleaning with ill-advised acidic liquids that de-colour blue ultramarine; cleaning with alkaline liquids that de-colour Prussian blue, exposing vermilion red to some salts; or the paint medium interacting chemically with copper-based pigments.

78. Hellen, Rebecca, and Joyce H. Townsend, 'Materials, technique and condition', in David Blayney Brown, Amy Colcannon and Sam Smiles, eds, *Late Turner: Painting Set Free*, exh. cat., London, Tate, 2014, 48–55.

79. Townsend, Joyce H., 'Do oil paintings darken when they are protected from light?,' *Turner Studies Newsletter* 107 (2007): 9–10; Townsend, Joyce H., et al., 'The yellowing/bleaching behaviour of oil paint – further investigations into significant colour change as a response to dark storage followed by light exposure', in Janet Bridgland, ed., *ICOM-CC 16th Triennial Meeting Lisbon Preprints* (Paris: International Council of Museums, 2011).

80. After the Tate Conservation Department was created in 1955, the Turner oil paintings were treated there, large groups having been already transferred from the National Gallery in 1905, 1910, 1929 and 1949. Unfinished paintings that had never been cleaned or varnished were rediscovered in the National Gallery's basement during the Second World War (see Hellen, 113), and subsequently surface-cleaned, after 1955, at Tate, but not varnished. Instead, the surface was lightly waxed, which protects the surface without creating a varnished appearance. These late-treated works thus appear now much as Turner saw them. The National Gallery conservation records for Turner oils were also transferred to Tate in 1955. These and National Gallery archives document first registration of the paintings, treatments (noted as only a few words) and unusual incidents in their histories. Some of the documentation goes back to c. 1860.

81. Thornbury, 175.

82. Egerton, 121.

83. Quoted in Butlin and Joll, BJ360 catalogue entry, from the *Spectator*, 9 May 1835.

84. Butlin and Joll, BJ401 catalogue entry.

85. Keune, Katrien, and Jaap J. Boon, 'Analytical imaging studies of cross-sections of paintings affected by lead soap aggregate formation', *Studies in Conservation* 52 (2007): 161–76; Jones, et al., 174–81.

86. The sources were untreated sewage and horse droppings from the main mode of transport. Carlyle, Leslie, and Joyce H. Townsend, 'An investigation of lead sulphide darkening of 19th-century painting materials', in Victoria Todd, ed., *Dirt and Pictures Separated* (London: UK Institute for Conservation of Historic and Artistic Works, 1990), 40–43.

87. Oil preparation methods in Turner's period have been investigated extensively by Dr Leslie Carlyle. The same lead white pigment, of stack process type, could end up looking more or less yellow, depending on the oil and medium it was used with. In some cases, the pure white pigment and pale yellow oil could end up a grey colour, darker than a mid-tone. Such studies are detailed in Townsend, et al., 'The yellowing/bleaching behaviour of oil paint'.

88. Townsend, 'Turner's *Regulus*', 109–24.

89. One of the unfinished works at Tate not cleaned until after 1955, its surface then protected with only a light coating of wax, and post-1987 by a frame with glazing.

90. Egerton, 122–23. The X-radiograph illustrated on p. 123 illustrates this rare example of a surviving Turner stretcher with diagonal corner-bracing. The evidence for such original stretchers is in most cases only preserved within crack patterns in the paint.

91. Ibid.

92. Cook and Wedderburn, footnote to p. 249.

BIBLIOGRAPHY

Alabone 2008
Alabone, Gerry, 'The picture frame: Knowing its place,' in Hermens and Fiske 2008, 60–69.

Baty 2017
Baty, Patrick, *The Anatomy of Colour* (London: Thames & Hudson, 2017).

Blayney Brown 2012
Blayney Brown, David, ed., 'Search the catalogue', in *J.M.W. Turner: Sketchbooks, Drawings and Watercolours*, Tate Research Publication, December 2012, tate.org.uk/art/research-publications/jmw-turner/search-the-catalogue-r1176978.

Blayney Brown, Colcannon and Smiles 2014
Blayney Brown, David, Amy Colcannon and Sam Smiles, eds, *Late Turner: Painting Set Free*, exh. cat., London, Tate, 2014.

Boon 1995
Boon, Jaap J., et al., 'The Opening of the Wallhalla, 1842: The molecular signature of Turner's paint as revealed by temperature-resolved in-source pyrolysis mass spectrometry', in Townsend 1995, 35–45.

Bower 1990
Bower, Peter, *Turner's Papers: A Study of the Manufacture, Selection and Use of his Drawing Papers 1787–1820*, exh. cat., London, Tate, 1990.

Bower 1999
Bower, Peter, *Turner's Later Papers: A Study of the Manufacture, Selection and Use of his Drawing Papers 1820–1851*, exh. cat., London, Tate, 1999.

Bridgland 1996
Bridgland, Janet, ed., *ICOM-CC 10th Triennial Meeting Edinburgh Preprints* (Paris: International Council of Museums, 1996).

Bridgland 2011
Bridgland, Janet, ed., *ICOM-CC 16th Triennial Meeting Lisbon Preprints* (Paris: International Council of Museums, 2011).

Butlin and Joll 1984
Butlin, Martin, and Evelyn Joll, *The Paintings of J.M.W. Turner*, 2 vols (New Haven and London: Yale University Press, rev. ed. 1984).

Carlyle 2001
Carlyle, Leslie, *The Artist's Assistant* (London: Archetype, 2001).

Carlyle and Townsend 1990
Carlyle, Leslie, and Joyce H. Townsend, 'An investigation of lead sulphide darkening of 19th-century painting materials', in Todd 1990, 40–43.

Cook and Wedderburn 1903–12
Cook, E.T., and Alexander Wedderburn, eds, *The Works of John Ruskin*, 39 vols (London: George Allen, 1903–12).

Cove 2017
Cove, Sarah, 'Fit for purpose: 30 years of the Constable research project', in Townsend and Vandivere 2017, 94–108.

Eastaugh 2004
Eastaugh, Nicholas, et al., *The Pigment Compendium: A Dictionary of Historical Pigments* (Oxford: Butterworth-Heinemann, 2004).

Egerton 1997
Egerton, Judy, *Turner: The Fighting Temeraire*, exh. cat., London, National Gallery, 1997.

Forrester 1996
Forrester, Gillian, *Turner's 'Drawing Book': The Liber Studiorum*, exh. cat., London, Tate, 1996.

Gage 1980
Gage, John, *Collected Correspondence of J.M.W. Turner* (Oxford: Oxford University Press, 1980).

Galassi, Warrell and Seidenstein 2017
Galassi, Susan Grace, Ian Warrell and Joanna Sheers Seidenstein, eds, *Turner's Modern and Ancient Ports*, exh. cat., New York, The Frick Collection, 2017.

Garlick and Macintyre 1979
Garlick, Kenneth, and Angus Macintyre, *The Diary of Joseph Farington 1793–1821*, 2 vols (New Haven and London: Yale University Press, 1979).

Hamilton 1998
Hamilton, James, *Turner and the Scientists*, exh. cat., London, Tate, 1998.

Hellen 2014
Hellen, Rebecca, '"Three days or more …": Turner's varnishing day practice and the physical evidence', *British Art Journal* 15:2 (2014): 47–53.

Hellen 2017
Hellen, Rebecca, '"Unfinished productions": History and process in Turner's 1820s port scenes of Dieppe, Cologne and Brest', in Galassi, Warrell and Seidenstein 2017, 110–19.

Hellen and Townsend 2014
Hellen, Rebecca, and Joyce H. Townsend, 'Materials, technique and condition', in Blayney Brown, Colcannon and Smiles 2014, 48–55.

Hermens and Fiske 2008
Hermens, Erma, and Tina Fiske, eds, *Art, Conservation and Authenticities: Material, Concept, Context* (London: Archetype, 2008), 60–69.

Houghton and Alabone 2011
Houghton, Ivan T., and Gerry Alabone, 'Understanding the framing of the Turner Bequest', *The British Art Journal* 12:1 (2011): 42–51.

Jones 2016
Jones, Rica, et al., 'Observations on drying crackle and microcissing in early and mid-18th-century British paintings', in Wallert 2016, 174–81.

Keune and Boon 2007
Keune, Katrien, and Jaap J. Boon, 'Analytical imaging studies of cross-sections of paintings affected by lead soap aggregate formation', *Studies in Conservation* 52 (2007): 161–76.

Killik 1925
Killik, William E., *A Short History of Winsor & Newton* (London: Winsor & Newton, 1925).

Moorby and Warrell 2010
Moorby, Nicola, and Ian Warrell, *How to Paint Like Turner* (London: Tate, 2010).

Moore 2015
Moore, Adrian, 'The framing of the Turner squares as a set', *The Picture Restorer* 46 (Spring 2015): 10–11.

Ormsby 2005
Ormsby, Bronwyn A., et al, 'British watercolour cakes from the 18th to the early 20th century', *Studies in Conservation* 50 (2005): 45–66.

Owen, Blayney Brown and Leighton 1988
Owen, Felicity, David Blayney Brown and John Leighton, *Noble and Patriotic: The Beaumont Gift, 1828*, exh. cat., London, National Gallery, 1988.

Riding and Johns 2010
Riding, Christine, and Richard Johns, *Turner and the Sea*, exh. cat., London, Royal Museums Greenwich, 2013.

Roy and Smith 1998
Roy, Ashok, and Perry Smith, eds, *Painting Techniques: History, Materials and Studio Practice* (London: International Institute for Conservation, 1998)

Russell and Abney 1888
Russell, William James, and William de Wiveleslie Abney, *Report to the Science and Art Department of the Committee of Council on Education on the Action of Light on Water Colours* (London, HMSO, 1888).

Shanes 2016
Shanes, Eric, *Young Mr Turner: The First Forty Years 1775–1815* (New Haven and London: Yale University Press, 2016).

Smibert 2019
Smibert, Tony, *Turner's Apprentice: The Essential Manual for Watercolour Success* (London: Thames & Hudson, 2019).

Smibert and Townsend 2014
Smibert, Tony, and Joyce H. Townsend, *Tate Watercolour Manual: Lessons from the Great Masters* (London: Tate, 2014).

Smiles 2006
Smiles, Sam, *The Turner Book* (London, Tate, 2006).

Solkin 2001
Solkin, David H., *Art on the Line: The Royal Academy Exhibitions at Somerset House 1780–1836* (New Haven and London: Yale University Press, 2001).

Solkin 2009
Solkin, David H., ed., *Turner and the Masters*, exh. cat., London, Tate, 2009.

Stoner and Rushfield 2012
Stoner, Joyce Hill, and Rebecca Rushfield, eds, *The Conservation of Easel Paintings* (Oxford: Routledge, 2012).

Thornbury 1877
Thornbury, Walter, *The Life of J.M.W. Turner, R.A.*, 2 vols (1862; London: Chatto & Windus, 1877; repr. 1970).

Todd 1990
Todd, Victoria, ed., *Dirt and Pictures Separated* (London: UK Institute for Conservation of Historic and Artistic Works, 1990).

Townsend 1993
Townsend, Joyce H., 'The materials of J.M.W. Turner: Pigments', *Studies in Conservation* 38 (1993): 231–54.

Townsend 1994
Townsend, Joyce H., 'The materials of J.M.W. Turner: Primings and supports', *Studies in Conservation* 39 (1994): 145–53.

Townsend 1995
Townsend, Joyce H., ed., *Turner's Painting Techniques in Context* (London: UK Institute for Conservation of Historic and Artistic Works, 1995).

Townsend 1996
Townsend, Joyce H., 'Turner's "drawing book", the *Liber Studiorum*: materials and techniques', in Bridgland 1996, 376–80.

Townsend 1998
Townsend, Joyce H., et al., 'Nineteenth-century paint media: The formulation and properties of megilps', in Roy and Smith 1998, 205–10.

Townsend 2004
Townsend, Joyce H., 'The materials used by British oil painters throughout the 19th century, *Tate Papers* 2 (2004), available at tate.org.uk/research.

Townsend 2005
Townsend, Joyce H., *Turner's Painting Techniques* (London: Tate, 1993; 4th ed., 2005).

Townsend 2007
Townsend, Joyce H., 'Do oil paintings darken when they are protected from light?,' *Turner Studies Newsletter* 107 (2007): 9–10.

Townsend 2011
Townsend, Joyce H., et al., 'The yellowing/bleaching behaviour of oil paint – further investigations into significant colour change as a response to dark storage followed by light exposure', in Bridgland 2011.

Townsend and Vandivere 2017
Townsend, Joyce H., and Abbie Vandivere, eds, *Studying the European Visual Arts 1800–1850: Paintings, Sculpture, Interiors and Art on Paper* (London: Archetype, 2017).

Townsend, Hellen and Warrell 2017
Townsend, Joyce H., Rebecca Hellen and Ian Warrell, 'Turner's *Regulus*: A tale of violence, abuse and accident, illuminated by technical study', in Townsend and Vandivere 2017, 109–24.

Wallert 2016
Wallert, Arie, ed., *Painting Techniques: History, Materials and Studio Practice* (Amsterdam: Rijksmuseum, 2016).

Wark 1997
Wark, Robert R., ed., *Discourses on Art: Sir Joshua Reynolds* (New Haven and London: Yale University Press, 1959; rev. ed., 1997).

Warrell 2007
Warrell, Ian, 'J.M.W. Turner and the pursuit of fame', in Ian Warrell, ed., *J.M.W. Turner*, exh. cat., London, Tate, 2007, 12–21.

Warrell 2014
Warrell, Ian, *Turner's Sketchbooks* (London: Tate, 2014).

Wilton 2006
Wilton, Andrew, *Turner in his Time* (London: Thames & Hudson, 2006).

INDEX

ACKNOWLEDGMENTS

Tony Smibert has provided the valuable perspective of an artist drawing inspiration from Turner's working methods since I first met him in 1996. He has shown me how to paint, how to look at landscapes with a view to creating landscape compositions, how an artist breaks the rules as soon as he becomes immersed in creative work, and how a right-handed artist uses his painting tools.

Many have contributed to this book, through professional expertise, discussion, their writings and shared technical examinations and conservation treatments. Stephen Hackney, former Head of Conservation Science at Tate, initiated the study of Turner oils there, and has always generously shared information, as well as his observations in earlier treatment reports, since my arrival in 1987. My doctoral research, mainly into Turner's oils, was supervised by Andrew Wilton, former Keeper of British Art, Tate, and the late Gerry Hedley.

That year also saw the opening of the Clore Gallery for the Turner Bequest at Tate Britain, which meant that numerous conservators and art historians, including a number of young curators who are now senior Turner scholars, were all actively working on the oil paintings, which were now displayed in their entirety, as well as the watercolours, which were being dismounted, imaged in colour in bulk, and stored to give better access and preservation.

Art historians Ian Warrell, Nicola Moorby, Gillian Forrester and Peter Bower have shared ideas over the years, while Juliet Beaumont-Jones and Christine Kurpiel have given access to many works on paper. Conservators Rebecca Hellen, Helen Brett and Amelia Jackson, as well as Rica Jones, Anna Southall and Roy Perry, have shared observations, fears and ideas on the Turner oils they were treating. Stephen Hackney and Rebecca Hellen have also commented on the text.

Leslie Carlyle, who investigates the history and behaviour of painting materials in the 19th century, has been a wonderful, constantly questioning co-researcher. Numerous conservation and research scientists have developed and applied advanced analytical techniques for Turner's challengingly complex paint: Jaap Boon, Marianne Odlyha, Brian Singer, Bronwyn Ormsby and Jennifer Pilc, along with their research teams. All are my long-term friends and collaborators, the ones who made Turner studies so rewarding, and I thank them all warmly.

To name all the rest who have contributed to our understanding of how Turner painted could fill the rest of this book, but they are all greatly appreciated. I shall limit myself to thanking the photographers who have contributed to the images of artworks here and so to many other publications on Turner, and to Turner scholars worldwide.